906 432 9685

Joost 1996.

Han van der Horst is a historian and publicist. He is a staff member of the Department for Communication of the Nuffic, the Netherlands Organization for International Cooperation in Higher Education.

The low sky
Understanding the Dutch

Han van der Horst

NUFFIC • SCRIPTUM

ISBN 90 5594 039 9

Contents

Foreword

THIS BOOK IS A RESPONSE to other people's surprise. I saw it in their eyes, the eyes of people who had come to the Netherlands for a short visit, usually for study or research, or on business. Sometimes they would say nothing, but more often they would ask questions. The Netherlands can be a very strange place for newcomers.

This book is intended for people who find themselves surprised by the Netherlands and by the Dutch. I do not wish to take away the surprise, because that can be a positive and creative emotion. But if you have some idea of the background to customs and forms of behaviour that appear unusual, bizarre or even scandalous, it may help you to understand them and to respond to them more effectively.

My work for the Nuffic means that professionally – and, frequently, in my personal life – I meet and mix with people from all over the world. Just which particular features of Dutch society will cause the familiar expression of surprise to appear on their faces depends very much on their particular social and cultural background. But, after a while, it is possible to identify certain patterns and these provided me with guidelines for what I should include in this book and what I should leave out. I must therefore thank everyone who has revealed to me at some point their surprise at the Dutch and the way they live. Without their openness, this book could never have been written.

But, of course, I cannot leave it there. For typical Dutch reasons, which I examine in detail later, I did not lay out the course of the book entirely on my own. I consulted with friends and colleagues, and gave them the opportunity to suggest improvements. This led to the formation of a kind of 'support group', a small team of people who read critically what I had written, asked questions and, where I threatened to become a little dogmatic, suggested what I should leave out or put in. This occurred at gatherings that, if sometimes a little chaotic, were always extremely fruitful and enjoyable. The group consisted of Jojada Verrips, cultural anthropologist at the University of Amsterdam, Niek Miedema, translator and publicist, Peter Schouten, documentary maker and a member of staff at the *Anne Frank Stichting*, and Marcel Oomen, director of the Netherlands America Commission for Educational Exchange. Their contribution to this book is of inestimable value.

Writing *The Low Sky* gave me a great deal of pleasure and I hope I succeed in passing some of some of this on to its readers.

[8]   Han van der Horst

Introduction

A REPLY TO DIRCEU BORGES

'You must not stay here', Dirceu Borges told his daughter after his first, brief encounter with the Netherlands. 'The sky is too low'. I remember that so well because Claudia and I once had a close relationship. We visited her family in São Paulo. I was more enthusiastic about Brazil than Dirceu Borges had been about the Netherlands. I sang the praises of the hot, steamy port of Belém.

'That is because it is exactly what you would expect a Brazilian town to be like', Dirceu said. 'Hot, dirty and a little run down. You like Belém because it fits your stereotype of Brazil.' Between us, unspoken, was De Gaulle's famous remark: *'Le Brésil, ce n'est pas un pays sérieux'*.

Dirceu Borges would get very angry about this. After a career in advertising he had built up – practically out of nothing – a number of modern companies one of which used advanced genetic techniques to breed cattle. He had also written several novels about rural life in the state of São Paulo. He knew about images and what people want to recognize in what they see. He had hit the nail right on the head with his explanation of my reaction to Bélem. I liked Brazil a great deal but, with the characteristic prejudices of most Dutch visitors to the country, my heart went out to the north and northeast, where the modernization that was sweeping the country had least affected the traditional way of life. The fact that so many of the people from the region were packing up and seeking a better future in the bustling metropolis of São Paulo did nothing to temper this view. Everything was simply a lot *nicer* in the northeast.

We saw what we wanted to see. The widespread poverty fitted neatly into the picture – Brazil is, after all, the Third World. This was what irritated Dirceu Borges. He was very sensitive about it, suspecting that it concealed a feeling of superiority. For us, Brazil was wonderfully romantic and different – from another time.

Dirceu deposited me in his Chevrolet Diplomat (Made in Brazil) and we set off up the *Anhanguera*, the motorway that connects São Paulo to the state of Minas Gerais. On the way we listened to *Sertaneja* on the radio. This was Dirceu's favourite music. It sounded to me like a cross between country and western and what we call in the Netherlands *smartlappen*, tear-jerkers of the first order. In any case, to me it certainly didn't sound Brazilian.

We passed enormous green road signs. Other than the fact that they would be blue in the Netherlands, the *Anhanguera* could have been a modern motorway anywhere in the world.

For fifty years or so, Brazil has been crossing its local cattle with the *zebu*, an Indian breed. This produces top quality beef cattle. Dirceu took the process a step further by inducing superovulation in the breeding cows, each of which developed twenty embryos. These were then transplanted into the wombs of 'normal' cows. It was this that Dirceu wanted me to see. We were racing towards his breeding plant in the Chevrolet. I could see it in the distance, its domes glittering in the sunlight. It looked for all the world like an Indian temple rising out of the flat countryside of the surrounding plain. As we drew nearer, I could hear the sound of gongs, which made it even easier to attribute it with a religious significance.

But inside there were laboratories and stalls for the livestock. The gong sounds I had heard came from a piece of decorative artwork that moved in the wind. A large sign in front of the door stated in no uncertain terms 'Nova India genética', the name of the company. I didn't understand at all; to me it all seemed rather kitsch. Dirceu explained. The building, he said, was its own advertisement. Here, after all, they were employing genetic techniques to upgrade Brazilian cattle with Indian *zebu*. There was an enormous colour photograph of the temple in the departure hall of the local airport. The name *Nova India genética* said enough. There was no need for complicated explanations. The building was the message.

I was now starting to understand why Dirceu had warned his daughter about the low sky in the Netherlands. It explained my initial reaction to the plant, the reaction of a full-blooded Dutchman. Dirceu was a romantic and romantics often have a very good feel for their surroundings. If he had built the temple in the Netherlands – at Wageningen, for example, where competitors of his are working at the Agricultural University – he would have been written off as a crank, *zebu* or not. A genetic breeding plant should look like a genetic breeding plant. The temple had lost him a number of customers. A building like this would have been seen as an expensive eccentricity in the Netherlands. That Dirceu Borges is a little crazy, a little abnormal, they would be thinking. Not someone to do business with. In the Netherlands, they would never have understood using architecture to transmit a message in this way. In the Netherlands, Dirceu observed a kind of 'flatness', a tendency to mistrust the unconventional, a fear of surprises. There was no place for adventurers.

HE WAS RIGHT ABOUT THE LOW SKY

But he was wrong, too. His analysis wasn't entirely correct, although there was something in it. He was right about the low sky. Too often, grey clouds hang above the land, filtering the sunlight so that the colours below become pallid and dull. My own plans all too often lost their way in a maze of endless consultations and meetings. When they did finally emerge from the mist, they had been trimmed down, thinned out and cut to size. My colleagues – average Dutch men and women, with whom I was trying to organize something or other – had indeed a rather exaggerated sensitivity to risks. They were rather fond of expressions like 'feasibility' and 'short of time'. They would start talking about the cost aspects, while – as Dirceu, the entrepreneur, would say – the money can always be found for a good idea. If it can't, it wasn't a good idea.

But with my plans, everyone would be working away at them as though their lives depended on it. Once they had been through the mill, they were usually a lot less ambitious. The scrolls, the bizarre lucarnes and the cupolas had, as it were, been talked out. But then the plans went through with the core intact. And without any problems with funding.

I even learned to take this into account. My proposals gradually became more ambitious rather than less. In that way, I told myself, more would survive the mill.

I had touched Dirceu deep in his soul with my predilection for the mildewed tropical city of Belém. He had touched me just as deeply with his low sky.

That is why I have called this book *The Low Sky*. I had the title before the first sentence had been typed into the computer. It had to be a kind of reply to Dirceu Borges. But also something useful, just in case he ever tried to set something up in the Netherlands. And also something that would interest a wider readership. The Netherlands has become, in effect, a country with a large immigrant population – no matter how and no matter what people may say to the contrary. The internal borders of the European Union are disappearing and the external borders are becoming more and more porous. Anyone who takes a walk along the Kalverstraat in Amsterdam or Rotterdam's Lijnbaan will find themselves in the midst of a large international and multicultural crowd.

THE QUESTION IS, THEN, WHAT IS 'DUTCH'?

A book like this could be seen as a kind of 'helping hand', perhaps a set of instructions for understanding the Dutch. The Dutch themselves are cautious about offering a helping hand. They think that everyone should be allowed to decide and find things out for themselves. They do not impose, wishing to be left in peace themselves unless they have given clear indications to the contrary. But a book is on a shelf in a bookshop – you can take it or leave it.

The question is, then, what is 'Dutch'? Clogs, tulips, St. Nicholas, the canals in Amsterdam, the Delta Project, a damp southwest wind in your face as you walk on the dyke, the flat expanse of the polders with their pedigree Frisian cattle. They are all part of the overall picture, but for ninety per cent of Dutch people they mean little or nothing at all. They are as typical of the Netherlands as Belém is of Brazil. Anyone who lives here for an extended period of time becomes acquainted with a completely different reality. These things are all typical but not representative.

The *Oude Maasweg* in Rotterdam is far more representative.

This is a rough translation of the first hit for the Amazing Stroopwafels, well-

'Ik zit hier op de snelweg	'I'm sitting on the highway,
met een lege tank.	with an empty tank
Regen klettert op het dak.	The rain beating down on the roof.
Ik zal nu wel naar huis toe	Now I'll have to hitchhike home,
moeten liften,	And with every step I'll be
'k denk aan jou bij elke stap.	thinking of you.
	The Transit gets smaller
In de verte blijft de Transit staan.	as I move away.
Ik kom nooit meer van je los.	I'll never be able to forget you.
Ik zie de Caltex in een nevel,	I can see the Caltex through the haze,

olievlekken op de Maas.	oil flecks floating on the Maas
Ik loop maar door,	I walk on,
maar ik kan nergens heen.	I've nowhere to run.
Het regent nog steeds	It's still raining
en ik voel mij zo alleen,	And I feel so alone
nu ik je nooit meer zie.	Since you went away.
Oude Maasweg, kwart voor drie.'	Oude Maasweg, a quarter to three.'

known in the Netherlands and world-famous in the Rotterdam area. We, the fans, never let them get away without playing this song. It summons up perfectly a kind of 'autumn' feeling that is Rotterdam to a tee. We have all seen the Caltex refinery through the haze. The Oude Maasweg passes through an area dominated by chemical plants, which runs along the banks of the Maas and considers itself the backbone of the Dutch economy. The lyrics of 'Oude Maasweg' have become a part of the spiritual baggage of a whole generation from that part of the country. The song is based on Leon Russel's Manhattan Island Serenade. The Stroopwafels acknowledge that debt by placing their own lyrics side by side with those of the original, which went as follows:

'Sitting on a highway
In a broken van
Thinking of you again.
Guess I'll have to hitchhike
To the station.
With every step I see your face
Like a mirror looking back at me,
Saying you are the only one
Making me feel
I could survive
And so glad to be alive.
Nowhere to run and
Not a guitar to play
Messed up inside,
And it's been raining all day
Since you went away,
Manhattan Island Serenade.'

In the Dutch version, the rain is heavier and more tangible. There is an implicit reference to environmental degradation. The geographical information is a lot more detailed and the pain is expressed in shorter – in my view, less poetic – words and phrases. Yet the two have a great deal in common. Large cities tend to be similar and New York undoubtedly has an 'Oude Maasweg' of its own. Countries and peoples have their own characters, but these cannot be captured in a superficial glance at their folklore. A global culture has also grown up, with its own image and its own symbols. It is a part of modern industrial society and is expressed in popular culture, fashion, new inventions and lifestyles. Except for its length, Rotterdam's Weena boulevard is interchangeable with the Avenida Paulista in São Paulo. Or the Jalan Thamrin in Djakarta or parts of the Thanon Sekhumvit in Bangkok, for that matter. In the final paragraph of his essay *De stad als kunststuk* , The city as a work of art, published in 1987, the Amsterdam cultural sociologist Abram de Swaan explains why this is:

'This is the city which can straddle an ocean and set the tone for the cultural life of this continent, which – as a genuine global metropolis – not only dominates the culture of its own nation, but is also the centre of everything that goes on throughout the continent and, ultimately, between the cultures of all the other continents. This is New York, the focal point of Atlantis, the cultural capital of Europe.'

In another article *Perron Nederland*, Platform Netherlands, De Swaan defines this influence, with New York at its centre (but explicitly not as the centre of cultural imperialism), as the internationalization of culture. He also uses the term 'global culture'. He writes:

'The internationalization of the Netherlands is taking place at two levels. Firstly, there is an increasing actual interdependence between the Netherlands and the rest of the world, particularly the countries around the Atlantic. Secondly, Dutch culture – and Dutch mass culture in particular – is increasingly taking its lead from global culture, and from American culture in particular.'

Previously, in *Verdriet en lied van de kosmopoliet*, The sorrow of the cosmopolitan, (1985), De Swaan welcomed this new global culture:

'Every week the dance halls are sold out because there is an African band playing. Twenty-five years ago, African musical groups also came to the Netherlands. The women danced bare-breasted while a man beat a drum. Everyone thought it was very interesting and authentic but that was as far as it went. The music played by the African groups who come here now is 'bastardized', a shameless mixture of tribal folklore, Islamic chanting, Caribbean carnival and pure American commercial sounds. More a mishmash than a synthesis, it is lively and loud and it never stops. This is the cosmopolitan culture, it has broken loose from its tribal roots, thrown off the shackles that bound it to the village…'

De Swaan concludes: 'The Netherlands is a station on that worldwide circuit. The function and value of the Dutch language and culture is that it allows you to step in or out of that world. A nation is but a platform for the outside world'.

As well as being a highly educated and well-respected professor, De Swaan is also a full-blooded Amsterdammer. Amsterdammers – and they are not alone in this – believe unconditionally that they live in the only truly cosmopolitan metropolis in the country and therefore have a direct line to all that is innovative and experimental in the world outside. For generations, the city has acted as a magnet for those who have had enough of conventional village life. Amsterdam sees itself as a window to the world. Things happen there first – or so the people of the city like to think – before they reach the rest of the country. This is true of many national capitals, of course, but in the Netherlands the distance between the capital and the provinces is small – both in the geographical sense and mentally. And the country is not only small but also highly urbanized, particularly in the west. It is the town, the city that sets the pace and that has its roots in historical tradition. The Netherlands has long been a centre of international trade, located exactly at the point where the German, French and Anglo-Saxon cultures meet. This in itself gives Dutch society the cosmopolitan tint that De Swaan describes so enthusiastically in his essays. The Oude Maasweg is a typical example of this cosmopolitanism – and by no means the only one. In the early 1990s thousands of television viewers became addicted to the first home-grown weekly soap opera, *Goede*

Tijden, Slechte Tijden – Good Times, Bad Times – which was, however, based on an Australian predecessor. And there are countless other examples.

This might lead you to think that De Swaan's cultural internationalization, his global culture (the product of New York, the world's cultural 'broker'), the whole mishmash together constitutes the reality within which the Dutch live out their lives. Readers of this book will recognize much that is also true of their own countries, and may think to themselves that things are not so different at home. Their responses may at times be similar, but they will not all respond to the same passages. The global culture has the same effect as herbs and spices. They mix and fuse with the ingredients of the dish, their flavour may even prove stronger, but they will never determine the taste entirely. And in this way, things that appear similar remain different. And, of course, once the spices have been added they can no longer be separated from the original ingredients.

If this were not the case, Dirceu Borges would never have noticed the low sky. And that is why this book is not about the tulips, the clogs and St. Nicholas. There are already plenty of books available for non-Dutch readers who want to know more about these. The same goes for cycling. The bicycle is an excellent means of transport as long as you don't have to go uphill. And there are few hills in the Netherlands. Other than that there is little to say about it.

This book takes another path, looking not so much at the way the Dutch look but at how they behave. It tries to give the reader an insight into the mentality that determines the way they live.

This is, of course, a dangerous undertaking. Even bees and ants, until recently believed to be robot-like creatures whose existence has meaning only within the colony in which they live, now appear to have more individual characters than was previously assumed. A person's responses are largely determined by his or her individual personality. Yet culturally determined behaviour does exist. The Avenida Paulista may look very much like the Weena, but my body language, the way I walk, is very different from that of the Brazilians. They recognize me immediately as a foreigner. From my posture, I might come from the south of the country, but they know I do not. I am different.

How can we obtain a better understanding of this? The Royal Tropical Institute in Amsterdam has been conducting research into other cultures for over a hundred years, not only in the field of sociology but also in medicine

[16]

and agriculture. It has rightly become a truly international institute with a wide experience of intercultural communication. In recent years, the institute has put this experience to practical use in a rather unusual way by offering courses to introduce foreigners to the Dutch way of life. The course identifies five traits that are characteristic of Dutch society: egalitarian, utilitarian, organized, trade oriented and privacy minded. Practically all of the phenomena which a foreigner who comes to live here for any length of time will be confronted with – and which may at first lead to amazement, shock, anger or despair – are dealt with under one or more of these five categories. In this way a picture is built up of the way the Dutch live together in society, of the Dutch man or woman as a social animal. Without forgetting, of course, that people – even more than social insects – resemble each other only with the most superficial of observations. They are all very much individuals and should never be seen as the exception that proves the rule.

NONE OF US IS A SLAVE OF THE CULTURE IN WHICH WE LIVE

This book devotes a chapter to each of the epithetic traits which the Royal Tropical Institute attributes to the Dutch. The sixth chapter looks at the cultural minorities who have established themselves in the Netherlands, particularly in the past thirty years or so, and who have become so much a part of everyday life in the cities that the urban face of the Netherlands has changed radically. These groups are the living proof that societies, cultures and mentalities are in a continual state of development and change. There are, of course, 'constants', collective experiences and the collective memories and mythology that they generate, but even their permanence should not be overestimated. This book is about change. It describes processes. I write this today, tomorrow the Netherlands will be a little different.

But that is what makes life so exciting. Even under a low sky, Dirceu.

Chapter 1

EGALITARIAN :

'LET THOSE WHO HAVE ABUNDANCE REMEMBER

THAT THEY ARE SURROUNDED WITH THORNS'

Act normally, that's crazy enough. Real wealth keeps a low profile. No one should dominate. The principle of consensus. The 'normal' image of the monarchy. Calvinist hard doctrine and soft practice. Sovereignty in one's own domain. The embarrassment of riches. The avoidance of risks. The welfare society. The new primacy of the individual.

FEW PEOPLE IN THE Netherlands have heard of Carel Nolet, but his 'Ketel 1' *jenever* is to be found on the shelves of any liquor store. Nolet's success is based on a clever marketing strategy. He lays heavy emphasis on the fact that his family company has been in business since 1695, leading the consumer to believe that what he is drinking is the product of three centuries of craftsmanship and experience. This is successful – and is reflected in the price of the product – as can be seen from the large number of requests received from people wishing to come and visit what is apparently a traditional company. The visitors find themselves in a highly efficient, computerized distillery, which produces not only Ketel 1, but also a whole range of other drinks.

And then, of course, there is the prize-winning videofilm. It cannot be shown without explanation. It was made for wholesalers in the United States, where Ketel 1 vodka has been on the market for a number of years. Carel Nolet appears in the film once only, driving in his Daimler. The guide explains that the Daimler was rented especially for the film. The boss does not, of course, really drive around in a car like that. He actually has a BMW. Toonder Studios, the makers of the film, had insisted that the Daimler was necessary for the

American market. If the director did not drive a luxury car – and a European one at that – the wholesalers might have their doubts about the company's solidity.

To Dutch eyes, the effect is exactly the opposite. The Daimler is proof that the director wants to show what an important man he is. He obviously has no loyalties towards the company. You can see from the car where the profits go to. With such an arrogant man at the helm, Ketel 1 won't last too long. This Carel Nolet is clearly not a serious business man. And above all, Ketel 1 is not cheap – why should we pay for the boss's car?

In a recent television commercial, Volkswagen made a direct appeal to this mentality. A series of cars filled the screen, each one larger than the last, finishing up with a powerful Mercedes. The captions told the story. 'The plant manager's car', 'The managing director's car' and 'The company president's car'. Finally a simple Volkswagen appeared on the screen, with the caption: 'The crisis manager's car'.

The visitors to Ketel 1 are easily convinced by the Daimler story. A clever idea, renting a limousine for a day to impress foreign customers. They are thinking to themselves: luckily we're not like that, here in the Netherlands. *Wij doen normaal, dan doen we gek genoeg.* We just act normally, that's crazy enough. But if we have to do something crazy to earn a few pennies abroad, so what? *Je moet iedereen in zijn waarde laten.* Each to his own. On the other hand, as all Dutch people know, *zuinigheid met vlijt bouwt huizen als kastelen.* With thrift and hard work you can build a castle.

NO HOVELS, BUT NO PALACES, EITHER

The phrases in italics are well-known Dutch sayings. At first sight they appear contradictory. The first is an appeal to conformist behaviour, while the second gives everyone the right to choose their own lifestyle, even though it may be a little strange. The third advocates a diligent and thrifty life – prosperity does not just fall into your lap, you have to earn it. But this is no excuse for extravagance. There are few castles in the Netherlands. There are no hovels but no palaces, either. Even the 'palaces' inhabited by the Royal Family are actually overgrown villas and are in no way comparable with Versailles, Sans Souci, Buckingham Palace or Windsor Castle. Even the House of Orange, with its centuries of tradition, does not escape the conformism of *'doe normaal, dan doe je gek genoeg'*. Even the monarch is subject to the restrictive law of the Daimler.

Yet the foreign visitor will see people in the street who clearly fall outside these conventional patterns of behaviour. Fabiola, a walking work of art, strides through the streets of Amsterdam, clad in glittering garments with a long train, giving him an androgynous appearance. Fabiola can do as he pleases, and often brightens up official public gatherings with his presence. The great success of the early nineties in the entertainment field was the 'gay' disco 'It'. The club rapidly gained a reputation throughout Europe as a result of the bizarre attire – or lack of it – of some of its guests, which frequently smacked of sado-masochism. Anything goes on the dance floor, the owner had said, with the exception of actual sexual intercourse. This is reserved for the professionals, who perform at It just to keep everyone in the right frame of mind. The popular press regularly publishes pictures of the goings-on at the club and what they show would certainly cause the average family man to raise an eyebrow. But there is one thing missing – jewellery. In the Netherlands, eccentric party-goers do not decorate their slave belts with gold or diamonds – even though their bank accounts might justify such extravagance. This would provoke an aggressive response from the wider public. As it is, the proceedings in It are followed with a kind of bemused interest, but not with anger or revulsion. *Ze zoeken het maar uit.* It's their business what they do.

This same popular press has no society columns of the kind that adorn the newspapers in most other countries. Parties given by ministers, members of parliament and captains of industry, the social life of the *haut monde*, are not considered news. This is firstly because they are generally of such modest proportions that they are not worth reporting and secondly because these people rarely allow journalists access to their private lives. The gossip press has to content itself with reporting on the parties given by popular entertainers who move in a circuit that takes its lead from Hollywood. Here, gaudy displays of wealth are the order of the day. Not only by the stars themselves but also by their rich companions, who have often made their fortunes in business and do not conform to the norms of behaviour adopted by those with 'old money'. These *nouveaux riches* arouse the suspicion of many 'normal' Dutch people. They believe there must be something not entirely above board about them or they would not behave in such a way. The general public were first introduced to this phenomenon in the early 1990s by a popular television programme,

Glamourland, which reported on the parties, receptions and other activities of the rich and famous. The programme's success lay in the fact that its presenter, G.J. Dröge – dressed appropriately in a smart dinner jacket – would poke fun at his guests. His superior attitude was in fact based on a saying from the Bible that every Dutch person knows, religious or not: *alles is ijdelheid* – all is vanity. The message was, these people should not be taken seriously.

Yet many regular customers at the It have done well for themselves. In the daytime, they are barely distinguishable from the rest of the crowd, going about their business in their nondescript outfits. This puts the apparent contradiction between the conformist motto *Doe normaal, dan doe je gek genoeg* and the more liberal *Laat iedereen in zijn waarde*, each to his own, into proportion.

[21]

FOR THE RICH, A LOW PROFILE IS A COMMANDMENT

The number of millionaires in the Netherlands increases steadily every year. Multinationals like Royal Dutch/Shell and Philips are largely based on Dutch soil. Financial consortia such as ABN AMRO and RABO are among the top twenty international banks. Per capita income is around thirty thousand guilders a year, a six-fold increase over the past 50 years. There is an incredible amount of wealth in the Netherlands, a large part of which is still concentrated in the hands of small minority. But these few, the super-rich, are not so easy to recognize. For the genuinely rich, a low profile is practically a commandment. In the thirties, many a minister still took the tram to the ministry. Although his modern counterparts may now have a chauffeur-driven car, this is by no means taken for granted. They justify themselves by referring to their overfull schedules and saying how easy it is to work in the back of a limousine. Captains of industry follow their example. They protect their privacy by living in large country houses, often in places like Wassenaar or Aerdenhout, favoured by millionaires but still modest by international standards. They exercise their influence through the boardroom and avoid the glare of publicity. Leading businessmen, such as Wim Dik of KPN, Jan Timmer of Philips or Wim Duisenberg of the Dutch Central Bank, appear in public only if they have something to say of financial or economic importance – perhaps to comment on their company's annual results. They then withdraw into anonymity, as far as possible from the limelight. And they always try to keep their own personalities at a distance. The average company director – and the same is true of politicians and top civil servants – will not often attribute his successes to his own talents. At least, not in public. He will insist to the contrary that it was a team effort, that it would never have been achieved without the dedication and hard work of those around him. He will insist that the company stands or falls by the efforts of its staff and employees. This he – and it is almost always a 'he'; women may be gaining ground in middle management, but have not as yet broken the glass ceiling especially in the world of big business – this he will do, at least if he is sensible, otherwise he will bear the brunt of contemptuous public opinion.

The families of these great men remain firmly in the background. The wife of Ruud Lubbers, prime minister for much of the eighties and early nineties, sought publicity now and again, mostly through the back door of the Glamourland circuit, and this resulted in the raising of a few eyebrows. She was a conspicuous exception to this rule. Not that the partners of the Dutch élite are content to spend their time flower arranging. They often try to build careers for themselves, but then in a way that has nothing to do with their partners. A Hillary Clinton would be inconceivable in the Netherlands, unless she used her maiden name and worked entirely separately from her husband. Few people know, for example, that politician Eveline Herfkens – who is currently a member of the Board of Governors of the World Bank – and colleague Ed van Thijn, sometime member of parliament, ex-mayor of Amsterdam and former minister, were married for several years.

It only became public knowledge at the funeral of Ien Dales, the interior minister, that she and Elisabeth Schmitz, a respected administrator and politician, were life partners. Even as this became known, voices in the media wondered whether this was not prying too deeply into the private lives of others and whether it was acceptable to subject the grief of Ms Schmitz to public scrutiny.

Respect for the privacy of others prevents the kind of curiosity which, only an hour's flight away to the west, ruins many a politician's career in London. But what about the It? You enter the club through a door in a blank wall. A bouncer keeps watch. It's guests are looking for others of similar inclination and the shoppers passing outside have no idea of what is going on behind that door. Nor – and this is the general view – is it any of their business. Public persons should be judged by their public acts and not by what they choose to do in their private lives. The conviction that this is not as interesting as it might seem is illustrated by the fact that so many Dutch people leave their curtains open at night, giving a clear view of their conventional, well-made furniture and their tidy, dust-free living rooms.

Perhaps this openness is a sign that so many Dutch people wish to show that they also act 'normally' in their private lives. This provides much food for thought. The Dutch word *kamertjeszonde*, for example, is a good starting point. The word, which has no English equivalent, is defined in the *Van Dale* dictionary, as 'vice, with a hint of small-mindedness, of being commonplace'. The suggestion is of petit-bourgeois suburbia, with small-scale lasciviousness going on behind closed doors. Yet those who place too much credence in such ideas are on the same thin ice as protohistorians who attempt to reconstruct an 'original society'. The fact of the matter is, the curtains are open and they reveal an overwhelming homogeneity..

Throughout the centuries, many travellers have been struck by these aspects of Dutch society. The way they have interpreted or commented on what they have seen depends to a certain extent on their own tastes. We find in their works enthusiastic descriptions of the Dutch sense of tolerance and democracy, evoking images of a multi-facetted and multicoloured society. But also of dull paintings of a conformist, colourless mass of people. A century ago, the Portuguese writer Ramalho Ortigão held the Netherlands up to his fellow countrymen as an example, for its openness and its progressive outlook. In the 1980s, his compatriot Rentes de Carvalho entitled a similar treatise 'Where the other God lives'. This was a cold-weather God, keeping watch over a puritan society which confuses its indifference with tolerance. *'Adieu, canards, canaux, canaille'*, Voltaire is supposed to have said, after a brief visit to the Netherlands. And German social researcher Ernst Zahn, a professor for many years at the University of Amsterdam, complains about an academic climate which reduces everything to the predictable. This is a long way from the magical attraction that gave Amsterdam a reputation, in the sixties, almost equal to that of swinging London or San Francisco, where you went with flowers in your hair. In that period, the Netherlands was seen as the focus of international renewal, where people experimented with new lifestyles, a first encounter with what was later to be called the 'post-industrial society'. The keyword for the time was *ludiek*, playful – in other words, the very opposite of 'normal'.

Yet, even in those years, the open curtains revealed a conventional three-piece suite and the grey glow of a television set (colour had not yet arrived). And Piet de Jong, the prime minister throughout that time, watched all the 'fun' with a bemused smile on his face. He was a conservative Catholic and an ex-submarine captain. His position was never under threat – not for a minute.

And yet – it must be said again – this conventional Dutch society demands a far lower price for unconventional behaviour than many others do. This mentality has developed over many generations and is closely related to the history of the Dutch state.

Today, the Kingdom of the Netherlands is a modern nation state with borders that are not under dispute – either within or outside the country. There is a single body of legislation. There is an almost complete consensus of opinion on the democratic and parliamentary principles according to which the country should be governed. A further uniting factor is that there is one generally accepted national language, standard Dutch. The architecture and the landscape also have an unmistakable character of their own, which becomes apparent as you enter the country from Belgium or Germany. You know immediately that you are in another country. And you know it not because of the empty customs hut you have just passed, a throwback to the time before the internal borders of the European Union were abolished. You can see it from the fields and the roads, the way in which the towns and villages are located in the surrounding countryside, from the behaviour of the car drivers and from the design and even the tone of the advertising billboards.

AN EXAMPLE TO CONTEMPORARY GENERATIONS

This Netherlands is in many respects a product of the nineteenth century. The standardization we see flashing past as we look through the car window has its roots in major nineteenth century inventions like the fly press, cheap paper, the railways, tarmacadam, education for the masses, the telegraph, the telephone, a daily postal service – in short, all forms of mass production. Nineteenth century ideologists, as it were, invented the Dutch 'character' and possessed the technical means to ensure that it became widespread. They provided the country with a history stretching back for two thousand years, including a whole era – the 'Golden Age' of the 17th century – that could serve as an example to contemporary generations. This was the century of Rembrandt and Spinoza, of voyages of discovery and of trading expeditions throughout the world, of heroism and of economic expansion, when Amsterdam was the financial centre of the western world (more than Wall Street would ever be) and when merchants from the west of the country largely controlled European trade. This past was indeed a source of inspiration, because the first seventy years of the nineteenth century were very difficult for the Netherlands. Together with Portugal and Ireland, it was among the most backward areas in Europe. The country was one big poorhouse and Amsterdam, the once so flourishing centre of world trade, now had a reputation across Europe as a paradise for cheap sex. Only a hundred thousand of the three million inhabitants of the country had a standard of living that would have been considered even minimally acceptable today and the average life expectancy was about thirty.

This deplorable situation came to an end suddenly and in spectacular fashion. The way in which it happened is closely connected with many of the idiosyncrasies of the Netherlands of the present day. This is also true, however, of the period that preceded it, a century decked with gold by a down-and-out generation and of the war that came before that, a war seen – entirely in the spirit of the previous century – as a war of national independence, yes, even a struggle between good and evil, between God and Satan.

The fact that Carel Nolet does not buy a Daimler is related to this whole complex of factors.

The idea of the Netherlands as an entity in itself is only a couple of hundred years old and has never been very strong. The growth of France, Germany and England into 'great' European nations went hand-in-hand with the development of strong, deeply-entrenched royal families. In the delta where the Rhine, Maas and Scheldt reach the sea – the area now covered by the Netherlands and Belgium – there was no single uniting monarchy and this gave local rulers greater room for manœuvre. The area was divided into a large number of counties and duchies which were to all intents and purposes independent. Although they were officially subject to the Holy Roman Emperor or the King of France, in practice they were hardly answerable to these higher authorities at all. Most present-day provinces have their origins in these small states and their borders are still often recognizable.

They were feudal states. Social relations were based on personal dependence, where the weak pledged their loyalty to the strong in exchange for protection and other privileges. These relations became increasingly hereditary in nature and could become incredibly complicated, not least because the counts and dukes – the 'great nobles' – seldom possessed the military power to actually enforce loyalty. They therefore found themselves increasingly forced to buy off their positions by granting new privileges to their subjects.

This situation became even more acute with the emergence of a new class of merchants, whose only aim was to accumulate money, something which the nobles, traditional landowners with a loathing for business, were chronically short of. At the estuaries of the Rhine, Scheldt and Maas – three arteries for transport and communications – trade flourished naturally. Anywhere where the minimum requirements for a safe existence could be guaranteed, settlements grew up of the kind that, these days, we would call 'towns'. Shortage of money and the pursuit of power forced the nobles to grant these settlements all kinds of rights, to the extent of allowing them a certain degree of self-rule in exchange for their loyalty or their cash. The oldest document in which the name Amsterdam appears, contains a privilege granted by Floris v, the Count of Holland, in 1275. He exempted the inhabitants of the city from paying tolls within his area of jurisdiction, undoubtedly with the ulterior motive of wooing them away from his competitors, the Lords of Aemstel.

From the 12th and 13th centuries on, many new settlements were granted charters. These were a complex of freedoms and privileges which practically amounted to self-rule, eroding even further the authority of the nobility. It is tempting to see this development as an early form of democracy, as a whole array of 'historical' ideologies later did with great enthusiasm, but this is a misconception. In the final analysis, it was a very complex system of special privileges and – even though the documents concerned referred to a specific region, village or castle – agreements between families. In the cities, too, power was concentrated in the hands of a small number of families. With a few exceptions, the members of the councils and other ruling bodies were recruited from this élite class. This did provide, however, a system of checks and balances. Things only went right if they attempted to reach some form of consensus.

Eventually, all the counties and duchies came into the hands of the Habsburgs, the family that also wore the crown of the Holy Roman Empire. It was a complicated process that took more than a century of strategic marriages and inheritances, which often had to be claimed by force of arms. The upshot was that by 1540, the area around the estuaries of the Maas, Rhine and Scheldt had a single sovereign lord, the emperor Charles v, who referred to these possessions as the lowlands or Netherlands. He, too, had inherited the whole complex of rights and privileges, which in effect restricted his power to the extent that here he reaped small benefit from his position as the most powerful ruler in Europe.

Charles v attempted to impose order and unity on this chaotic situation. He appointed a regent for the whole region, who resided in Brussels. He also appointed in each county or duchy a lieutenant or Stadholder, who was authorized to use the royal seal and who – with lines of communication being so slow and difficult – enjoyed considerable freedom to make his own decisions. Generally speaking, the emperor chose important nobles for these positions who had a personal connection with the region. One of these was William of Nassau-Dillenburg, Prince of Orange, who had grown up at court in Brussels. He was chosen because his family owned large estates in the Duchy of Brabant, of which Brussels was the capital at that time.

Anyone studying the European history of the sixteenth and seventeenth centuries will come across countless disputes between centralized monarchs and subjects claiming rights dating back to the Middle Ages. Generally speaking, the monarchs won these disputes. France and Spain are the most striking examples of such victories. In the Netherlands, however, the reverse happened. The outcome of what the Dutch proudly refer to as the 'Eighty-Years' War' (1568–1648) was that these medieval rights and privileges continued to be the basis of their polity.

After Charles v had abdicated, the Netherlands passed into the hands of his son Philip, better known as Philip ii of Spain. The Spanish crown had succeeded in depriving most of its subjects of their *fueros*, their privileges. Philip ii, a consistent man, instigated a similar process in the Netherlands. He also attacked Protestantism with far greater vigour than his father, enforcing a long-existent law under which the practice of religious beliefs other than Roman Catholicism (heresy) was punishable with death by fire.

In the Netherlands there was a certain amount of sympathy for the reformist tendencies in the church that were springing up throughout Europe after Luther's protest in 1517. Not that there was any real schism to speak of, but the new ways of thinking were finding support in leading circles in the city and in the countryside, and even within the church itself. It was a little like the 1960s when, without actually being a communist yourself, you could summon up a certain appreciation for 'Uncle Ho', Chairman Mao and Che Guevara.

Erasmus, the internationally renowned thinker, was in some ways a typical example of this tendency. For many years, people did not know whether he should be considered a reformer or a trusty catholic. These élites therefore tended not to make too great an effort to persecute genuine Protestants, travelling preachers and manifest heretics, in spite of pressure to do from far-off Spain. This even applied to the followers of John Calvin.

CALVINISTS WERE SUBJECT TO A STRICT CODE OF BEHAVIOUR

Most of them live in the country, but anyone who is sufficiently acquainted with them, can recognize them in the larger towns and cities, too. They are the followers of the 'black-stocking' church. On Sundaymornings, you can see whole families hurrying along the street, the women in long dresses with their heads covered, the men in overwhelmingly dark suits, with perhaps a slightly more cheerful grey here and there. The traditional black stockings may have been replaced by slightly more colourful designs, but the general feeling is one of humility and a sense of guilt.

They are on their way to the first of the two hour-long church services they always attend on this, the Lord's Day. There they sing His praises in long drawn-out tones, but the focal point of the service is the sermon. The minister rebukes them all without mercy, his talent for oration, the fruits of centuries of development, reducing him to tears. 'Let but one be saved!' the preacher calls out in desperation, for their God is above all a wrathful judge who ruthlessly separates the chosen from the great mass of sinners who shall be cast into the fires of hell.

The believers listen with fear in their hearts as the minister preaches hell and damnation. Occasionally one of the congregation feels that he has been touched by the finger of God and knows that he shall be saved. But this happens very rarely and most live out their lives in terrible uncertainty.

They avoid all that 'conforms to the world', since this surely leads to eternal damnation. By this they mean all that gives life its colour – fashionable clothing, going out, films and – although this is shunned to a lesser extent these days – the television. Right up to the 1950s, the inhabitants of St. Philipsland, an isolated community in Zeeland, believed – on the basis of the Bible – a mains water supply to be too worldly. A number of 'black-stocking' communities still forbid inoculation against sickness, since this is against God's will. This strict faith has as many as six hundred thousand followers in the Netherlands, largely concentrated in a wide band stretching from Zeeland in the southwest to Overijssel in the northeast, where they sometimes impress their heavy stamp on entire rural communities. They consider themselves the true descendants of Calvin. They believe that, unlike the large Protestant communities, they have not prostituted his legacy to the world and its sinful temptations.

Johannes Calvijn

Next to Martin Luther, Calvin was the most influential reformer in the history of Christendom. Not only for his theological teaching but for the new form of organization he developed for the church. His spirit and his beliefs had far-reaching effects in the Netherlands.

Man, said Calvin, is by nature bad. Through the mercy of God alone can a chosen few be saved. But this is not a reward for their merits. Calvin believed that God determined in advance which fortunates would inherit the kingdom of heaven and who would be cast down into hell.

And yet, each of us is responsible for his own fate and his relationship with the Almighty. All of this is laid down in the Bible, the only source of knowledge of the divine.

This led to a strict code of beliefs and behaviour which left no room for Catholic pomp and circumstance and certainly not for the frivolity of Rome. Calvinists had to lead their lives according to this code. Most of life's small pleasures, such as playing cards or dice, dancing or going to the theatre were seen as cardinal sins. And, in imitation of the Sabbath of the Orthodox Jews, Sunday was a day of complete rest.

Diligence and the exercise of one's duty, on the other hand, were virtues, as were simplicity in clothing and behaviour. Most Protestant churches in the

Netherlands consider themselves Calvinist, but it is only the smaller and more radical communities that still embrace it in its purest form. Calvin designed a model for the church in which preachers were appointed by elected church councils of true Calvinists. These councils were empowered to place all of the members of the church under their supervision. This meant that they could impose a wide variety of punishments on those who did not adhere to the code of behaviour or who held deviant opinions. It was a typical model of leadership by a disciplined vanguard and bore close resemblance to the organization devised three centuries later by Lenin to bring about the victory of Bolshevism. And it was a perfect breeding ground for conspiracies.

After all, Calvin intended that, organized in this way, the church should exercise a kind of supervision over worldly governments, whose sole guideline should also be the word of God. His ideal was identical to the situation in present-day Iran, where the Shiite mullahs have considerable power over their political rulers.

The effectiveness of this form of organization became clear when events became far too complex and began to move too fast for a simple book such as this. In outline what happened was that in 1566 – a year of crisis and famine – the dissatisfied populace, led by Calvinists, began to destroy the interiors of churches because the statues of the saints were considered a form of idolatry. In response to this unrest, which was particularly fierce in Flanders, Philip II appointed a new regent in Brussels, the Duke of Alva. Alva is still considered one of the great villains of Dutch history. During the German occupation, many made the comparison – and not without reason – to Adolf Hitler. He arrived with an army of occupation, introduced a special court for religious offences and forced the local elites – who had petitioned the king to be tolerant – to make a clear choice, for or against. Just to show he meant business, he had two prominent figures who had signed the petition beheaded. A third, William of Orange, escaped to Germany just in time.

AND DRIVE THE PLAGUE THAT TRY US AND TYRANNY AWAY

Alva the Tyrant's foulest deed, however, was the 'tenth penny' tax on commercial transactions, which he imposed on the orders of Philip II. The tax ignored all existing rights and privileges and is better remembered by later generations than Alva's religious persecution. There is another Dutch expression that expresses this indignation: *pijn doen in iemands portemonnee*, to hurt someone through their purse. Intervention of this kind invokes great emotions among the Dutch.

The Calvinist vanguard now came into its own, part of it transforming itself into a guerilla movement with little difficulty. They were known as the *'geuzen'*. *'Geus'* is a bastardization of the French word *'gueux'*, meaning beggar. This was a reference to those who had signed the petition asking for tolerance. There were *'Bosgeuzen'*, who operated from the safety of the forests, and *'Watergeuzen'* who attacked from the sea. William of Orange and his brothers used their wealth to assemble armies of mercenaries which they used to make unsuccessful attacks against Alva's troops. It was finally the *Watergeuzen* who gained a foothold in a number of towns in the County of Holland from 1572 onwards. This led to a series of disconnected revolts throughout the Netherlands which were not initially directed against Philip II but against his unjust servants. William of Orange more or less declared himself leader of the whole movement. Around this time, an anonymous bard wrote the battle hymn *'Wilhelmus'* which, in 15 verses, encapsulates the ideology of the revolt. It is now the official national anthem of the Netherlands and every Dutch man, woman and child knows the first few lines:

'Wilhelmus van Nassauwe ben ik van Duitsen bloed
den vaderlande getrouwe, blijf ik tot in den dood.
Een prince van Oranje, ben ik vrij onverveerd,
de koning van Hispanje heb ik altijd geëerd.'

'William of Nassau, scion of a Dutch and ancient line,
I dedicate undying faith
to this land of mine
A prince I am, undaunted, of Orange, ever free,
To the King of Spain I've granted a lifelong loyalty.'

The part about the king is sung out in long, sustained tones and is little understood by current generations. This is, however, not true of the sixth verse, the only part of the rest of the anthem with which many people are familiar:

'Mijn schild ende betrouwen

zijt gij, o God, mijn heer,
op U, zo wil ik bouwen,
verlaat mij nimmermeer.
Op dat ik vroom mag blijven,
Uw dienaar, t' aller tijd,
De tyrannie verdrijven,
die mij het hart doorwondt.'

'A shield and my reliance,
O God, thou ever wert.
I'll trust unto Thy guidance
O leave me not ungirt.
That I may stay a pious
Servant of Thine for aye
And drive the plagues that try us
And tyranny away.'

These two verses contain three crucial elements: the central role of William of Orange as the leader of the movement, the appeal to God for help and the desire to drive out tyranny.

The people of the Netherlands still use these diverse elements of the revolt as a basis for their own ideologies. *Het Parool*, a social democratic newspaper with its roots in the resistance to the Nazi occupation, carries the words *'vrij, onverveerd'* – undaunted, ever free – under its header. *De Rotterdammer*, a defunct Calvinist daily, appeared under the motto *'Mijn schild ende betrouwen zijt gij, o God, mijn heer'* – A shield and my reliance, O God, thou ever wert. And the success enjoyed by movements such as Amnesty International in the Netherlands, the large numbers of people that take to the streets to demonstrate against military dictators like Augusto Pinochet, clearly illustrate that for many people 'driving tyranny away' is a serious business.

Revolt always leads to radicalization. If the opposing party then becomes more acceptable to the more moderate elements by adopting a conciliatory approach, a new situation arises. Philip II created such a situation through a rather clever combination of violence and concessions. In 1579, those provinces which still refused to be reconciled signed the Union of Utrecht in the city of that name. Two years later, they solemnly released themselves from their Oath of Allegiance to their king. They based this act on a revolutionary ideology – that monarchs did not receive their authority from God, but from a contract with the lower levels of government, who were entitled to displace the sovereign if he (or she) should resort to tyranny.

The signatories to the Union of Utrecht repudiated Philip ii. It would also have been logical to abolish the office of stadholder, the king's representative in each of the provinces, but this did not occur. After all, William of Orange, the unofficial leader of the revolt was a stadholder. The office remained intact until the end of the Republic in 1795. And the position was always filled by a member of the family of Orange, so that it gradually acquired the characteris- tics of a monarchy. In practice, sons succeeded their fathers, although there were occasional long periods during which the Province of Holland had no stadholder because many regents were afraid of the power of Orange. The family also enjoyed considerable support among the common people who, in their turn, saw the successors of William the liberator as their protectors against the urban patricians who sat on the Council.

Philip ii wrongly saw William of Orange as the evil genius behind all this. He declared the prince an outlaw and then sent terrorists after him. In 1584, they succeeded. The prince was the first of a long line of politicians through-out the world to die by the gun. The bullet hole in the wall can still be seen in Delft. The Union of Utrecht, an alliance between a number of former counties and duchies, lasted until 1795.

As time passed it began to function as a kind of constitution, eventually forming the administrative foundation of the 'Republic of the United Provinces', as the country was known in the seventeenth and eighteenth centuries. It was, however, a rather unstable foundation, based as it was on the preservation of rights, privileges and exceptional provisions that dated back to the Middle Ages. Right up to the 1960s, first-year history students were driven to distraction by a compulsory examination on the Union of Utrecht, in which the exceptions completely outnumbered the rules.

The same was true of the constitutions of the individual provinces, whose extremely complex structure more or less gave them the form of feudal states. And, to complicate the situation even more, they also acquired territories that were subject to their authority. There was no central rule to speak of. The provincial governments, known as States, sent representatives to The Hague, where they formed what was known as the States General. But they were only able to take decisions on which there was unanimous agreement. All in all, the Republic consisted of hundreds of small territories, each with its own area of jurisdiction.

IN A SYSTEM OF THIS KIND, THERE WAS LITTLE TO BE ACHIEVED BY *HAUTEUR*

In a system of this kind – if it can even be described as a system – there was little to be achieved by *hauteur*. It was better to adopt a cautious, conciliatory approach accompanied by a discreet shake of the purse when required. The fact that this actually resulted in cooperation was related to two factors: firstly, the existence of a common enemy (there was usually one of some kind) and secondly that, in spite of the king's authority being repudiated, the system of stadholders had been maintained. The position was always held by a member of the family of Orange, who successfully managed to increase their power from generation to generation. To achieve this, however, they had to strike up alliances, since they were never able to break down the complex structures of authority. It was also to their advantage that Orange could generally count on the support of the mass of the people. If necessary, they would not hesitate to use the threat of popular uprising as a political factor. The popularity of the royal family today has its roots in this tradition.

Yet none of this provided sufficient cohesion to prevent the eventual disintegration of the Republic. There was a third factor – the Province of Holland. Holland was by far the richest of the seven provinces and bore a good seventy per cent of the joint costs of the Republic. This gave it a dominant voice in affairs of state.

The radical Calvinists had succeeded in setting the tone of the revolt. But as the situation stabilized more and more on the side of the Union of Utrecht, they began to lose their grip on the local élites. As with their grandparents in the time of Charles v and Philip ii, the members of the élite largely agreed with Calvin's views but many of them were not prepared to subject themselves to his theocratic model, to allow their lives to be run at a distance by the church councils and the strict preachers, who denounced them as 'libertines'. The Calvinist preachers were unable to achieve the 'mullah-like' power they sought and the administrative élite continued in practice to be libertines. They gradually acquired a dominant influence on the church and ultimately relegated the stricter preachers to the sidelines.

In any case, it would not have been feasible to impose an inflexible orthodoxy, with all its consequences, on a chaotic republic where the only way to achieve anything was by compromise and a genuine respect for the other party. The decentralization, which was sometimes pushed to the point of total absurdity, did demand a tolerant attitude. Anyone who refused to accept this was soon marginalized. Conspicuous characters achieved little in such a system.

Those who did not know how to bend the countless rules and regulations to suit the demands of the immediate situation also achieved very little. This led to the development of a flexible administrative structure that did not bother itself with grand ideas, but focused on the search for practical solutions to the problems of the moment. In all of this, the Province of Holland took the lead. This was because power was concentrated in the hands of the urban élites, who had built their wealth on fisheries, trade and, to a lesser extent, industry. Today, Rotterdam is the largest port in the world. This is not because the Netherlands has such a large volume of imports and exports, but because it is perfectly situated at the mouth of the Rhine to distribute goods to and from the rest of the continent. The Province of Holland – and Amsterdam in particular – played a similar role in the seventeenth century. It was a European distribution centre, not only for bulk goods like timber, grain, fish, sugar and tobacco, but also for luxury articles including East Indian spices, Chinese silk and muslin from India. This gave Holland the highest standard of living in the whole of Europe, a position it managed to maintain well into the eighteenth century.

The role that Amsterdam had at that time in Europe was similar to the position enjoyed by present-day Hong Kong with respect to China. It was a glittering metropolis, bulging with wealth, where the economic strings of the whole continent came together, an emporium stacked full of products from throughout the world, a city that earned a living from trade, the provision of services and the processing of raw materials. It was also a pocket of free-thinking liberalism, where a wide variety of lifestyles and principles were tolerated, for without this the city would have been unable to flourish.

The city's élites depended on trade for their wealth. To use a modern term, they had to assure for themselves the right business climate. This meant that people had to be certain of their money under all circumstances. The Amsterdam bank issued coins with a guaranteed precious metal content. There was a whole complex of laws and regulations which, as far as was possible given the constraints of the period – protected businessmen against fraud. Crimes of violence, theft, robbery and other offences against property were subject to draconic punishments, although the chances of being caught were relatively small. Property was sacred and inviolable.

On the other hand, the city's government showed great tolerance, particularly where it might promote prosperity. The rapidly growing province of Holland attracted large numbers of immigrants from throughout Europe. As long as they brought money with them, they were welcome. At the beginning of the seventeenth century, Portuguese Jewish merchants who had been driven from their own country had no trouble in settling in Amsterdam. They were even given a form of internal self-rule. Their synagogues are still among the most splendid buildings in the centre of the city. Destitute refugees from war-torn Germany, however, did not fare so well. The *schutterij*, a kind of citizens' militia (who were immortalized in Rembrandt's painting 'The Night Watch') would descend on them from time to time and force them out of the city or press-gang them into serving with the war fleet.

TOLERANCE BECAME SECOND NATURE

But the government in Holland interfered as little as possible with people's private lives – at least, in as much as it only affected them personally. There was a fairly large Catholic minority throughout the Republic, whose freedom of movement was limited by discriminatory regulations. This was due to the efforts of the Calvinists during the early years of the revolt. The Catholics had lost their churches and were not even permitted to practice their religious beliefs, at least not officially. As long as Catholic churches were not recognizable as such from the outside, the government generally turned a blind eye. In practice, in spite of clear legislation to the contrary, tolerance had become second nature for political leaders in the Netherlands. And just as then a Catholic church was tolerated as long as it looked like a barn or a house, small-scale entrepreneurs may sell soft drugs today, as long as the outlet looks like a coffee shop. In the same way, modern governments have tolerated organized prostitution since 1911 and, occasionally, illegal gambling.

But, as it should be, the government always has the law to fall back on.

Catholics who were too outspoken in the Golden Age found this out to their regret. As have hash dealers whose coffee machines have, in the eyes of the authorities, become a little too symbolic. There is a rule of thumb that no one in a coffee shop may have more than 30 grams of hash on their person. Anyone who causes a nuisance – there may be complaints from the neighbours, perhaps there is too much violence on the street or there are indications of dealing in hard drugs (which, in spite of all the stories to the contrary, is strictly forbidden in the Netherlands) – anyone who causes a nuisance finds themselves in serious trouble. And very easily, because tolerance also leaves room for arbitrariness and this is a very effective means of defining clear limits. It would be an exaggeration to attribute this tolerance to the libertine mentality of the urban élites. They often had little choice. As I have already said, the Republic was in reality divided into hundreds of separate regions, each with their own laws and regulations. The power of the government seldom extended more than a few kilometres. You did not have to

iedieniedienwiet   nederwiet

run far to escape the strong hand of authority. When, in the eighteenth century, a richly varied press developed, the governments proved to be no more tolerant than their counterparts in other countries. Publishers would move offices a couple of kilometres away where the authorities were less hostile to their political views. In the administrative chaos of the Republic, tolerance was the only alternative.

REGENT: TODAY THE WORD HAS NEGATIVE CONNOTATIONS

Since the seventeenth century, the word *regent*, regent, has been used in Dutch to describe these local and provincial administrators, who were so concerned with compromise. Today, the word has negative connotations. If a contemporary politician is described as a 'regent', it is a permanent slur on his record and an obstacle to his further political career. A common definition is: 'a regent is someone who thinks that the people do not know what is good for them. The regent knows better'.

This is a direct reference to the Republic of the United Provinces. In the account given above, I deliberately avoided use of the word 'democracy'. The system I have described had little to do with democracy. Administrators were appointed overwhelmingly by co-optation. Those on the councils filled vacancies from their own ranks. This ensured that political power remained essentially concentrated in the hands of a small number of leading families. To the outside world, these regents were the *hoogmogende heren*, their 'high and mightinesses', their official title. They always acted jointly, expressing their power collectively. This not only gave an impression of power being imposed from above, but also that it was being exercised by a single entity. Michiel de Ruyter, the admiral of the fleet and the bearer of many foreign titles and distinctions, was permitted to sit while reporting to the *hoogmogende heren* rather than stand. This was considered a greater honour than the title of duke, bestowed upon him by a foreign admirer of royal blood.

As a group the regents gave an impression of great arrogance, but they could not allow themselves to stand out too much as individuals because to do so would endanger the good relations and the culture of compromise in the group. Overly ambitious regents, particularly those who did not try to hide their intentions, were promptly put in their places by their fellows.

We can see the result of this system if we look at the many portraits of regents hanging in the country's museums. They appear self-confident, but not threatening. They are well-dressed, but not conspicuously so. The paraphernalia is modest. Here, too, the order of the day is *doe gewoon, dan doe je gek genoeg*. Yet the paintings also capture the aura of excellence that surround these high and mighty gentlemen; they feel that they are better than the rest of humanity. They are in control, they know the rules of the game as no other. They have earned the right to take themselves seriously and they clearly do just that. They may be humble, but they are the *hoogmogende heren*. And it is wise not to forget that.

The regents' houses have the same aura. They are always imposing buildings with three of four storeys, but they stand neatly in line alongside the canals of the city. This gives them a certain feeling of equality. Great attention has been devoted to the façades. There are steps up to the front door and decoration on the walls. But it would be wrong to call them ornate. Even in the bend of the Herengracht in Amsterdam, roughly between the Leidsestraat and Wolvestraat, which was the richest part of the whole country until deep into the nineteenth century, there is no extravagance. The regents had houses, not palaces, even though they were often financially better off than the average European noble, who would commission a 'Versailles' all of his own. The German scholar Max Weber, one of the founding fathers of sociology, linked all this to Protestantism. In his *'Die protestantische Ethik und der Geist des Kapitalismus'*, The Protestant Ethic and the Spirit of Capitalism, he explained how the cult of simplicity preached by Calvin not only created the mentality to invest in new and profitable activities but also the money, which was saved [39] rather than squandered on 'wine, women and song' and other examples of Roman Catholic frivolity – such as buying a Daimler. It is an attractive theory, especially for self-aware Calvinists, although it has lost some of its power over the course of time. But Weber's vision – if it is not adopted exclusively and fanatically – continues to be illuminating. The Protestant ideal of self-control was certainly very suited to the calm consultation, the unflappable manner, the cautious step-by-step approach that was required to obtain a share of power in the Republic.

IN TIME THIS ATTITUDE DEVELOPED INTO A KIND OF GENTILITY

In time this attitude, as adopted by the members of the élite, developed into a kind of gentility. The word itself summons up not only good breeding and respectability but the affectedness that can accompany it. It is very close to what is called in Dutch *'uit de hoogte'*, roughly the equivalent of the English word 'snooty'. It is possible to identify people with a 'snooty' accent. It usually goes together with certain formal gestures, a controlled manner of speaking and expensive-looking, but never flamboyant, clothes which are in no way the height of fashion – more probably they are hopelessly outdated.

This gentility concealed much social decay and corruption, which manifested itself only when, in the eighteenth century, the Republic went through a period of economic stagnation and began to fall behind later economic starters elsewhere on the continent, sharing a similar fate to today's England, once the motor of the industrial revolution. In the same century, the arrival of the 'patriot movement' presented a clear opposition to the regent system and, later, the stadholdership held by the family of Orange. After the storming of the Bastille in 1789, the patriot movement identified closely with the ideals of the French Revolution. When French troops occupied the Republic in 1795, the patriots took power and the stadholder, William v of Orange, fled to England.

The eighteen years that the Netherlands was under French influence, initially as a vassal state and later as part of Napoleon's empire, did bring about a revolution. Under the watchful eye of Paris, order was brought to the chaos of the Union of Utrecht. A single body of legislation was created – which simply entailed the wholesale adoption of Napoleon's civil and criminal codes. The confederation made way for a single state with provinces and municipalities. The state and the government acquired the basic structures they still have today. It is due to the patriots that every Dutch citizen is equal before the law. It not only put Jews and Catholics on the same footing as Calvinists, it also abolished all the old rights and privileges with one stroke of the pen.

When, in 1813, it was clear that Napoleon's days were numbered, a small group from the Hague élite decided that it would be advisable to commit a kind of *coup d'état* before Prussian or Russian troops moved in to occupy the country. They put all their cards on what they hoped was the still strong loyalty felt by the mass of the population for the House of Orange. Their true feelings about the common people are suitably expressed in one sentence from their proclamation: 'The people shall be given a day of festivity at the expense of the treasury'. In those days, this meant free drink for all. The people were not intended to take any initiative themselves. William Frederick, the son of the last stadholder, returned to the Netherlands and found himself proclaimed sovereign prince and then King of the Netherlands. For the first fifteen years, this also included what is now Belgium. The union was not successful and in 1830, the Belgians instigated a revolution of their own and cut themselves loose from the new kingdom.

William I – for this is how he has gone down in history – did not wish to return to the dark days of the old republic any more than the 'gentility' among his supporters wanted to. He preserved the system introduced by Napoleon almost intact, including the existing structure of government. In his residence in The Hague, the new king tried to surround himself with the trappings of a real monarchy, as recent dynasties are wont to do. The centre of The Hague still has a whole collection of statues of people largely forgotten by history – such as the Prince of Wied, who commanded William's army – which bear witness to this failed attempt to create a sense of grandeur. Even Noordeinde – William's palace, now used as an 'office' by Queen Beatrix – is too small and far too modest, standing as it does in a narrow street, to be an adequate symbol of the monarchy.

ORANGE CANNOT AND SHALL NOT RULE A NATION OF SLAVES

During the German occupation, the illegal newspaper *Oranje Bode* described the difference between Wilhelmina, the Dutch queen in exile in London, and Adolf Hitler. 'She is – and wants nothing other than to be – our Queen, the [41] royal mentor of an independent people. This healthy relationship between the monarch and her subjects is the source of an indestructible strength. Orange cannot and shall not rule a nation of slaves, that bows to a repressive tyrant only under protest. The German people may allow themselves to be browbeaten and oppressed, they may groan as they feel the weight of the despot's foot on their neck, but such a position does not suit the people of the Netherlands.'

The House of Orange has never derived its reputation from a spectacular Royal Court or from any other form of grand spectacle. Those that did take steps in that direction soon felt the pressure of disapproval and clearly it was not really in their blood. The message from the *Oranje Bode* – particularly what it says about the Germans – obviously has to be seen in the context in which it was written, but it does hit the nail on the head. The reputation of the Orange dynasty is based on the fact that it protects freedom. It is associated not with power but with justice. Orange stands above all other parties and guarantees the freedom of each individual to be himself.

It is not difficult to elicit praise for the Royal Family from the Dutch people. The Queen, they will assure you – and this is the highest praise possible – is a normal person. In spite of their lofty position, the royals have no pretensions. They are normal.

The real national day of celebration in the Netherlands is *Koninginnedag*, the Queen's official birthday. Beatrix was born on 31 January 1938, in the middle of winter. It was therefore decided that *Koninginnedag* should continue to be held on the previous Queen's birthday. Juliana, Beatrix's mother, was Queen from 1948 until she abdicated in 1980. Her birthday is in spring, on 30 April, when there is a better chance of good weather. This is crucial, because

Koninginnedag is celebrated out of doors. There is a carnival atmosphere, and street markets are held in many towns and villages. Amsterdam in particular celebrates on a grand scale. For this one day, anyone can sell whatever they like without a licence, and the whole city turns into one gigantic open-air market. It attracts enormous crowds, which regularly exceed a million people.

Of the celebrations organized in every community in the country, the Queen selects two which she visits personally, accompanied by her whole family. This is broadcast live on television and tops the viewing list year after year. It is, of course, fantastic publicity for any town or village that is chosen to host the royal visit, and competition is fierce. A glance at the places visited by the Queen over the past decade leaves the impression that they are frequently communities that would otherwise rarely be in the news.

The Queen arrives in the middle of a public celebration that has all the trappings of a funfair, and the whole family spontaneously joins in with the activities. The princes test their strength against the members of the local sports clubs, while the Queen speaks graciously to the children. The whole folkloristic circus leads the onlooker to conclude with surprise that the people and the Royal Family are one. Yet everything, even the 'spontaneity', is planned to the last detail. This is not to say that it is mere playacting. Everything is sincere, the entire community displays its support for the monarchy and the Royal Family feels the closeness of its ties with the people. All barriers between ruler and rules have been removed.

In spite of this, however, there is still something a little 'sacred' about each and every member of the House of Orange. Dutch Calvinists of the old school undoubtedly believe that God has made a special covenant with the people of the Netherlands, in the same way that Jehovah did with the Jews, and that the House of Orange is an expression of that pledge. This inevitably puts a distance between monarch and people and, in their presence, nothing must go wrong.

Local administrators and leaders of industry always get into an advanced state of panic if the Queen accepts an invitation for a working visit or to join in the *Koninginnedag* celebrations. They will treat Her Majesty as a normal person and, in doing so, will leave nothing to chance. And that is what makes the whole thing so special. The stories of companies that have new toilets installed just in case Her Majesty feels the call of nature during her visit are legion. Speeches and guided tours are planned in the minutest detail. Extensive instructions are drawn up to indicate who will be introduced to the Queen at what particular moment and the exact words that will be used.

This is because the encounter will be unforgettable. My mother still remembers the day that Queen Juliana looked me directly in the face – I was then a four-year-old child – as she passed in a limousine on her way to launch a new ship at a nearby shipyard. My mother and I were part of an enthusiastic crowd lining the route. *Juliaantje* – the Queen was often referred to by this affectionate name – was wearing a small black hat and she waved as she passed. Our eyes met for a moment, perhaps three seconds, but my family still speak of it now and then. My brother has now surpassed me, however. On the mantelpiece – after the television, the centrepiece of the Dutch living room – hangs a colour photograph in which he is explaining a piece of electronic research on which he is working to none other than Queen Beatrix.

All this has turned the contact between the monarch and the people into a ritual and it makes membership of the Royal Family an extraordinarily difficult task. It is the only position in the Netherlands that is not earned by merit or ambition. It is inherited – and the psychological pressure this brings must be overwhelming. Now and then, commentators may be heard to say that it is inhuman to demand such a price of any family. They are denied a normal life not only in appearance, but also in reality.

The only advantage of this extraordinary position is that the House of Orange has protected its privacy from the glare of the gossip magazines with greater success than other European royal families. Not that Dutch paparazzi have more integrity than their international colleagues, it is simply that their readers would not tolerate such malignant gossip. Anyone who speaks ill of the Royal Family is met with an effective rebuff from a massed public opinion. 'The Queen cannot defend herself' is a common response. Gossip and other forms of criticism of the Royal Family are therefore seen as cowardly attacks on defenceless people. The Queen stands above all parties and is therefore above criticism. And perhaps most Dutch people feel that an attack on the Royal Family is an attack on the society they are a part of and the 'unity in diversity' which is its main distinguishing characteristic.

Furthermore, the Queen is still seen as the protector of the weak. Simple citizens who lose their way in the maze of bureaucracy and feel that – intentionally or unintentionally – they have been badly treated, frequently threaten to write to the Queen. The royal household does not encourage this but always ensures that complaints are forwarded to the correct address. The same traditions can be heard in the Queen's annual Christmas message. Beatrix, like Juliana before her, always draws attention to the most pressing social problems – without, of course, offering any solutions since her constitutional position forbids this. Her ministers are considered responsible for everything the monarch, in her inviolable position as Head of State, says or does.

William I accepted the throne in 1813 only on the condition that a 'wise constitution' would be introduced. The new constitution created a governmental structure, based on the English system, with a *Tweede Kamer* as a 'House of Commons' and an *Eerste Kamer* for the nobility so enthusiastically created by William I from among the descendants of the leading regent families. The entire system depended on indirect elections, so that only the very rich had any influence on the government and even this extended little further than a limited share in decision-making. William I had in effect almost unlimited power, but he exercised it with care, showing reasonable respect for what we would today call human rights.

His kingdom was in a state of crisis. The French revolutionary wars had destroyed the foundations of the outdated economy and the Netherlands had become one of the poorest and most backward countries in Europe, almost on a level with Ireland. The old money was still there, but it was often invested abroad. William I, familiar with the industrial revolution that had swept England, tried to introduce modernization here and there but it did not really take hold. He called in experts from England to introduce technological change in very much the same way that 'development workers' do today in the Third World. And largely with just as little success. Modern historians estimate that, in 1850, only 4 per cent of all machinery in the Netherlands was powered by steam. In England, this had long been around 50 per cent.

The élites were happy with the status quo. It was only after William had long gone to join his forefathers that they were confronted en masse with the backwardness of their country. The cause of this was Thomas Cook, founder of the famous travel agency.

THEY WERE SHOCKED, AND THEY WERE EMBARRASSED

In 1851, Cook organized group trips to Crystal Palace in London, where the first World Exhibition was being held. It was the Dutch élite's first acquaintance with organized tourism and they were unable to resist the temptation. A large number of them therefore made the trip to Crystal Palace, the temple of steam power, of miracles and progress. The Dutch stand, with its traditional trades and products, was a pale contrast to all the latest technical achievements they saw around them. They were shocked, and they were embarrassed. Those who had not gone to London were able to read all about the exhibition in detailed series of reports in the *Algemeen Handelsblad*, the largest liberal newspaper of the time, whose tradition survives today in the quality daily NRC *Handelsblad*.

They observed, for example, that, whereas the British presented their products as 'new' or 'improved', Dutch companies preferred mottos like 'tried and trusted'.

[45]

In 1851, the Netherlands had a progressive liberal government. The most outspoken advocate of liberal ideology was Leiden professor Johan Rudolf Thorbecke. His theories provided the foundation of the new constitution drawn up in 1848 and 1849 when King William II, alarmed by the revolutions in Naples and Paris and a small number of demonstrations at home, was – in his own words – 'converted from a conservative to a liberal overnight'. The new constitution preserved the monarchy, but also established the inviolability of the king. All responsibility for government rested on the shoulders of the ministers, who were accountable to a parliament where the *Tweede Kamer* was directly elected. Not by the 'people', but by men who paid a specified minimum of taxes. In practice this was the richest one hundred thousand in a country with a population of approximately three million. It was no democracy. It was a kind of oligarchy, but it was a first step on the road to universal suffrage. Thorbecke himself did not exclude the possibility that suffrage would be extended in time.

Shocked by what they had seen in London, the élites began to work on modernization of the infrastructure, the basis for which had already been laid by William I. In the twenty years following 1848, the country acquired a complex network of railways. New canals were dug, legislation was updated and telegraph poles sprung up across the country. An efficient and fast postal system was set up, complete with postage stamps. Mass education, introduced during the French occupation, expanded enormously. The tax on newspapers and periodicals, introduced to ensure that political comment remained the prerogative of those with money, was abolished. The country became one of the last in Europe to abolish corporal punishment and simultaneously the first to do away with capital punishment. The guiding principle of the government's economic policy was – and has remained – free trade, and as much of it as possible.

This was all possible because, even though poverty was widespread, the state itself was reasonably wealthy. The colony of the Dutch East Indies was organized such that it made a healthy profit, which was transferred to the treasury in The Hague every year. It prepared the country for its own industrial revolution, which started about 1870. During the last thirty years of the last century the country went through a period of phenomenal economic growth, very similar to that currently being experienced by the 'tigers' of South East Asia. This was also partly due to a favourable wind blowing in from the east. After achieving German unity in 1871, Bismarck, the Iron Chancellor, was pursuing an active industrialization policy which was also having beneficial effects on the Dutch economy. Its location on the mouth of the Rhine made the Netherlands Germany's main gateway to the outside world, and particularly for the industrial region along the Ruhr. Since then, Germany has been by far the Netherlands' largest trading partner and it is often said now that the government in The Hague and the Dutch central bank can do little more than meekly follow the policy of their neighbours to the east.

Accustomed to two centuries of stagnation, the major cities – The Hague, Rotterdam, Amsterdam and Utrecht – saw their population increase fivefold in a period of twenty-five years. The population of the entire country grew phenomenally, but the economy grew even faster. The general state of public health – around 1870 the average age was still about thirty – improved quickly. This was due not so much to better medical care, but to improved sanitation as a result of new mains water supplies and sewers. Almost all children now had the opportunity to at least attend primary school, where they learned to read, write and do arithmetic. Without the crippling taxes, daily and weekly newspapers became accessible to the mass of the people. Papers aimed at this new market thrived alongside élite newspapers like the *Algemeen Handelsblad*. Among these was *De Echo*, famed for its exciting stories, published in a series of separate episodes. There were also hundreds of local papers which – primitive and fragmentary as they would appear to us today – brought the world into people's homes.

And in the cities, the steam engines pounded away, the chimneys belched smoke, the machines rattled and the riveting hammers battered away.

In 1879 a new weekly newspaper appeared in Amsterdam. It was called *Recht voor Allen*, 'Justice for All', and it was published by a Lutheran preacher who had lost his faith in God, Ferdinand Domela Nieuwenhuis. In the same year another preacher, whose faith had been re-kindled with a vengeance, founded the first modern political party in the Netherlands. The preacher's name was Abraham Kuyper and he called his creation the *Anti-Revolutionaire Partij*. The whole socialist movement in the Netherlands – from the most moderate to the most radical – considers Domela Nieuwenhuis as its founder. Abraham Kuyper was what we might today call a fundamentalist.

[47]

Like most people living in the Netherlands at the time, Kuyper had to survive during a period of sweeping social change, when many fled the growing unemployment in their villages to seek what work they could find and live in squalid little rooms in a large, anonymous city. There they would read papers like the *Geïllustreerd Politienieuws*, with its exaggerated tales of crime and decadence – accompanied by the goriest of illustrations – which would destroy any sense of security they might have retained. In the big city, God and his commandments no longer had a secure footing; traditional guidelines for behaviour no longer seemed to work, or at least were certainly not applied by the rich and successful, who would pass you by on their way to the stock exchange or a fancy restaurant, or stroll by with a beautiful fiancée on their arm dressed in the height of fashion. From a small world, you had been thrown into a very large one. And that makes you feel insecure.

SOVEREIGNTY IN ONE'S OWN DOMAIN

Kuyper knew instinctively where that security was to be found – in the Bible, in the words of Calvin. Old as they were, Kuyper felt that they still provided the answers. It was not this orthodox belief that made Kuyper's thought new, it was his ability to combine it seamlessly with the new technology born of modernization and the industrial revolution. Kuyper placed his simple, straightforward faith at the centre of the modern age. It provided a solid basis which allowed people to function in these unsettled times. He had a daily newspaper and a weekly magazine which he used to distribute his views among the people. He took advantage of the rail network and the daily postal service to set up mass organizations across the country. He founded the Free

University to further education with the blessing of God. Kuyper was, in all senses, a modern man and a child of the nineteenth century.

AN EXTREMELY WIDE CHOICE OF SCHOOLS

Anyone who is looking for a school for their children will still be confronted with Kuyper's life's work. A glance in the telephone directory will show you just how much choice there is. In addition to the schools run by the state or the local authority, there is a whole range of others, the majority of which prove to have a religious background of some sort. And this is just as true of small rural communities as of the big cities. Until a few years ago, most publicly-run schools promoted themselves with the motto: 'Altogether to the public school'. In practice, however – as the telephone directory proves – the exact opposite is often true. Protestant, Catholic and, these days, a small number of Islamic or Hindu schools are not privately run. They are entirely funded by the state. They must comply with government quality standards and receive regular visits from the Education Inspectorate. But they are free to choose their own spiritual direction, or rather this is decided by the school board, known in official texts as the 'competent authority'. Parents in the Netherlands may therefore choose a school which reflects their own beliefs. If they have no strong religious convictions, or if they wish their children to grow up with friends from all kinds of backgrounds, they can send them to the state or municipal school, which has no religious basis. The law contains a whole range of provisions to ensure that the ministry of education does not give preferential treatment to these public schools. If anything, they guarantee the contrary. The heads of schools in the public sector frequently complain that they have less elbow room than their colleagues at the 'religious' schools.

Parents who cannot find a school that suits their religious tastes are free to set one up themselves. The law specifies all kinds of quantitative requirements that have to be met and the lessons must be given by qualified teachers. If these requirements – which are not overly strict – are complied with, the government is bound to provide the funds for the new school. And that is exactly what Abraham Kuyper had in mind.

As a Calvinist, Kuyper was condemned to constant opposition to the liberal state, dominated as it was by a free-thinking élite. He accused them of imposing an a-religious neutrality on the population. Their main instrument was an increasingly mass-oriented system of education which, as the law demanded, brought children up to believe in 'generally accepted Christian and social virtues'. As an alternative to this, Kuyper presented his political ideology of 'sovereignty in one's own domain'. Education was emphatically and primarily the responsibility of one's own immediate circle. Parents should be given the opportunity to set up schools in which they would determine the nature of the education to be given, but which would be funded by the government. His Calvinist Anti-Revolutionaire Partij, named to express its resistance to consequences of the French Revolution, adopted this as the centrepiece of its political programme. But Kuyper's teaching went further. Sovereignty in one's own domain meant not only the church, education and politics, but a whole range of social relations, such as trade organizations, interest groups and cultural and recreational societies.

Kuyper directed himself not so much at the élite as at the social groups below them. He called them the *'Kleyne Luyden'*, the 'little people', a term from the Eighty-Years' War. Much of his inspiration was drawn from this period, when the struggle against the Spanish produced much revolutionary rhetoric. To achieve his goals, Kuyper needed the votes of the *kleyne luyden*. He therefore actively promoted extension of the right to vote. This set in motion a process which in 1922 resulted in universal suffrage for men and women. Only then could the Netherlands rightly call itself a democracy.

Abraham Kuyper's teaching proved to be a suitable model for the Catholics – then about 30 per cent of the population – who replaced their converted barns with proud neo-Gothic cathedrals but who still – rightly – frequently felt themselves to be second-class citizens. In the final quarter of the nineteenth century and the first ten years of the twentieth, they set up a similar network of political, religious and social organizations – but then with a relatively strict Catholicism as the guiding principle. They found their own Kuyper in the person of politician-journalist-priest Hermanus Schaepman. In the *Tweede Kamer*, the Calvinists and the Catholics formed a tactical alliance which was primarily intended to achieve their common educational objectives. They were successful in 1917.

This was all essentially an offensive against the forces of revolution, with the liberals as the main victims. A rowdy socialist movement grew up around *Recht voor Allen* and Domela Nieuwenhuis, which may have caused much fear and consternation but, in the beginning, could in no way equal the organizational talent of the Protestants and the Catholics. It was not until lawyer-poet Pieter Jelles Troelstra set up the *Sociaaldemocratische Arbeiderspartij* (SDAP), based on reformist ideals, that the movement achieved any real form of genuine organization. The socialists rather grudgingly gave in to this growing tradition and formed their own network of similar organizations. They kept their distance, however, from education, although plans were made to set up schools based on social-democratic principles. Circumstances forced them, too, to adopt 'sovereignty in their own domain'. Once democracy finally arrived, there was little left over for the liberals than just under ten per cent of the electorate.

In 1901, the Catholic–Calvinist alliance won the elections. Abraham Kuyper formed a cabinet which he led with a firm hand, so firm in fact that he can be considered the first modern prime minister of the Netherlands. Since then, with an occasional short intermezzo, Christian parties have been dominant in successive Dutch governments. They were exiled to the opposition bench for the first time in 1994.

GREAT TOLERANCE FOR OTHER WAYS OF THINKING

Sovereignty in one's own domain is connected in a certain way to the old divisions of the Republic, which forced the regents to develop their culture of compromise. There were various 'domains', particularly within the Protestant part of the population, where the different versions of orthodoxy led to division.

Abraham Kuyper thought that the Dutch Reformed Church was too tolerant of different beliefs and forced a schism that has not yet been healed. None of these groups held the upper hand and their leaders were forced to seek common interests and forge compromises to enable coalitions to be formed. Sovereignty in one's domain therefore demanded great tolerance for other ways of thinking. Dissenters may have got hold of the wrong end of the stick, but they had the right to organize within their own group in any way they wished. Generally speaking, the leaders of these groups tried to emphasize their differences among their respective members, but in government, they worked together closely. This included cooperating with the liberals and, later, with the social democrats. The whole system rested on a network of local Kuypers, Schaepmans and Troelstras who played crucial roles in the development of their own particular town or region and who – along with national leaders – frequently had streets named after them. Where the founders, the forerunners of these movements were visionaries, their successors were often businesslike administrators, who rarely sought the front of the stage and who, in their attitudes and their way of government, continued the tradition of the old regents. If this were not the case, they could not have functioned as they did.

DUTCH SOCIETY RESTS ON A NUMBER OF SEPARATE ´PILLARS´

Political scientist Arend Lijphart, who was a professor at Leiden University, made the study of this system his life's work. He gave us the word which has come to describe this system: *verzuiling*, 'pillarization'. The symbolism is clear – Dutch society rests on a number of separate 'pillars'.

The word 'pillarization' has taken on negative connotations in current debates on the nature of Dutch society. It implies a segmented community, where large groups of the population allow themselves to be manipulated by front men who, by virtue of their strategic positions in a number of important networks, hold the real power in their hands. It also has a little to do with spiritual repression. The 'Roman Catholic Goat-breeders' Association' is a frequently heard cliché in any discussion on pillarization. As late as 1954, the bishops issued a charge forbidding Catholics to be members of the social-democratic party or trade union movement. 'The Catholic should take it and read it with respect' wrote the largest Catholic newspaper *de Volkskrant*. And that is what happened. Significantly, the charge had no effect at all on the close political cooperation between the two parties.

So why does the word 'pillarization' now have such negative connotations? It is because the extensive networks, the foundations for which were laid by people like Kuyper and Schaepman, still exist to a certain extent, while the corresponding structures of belief have been diluted. This process started in the 1960s and is still continuing.

THE 1960S WERE A CULTURAL-HISTORICAL WATERSHED

The 1960s were a watershed in the cultural history of the Netherlands. This may seem a surprising claim at first, since there is another period that would perhaps better deserve the description – the time of the German occupation between 1940 and 1945. This was without doubt the most traumatic collective experience since the Eighty-Years' War and many Dutch people have made the comparison. The German occupiers were not content with sending in troops and using the country's resources for the war effort, they also tried hard to reorganize Dutch society along national-socialist lines. The ideology of pillarization proved strong enough to resist these attempts. Although the Nazis succeeded in taking over most social organizations, they simply folded; membership fell to practically nothing, only to pick up again after liberation.

After the war, a coalition of liberals, social democrats and members of the resistance tried to preserve the unity built up during the Nazi occupation, by setting up a mass organization known as the *Nederlandse Volksbeweging* – the Dutch People's Movement – and a new *Partij van de Arbeid* (PvdA – the Dutch Labour Party), but the attempt failed. The PvdA survived and became the core of the traditional 'red' pillar, but proved to be nothing more than the old SDAP in a new jacket. After the Germans had been defeated, the pillars returned to Dutch society more deeply entrenched than before.

Even so, the system would not last twenty years. So what happened in the sixties that made the decade so important and why did it happen just at that time? The most plausible explanation lies in the development of the national economy. The economy had been growing in fits and starts since 1870, but the population had kept pace. After about 1890, per capita income ceased to grow and stayed that way until the start of the 1950s. It was then between a fifth and sixth of what it is today. Nevertheless, generally speaking, public welfare improved considerably during those fifty or sixty years. Thanks to the arrival of mass production, the prices of a number of consumer goods – such as good quality, ready-to-wear clothing – fell. In addition, national income was distributed more equally. This had a lot to do with the fact that the 'pillars' were in many respects emancipation movements. The most important thing for Kuyper, Schaepman and Troelstra was to improve the lot of their respective mass of supporters. This meant not only that they should get an education of their choice, but that it should be of good quality. And that meant that the people themselves had to be better 'developed'. In 1892, Abraham Kuyper caused quite a furore when he organized a number of large-scale social congresses to address the problem of poverty. The Catholic and Calvinist leaders did not share the social democrats' belief in the class struggle. But improving the lives of the less fortunate among their congregations was another matter. In this way, they were advocating a kind of 'common interest' philosophy, in which each individual receives his due and the fair distribution of national wealth is a matter of consultation. The many local Kuypers and Schaepmans – often preachers and priests – were also very good organizers. They brought workers, small businessmen and members of certain professions together to work on improving their common lot. It is typical that the final 'block' in the Catholic pillar was the *Sint Adelbertsvereniging*, an organization of rich believers. The Catholic trade union had preceded them by a quarter of a century. With hindsight, it is clear that this was all a matter of achieving emancipation for certain groups, not for individuals. On the whole, the result was that hunger and misery practically disappeared in the Netherlands in the first thirty years of the century. The standard of living of the majority of the population would be considered very modest in modern terms and probably unacceptable to many Dutch people today, but – generally speaking – group emancipation was accompanied by an improvement in welfare.

Within the group there was little opportunity for individuals to indulge in unconventional behaviour. This was simply due to lack of money. A modest financial position encouraged conformity. It is not advisable to place yourself outside the rest of the group because you might need them one day. The pillarized society possessed a wide range of sanctions for eccentric behaviour. Priests and preachers alike would tell their congregations from the pulpit – and this was still common practice in the 1950s – that they should give their custom only to fellow believers. And they would also make it clear that certain people were no longer considered to fall within this category. Socialist literature in particular is full of examples of members of the religious pillars who had been ruined after displaying too great a sympathy with 'red' ideas. In short, for most people, non-conformity was a luxury they could not afford.

DONALD DUCK

Around 1950 the average Dutch family – the father would be a skilled worker, the mother would be a housewife – would have furniture of a reasonable quality. The man's wages would be sufficient for them to afford good food and clothing. They would have a daily newspaper, an illustrated weekly magazine, a comic for the children. In the living room, there would be a bookshelf with a row of books, sensible novels from the publisher associated with the family's 'pillar', which were often distributed through some kind of subscription scheme. And that was about it. The one large and expensive article in the house – for which newly wed couple would first have to save – was the radio. A refrigerator, a record player or a washing machine were simply out of reach of most of the population. Not to mention a television set to pick up the modest range of programmes that were broadcast from 1951 onwards, largely at the insistence of Philips. The possibility of owning a car was beyond their wildest dreams.

And yet, many children knew of the existence of these luxury articles. They were introduced to them in the pictures of a new comic, the *Donald Duck*, which first appeared in 1952 and reached circulation figures unprecedented for the time. The comic was a colourful confrontation with the American way of life, which had also made its presence increasingly known since the liberation in films, swing music and popular culture. From an international standpoint this American way of life was the alternative to the tyranny of Stalinist communism, the outer borders of which were only three-hundred kilometres to the east. The entire country – with the exception of the communists themselves, of course, who never had the support of more than 10 per cent of the population – was united in its abhorrence of this godless ideology. But the focus on consumption, the outward display of wealth and the enjoyment of the fruits of welfare that are such an important part of the American way of life were not well suited to Dutch frugality, the compromise culture and the considerably more restrained ways in which the regents traditionally enjoyed their wealth. The people were warned against such excesses in the media and from the pulpit. And at the end of the forties, the Ministry of Education, Art and Science started a campaign against the decadent influence of comic magazines. The problem for the established powers was that a consumption-oriented way of life was starting to come within reach of more and more people. The Netherlands shared in the welfare explosion that swept Western Europe in the second half of this century. After being stable for more than half a century, per capita income – as already mentioned above – increased more than fivefold. The state creamed a large percentage of this off through high taxation, but this was used primarily to redistribute welfare through a system of subsidies that largely benefited the 'pillarized' institutions and by gradually expanding the welfare state.

I was born into a typical Dutch family, where the radio was the greatest luxury. Between 1958 and 1964, we acquired first a television, then a washing machine, a refrigerator, an electric oven and, lastly, a DAF, the newly introduced Dutch family car. This was not because my father had such a thriving career – he was a typographer at a medium-sized printing company. Everything was paid for from his regular wage increases. The money left over after the family's basic expenses had been met was saved up to allow us to buy more luxuries, because illness, accidents or unemployment would all be covered by the system of social security. This was all the work of the post-war governments, in which Catholics, Calvinists and socialists worked closely together, building up the role of the state. This is related in part to the sense of community in the Netherlands, which will be examined more closely later in this chapter, but also to the definitive establishment of the pillars as the basis of Dutch society, as envisaged by the political leaders in each group.

At first, the social organizations they set up – including hospitals, *kruis-verenigingen* (which provided home nursing services), night schools and children's homes – were self-financing. The striking exception to this rule was education which, although pillar-based, had been largely dependent on state subsidies since 1917. The pillars attempted to extend this form of funding to cover the remainder of their respective networks, since this was a greater guarantee of continuity. This did mean that the organizations became more distanced from their ordinary members, but few objected. An increasing proportion of the social care system therefore became dependent on state funding. This in turn led to expansion of their tasks. Obligations which in many societies are the responsibility of the family, such as caring for the seriously ill, helping parents or destitute cousins, were rightly taken over by special organizations. A woman who has just given birth would (and still does) receive professional help in the home for ten days or so. Parents who are no longer able to live on their own can move into old-people's accommodation with hotel-like service and a wide range of medical facilities.

The organizations which provided these services gradually became more anonymous and bureaucratic. They were there. You could call on them if necessary. They were generally good at what they did. But in a certain way they were also far removed from the normal people.

Meanwhile people saw the world everyday on their televisions. They could afford a holiday abroad. And as their income increased they became more self-aware. Because the social organizations worked so well, the people of the Netherlands were able to think and act more as individuals, who thought for themselves and were no longer just a part of the group. This was the paradox of the success of the pillars.

Today many Dutch people applaud these changes. One of their spokesmen is Marcel van Dam, a former PvdA politician and currently head of the VARA, a national broadcasting company with its roots in the 'red' pillar. Van Dam calls this development the continuation of emancipation. There are others who regret the change. Calvinistic politician Elco Brinkman rejects the individualism which allows social responsibilities to be shouldered by state-funded organizations, replacing it with the concept of a 'caring society' where the state withdraws from the social stage and draws the attention of individual citizens to their responsibilities to their family and to the group as a whole.

For whatever reason, in the sixties the established powers within the pillars quickly began to lose their grip on the ordinary members. This was first noticeable in the media. The Catholic, Calvinist and socialist press suddenly lost out to non-pillarized rivals. The latter had been in existence for a long time and had a reasonable share of the market, but always within certain limits. Today there is not a single daily newspaper in the country that calls itself Catholic – in the 1950s there were still more than thirty. The most interesting example of this development is *de Volkskrant*. Today it is a quality left-wing newspaper, which competes with the traditionally liberal NRC *Handelsblad*. *De Volkskrant* was originally the paper of the Roman Catholic trade association and was always loyal to the political and religious leaders of the Catholic 'pillar'. The more the faithful ignored the orders of the church, the more *de Volkskrant* went its own way so that it could ensure the continued support of the children of the original subscribers, Catholic craftsmen. These post-war craftsmen were the first generation able to offer their children a better education than they themselves had had. The rapidly growing prosperity also brought better educational chances. The government introduced a system of study grants but perhaps even more significant was the fact that parents could now believe to give their children a secondary education. They no longer relied on them to work from the age of fourteen, the age at which the Dutch traditionally started work. This development was encouraged on all fronts because the economic growth of the country demanded a more skilled workforce. The young generation – who had experienced nothing other than progress – took this all for granted. They could even afford to object to the society their parents were part of, without having to forego its benefits.

THEY LET THEIR HAIR GROW

After the Beatles first spectacular visit to Amsterdam, you could clearly recognize these young people – they let their hair grow. They emphasized the normality of their prosperity by wearing denim jeans in their spare time.

Jeans were traditionally the symbol of hard, unrewarding work; in the sixties they became a symbol of the new freedom. The younger generation adopted, as a kind of cultural banner, the very clothes their parents had hoped they would escape forever. They mocked traditional norms and values of moderation, particularly where relations between the sexes were concerned. The contraceptive pill – which had been readily available since 1963 and was so popular that the demographic trend towards population increase was reversed – made close physical contact far less risky. All this led to a shift in cultural values and norms. *De Volkskrant* reported these changes in detail and with decreasing antipathy. When it moved to a new building, it celebrated by dropping its subheader 'the Netherlands' Catholic daily'. Since then, the paper no longer defines its position, but it has become the mouthpiece for many who have left the pillars behind them. It does this in a very special way. It advocates cultural individualism but not personal egoism. In typical Dutch fashion, the editors take the side of the weaker groups in society. They believe – and this again is typically Dutch – that the 'strongest shoulders should bear the heaviest burden'.

De Volkskrant currently has a circulation of nearly three hundred and fifty thousand. During the heyday of pillarization it was a hundred and seventy thousand. The Calvinist daily *Trouw* experienced a similar development, maintaining a readership of over a hundred thousand in spite of remaining more faithful to its religious foundations. The rest of the pillar-based press – including the once enormously strong socialist publications – has disappeared without a trace. *De Volkskrant* won the day by taking its leave of the pillar system at the same time as its readers.

At first glance, it appears to be a remarkable combination – extreme liberalism in the private sphere together with almost its complete opposite when it comes to the organization of society as a whole, where countless hands join forces to help pull individuals out of any miserable situation they may find themselves in, no matter what the reason. Yet, through Dutch eyes, this is not so strange. The wet earth of Holland has proved fertile soil for paternalism. The roots of Dutch society lie in the Christian faith and, like the Koran, the Bible devotes considerable attention to the poor. Charity is one of the greatest virtues, as is hospitality to strangers and the protection of widows and orphans. As early as the Middle Ages, we find examples of wealthy citizens wishing to do something for the poor. This was usually rather structured and frequently took the form of an inheritance, since leaving money to the poor was a surefire way of entering the kingdom of heaven. A good example of this was the hospice for the poor in the provincial town of Schiedam, which was mentioned in the town charter in 1275. It was intended, in the words of a later document, for the poor of Christ, the old and decrepit, the sick and others who belonged in such an institution. Its name, the St. Jacob's Hospice, illustrates its religious connotations.

The hospice was an excellent cause to leave a 'little something' to. In this way, St. Jacob's acquired several estates in the Schiedam area. The costs were covered by interest earned from capital. In addition, the town council had introduced a primitive sort of tax to support the institution. St. Jacob's therefore not only received the best garments of the wealthy and deceased, but also a small percentage of every piece of peat sold in the town.

The Calvinist victory in the Eighty-Years' War led to the disappearance of the whole official infrastructure of monasteries and Roman Catholic brotherhoods. Generally, their properties fell to the local authorities who allowed the charitable activities to continue under their supervision. The strict Calvinist church organization also had to contend with brothers and sisters who were less well off and unable to fend for themselves. It was against the nature of religious communities to leave such people to their fate. Their support became the special area of expertise of a new kind of church official – the deacon. Care for the poor and sick therefore became the responsibility of church and civic officials. Even the most humble of local authorities were represented in the board of governors of some charitable institution or another. Particularly in the cities, these activities expanded to such an extent that they became inextricably bound up with the administrative tasks of the municipal authorities. This was in no way a matter of what we would today call social justice. It was Christian duty to provide charity, but it could never be enforced, particularly by those who received it. The general rule was that help was given only to those who really needed it. This did not include people without work, but the infirm, children and old people who were unable to rely on their families because they had, for example, been lost during an epidemic.

Foreign observers were impressed by these activities. Compared with the rest of Europe, they were very extensive although it should not be forgotten that, especially during the Golden Age, the standard of living was so high that there was plenty of wealth over to put to good use. Furthermore, the charitable works were not exactly kept a secret. It was a status symbol to care for the weak and the sick. This was expressed in the size of the buildings built for these purposes. The St. Jacob's Hospice is still a dominant landmark in the centre of Schiedam; its façade, in classical Greek temple style crowned with a bell tower, conceals the chapel. On either side, there are high wings, which formerly housed the elderly (this became the hospice's speciality). The enormous building was erected in 1789, when Schiedam was flourishing and could afford such extravagance. The hospice is now a spacious museum of modern art. Many Dutch cities possess historical buildings of this nature. Amsterdam, for example, is graced with the *Maagdenhuis*, formerly a home for orphan girls and now the administrative centre of the university. Then there are the *hofjes*, the equivalent of an English 'court'. These consist of rows of small houses around a central square, often covered with grass. The court is sealed off from the outside world by a door or gate. They were frequently founded at the bequest of a wealthy citizen who would leave sufficient money in his will to cover the building and running costs. As a rule, the patron would stipulate for whom the houses were intended, perhaps widows of limited means or decrepit couples of a certain religious persuasion. These courts can still be seen in most Dutch cities, where they have been beautifully restored and seldom fulfil their original function. They were – and are – showpieces in the historic centres of the cities.

The splendid façades, however, concealed little luxury. Elderly people who wished to be taken in at St. Jacob's had to exchange all their worldly goods for their bed and board. If they had no possessions, they had go from door to door – as long as they could walk – begging for alms in an attempt to recover at least a part of the costs of their upkeep. This practice was still common until well into the twentieth century. Many of the courts also had a system of 'purchasing', whereby future residents paid a fixed amount to guarantee for themselves a place in later life. They also made regular contributions to the court, the value and nature of which differed from case to case. One might be obliged to donate a certain quantity of peat every winter to fire the stove, while others might be required to turn over all their possessions. The rich therefore paid more than the poor for the same service. And the orphans were always recognizable by their clothing – it was necessary that they were seen to be needy and dependent on charity.

THE EMBARRASSMENT OF RICHES

And yet there was more behind this care for the needy. The British historian Simon Schama prefaced his cultural history of the Dutch Golden Age, *The Embarrassment of Riches*, with a quotation from John Calvin: 'Let those who have abundance remember that they are surrounded with thorns, and let them take great care not to be pricked by them'.

Charity, so splendidly displayed in the courtyards and palace-like façades, enabled the rich to allay the sense of guilt that their material success brought with it. For no matter how libertine their lives may have been in practice, the Calvinist threat was constantly in the background – that many were called but few were chosen; that their prosperity and wealth could turn against them.

In Schama's words: 'The profusion and munificence of charitable institutions in the Netherlands as elsewhere in baroque Europe, has been classified by modern historians as an exercise in 'social control'. And there is no doubt that part of its momentum derived from prudential consideration. Where elites governed by persuasion rather than coercion, philanthropic donation on a large and obligatory scale was a small price to pay for cushioning themselves against the threat of popular revolt. But this kind of manipulative explanation omits as much as it explains. In particular it pays little attention to the almost perfervid urge with which the Dutch were commanded to honour their good fortune by sharing some of it with the less well off.' And: 'It was rather a moral balancing act that permitted the retention, not the repudiation, of riches, on condition that they were yielded to communally determined ends'.

Yet there is in this charity an even more important element of social control than Schama will admit to. Anyone who reads the regulations of the charitable institutions will be surprised to notice how strictly life there was regulated and how much attention was devoted to preventing abuse. It is striking that the more money the regents pumped into the institutions, the richer they became, while their residents led an exceptionally sober life. The St. Jacob's Hostel even had a small prison in its cellar for any of its elderly inmates who proved difficult to handle. Another striking example is an appeal to the citizens of Amsterdam – dating from the 1840s – to support schools for the children of the poor. The argument was that there the children would learn obedience and gratitude. About this same time, preacher and man of letters Bernard ter Haar published a poem in which he thanked God that he owned a fur coat after seeing a woman shivering in the cold. There was nothing cynical about this – it was perfectly genuine. It had already been noted in the Middle Ages that the poor had been created by God for a reason – to give the rich the opportunity to love their neighbours. On the other hand it is dangerous to judge situations and customs from the distant past according to twentieth century values. This happens a great deal in the Netherlands because regimes like the one at St. Jacob's with its compulsory begging and its prison cell live on here and there in the collective memory. They are horror stories that people like to tell to contrast that time with the present, when a system of social security is a right, which is fiercely defended by *de Volkskrant*, *Trouw* and their readers.

Our comprehensive system of social security may have been set up in the past 50 years or so, but the basis was laid much earlier – during the heyday of pillarization and under the influence of rapidly growing socialism. This latter pillar always rested on the fundamental belief in 'a fair day's pay for a fair day's work' but also that everyone was entitled to protection against the effects of unemployment, illness and age. The Catholic and Calvinist pillars had a slightly different solution to these problems, usually in the form of collective savings or insurance schemes rather than leaving it up to the state, but the result was the same – the less fortunate had to be protected against the vagaries of fate. In practice it was the liberals, followed later by Catholics and Calvinists, who developed the first forms of social security. Unemployment

[61]

insurance was introduced, which was run by the 'pillarized' trade unions and subsidized by the government. And it did not stop there – the government also provided a meagre benefit for the long-term unemployed who were no longer eligible for support from the insurance schemes.

MOST BENEFITS WERE BASED ON AN INSURANCE SCHEME

The welfare explosion after 1950 gave the still-pillarized government the opportunity to restructure this whole complex system of social support. True to tradition, it decided on a compromise – people were entitled to support, but most benefits were based on an insurance system. The first example of this was the *Algemene Ouderdoms Wet*, known popularly as the AOW, which guarantees every individual over the age of 65 a pension approximately equal to the minimum wage. Individuals contribute to the scheme on a pay-as-you-earn basis. The money is, however, not pooled in a fund and invested to accumulate sufficient capital to pay each person's pension as long as is necessary. The pensions are financed from the compulsory contributions paid into the scheme by younger generations. This is known as an 'apportionment' system – the total contributions from those paying in are divided up among those entitled to the benefit in question. The *Wet Arbeidsongeschiktheid* (WAO), which provides disability benefits, works on the same principle, as do the *ziekenfondsen*, the national health insurance schemes. Under this system, those who pay contributions do not accumulate any rights. The government is entitled to repeal or amend the legislation, change the levels of benefits, the conditions for eligibility or the period during which benefits are received – and has done so in recent years, acquiring for itself the reputation of a bad insurer. There is little understanding among the general public for the apportionment system; after all, this is not the basis of the normal commercial insurance schemes that most Dutch people are accustomed to.

Negotiations between employers and employees very rarely lead to open conflict. This has its roots in the organization of the Catholic and Calvinist pillars, where trade unions and employers' organizations would share a common ideology of listening to each other and of close collaboration. This mentality was later adopted by liberal employers and the socialist part of the union movement. These negotiations, in which working conditions are usually equally as important as wage levels, are conducted per economic sector and

[62]

result in Collective Labour Agreements (known in Dutch as CAO's) which apply to the whole sector. In addition to agreements on wages and salaries, the CAO's also contain provisions for training, hiring, dismissal and redundancy. Trade union negotiators are usually prepared to accept moderate wage settlements in exchange for other concessions, such as the preservation of jobs.

These days, nearly every sector has its own pension fund, into which both employers and employees pay high contributions. These funds have become the leading players on the capital markets. They are private enterprises, and those who pay into them accumulate rights based on the number of years they pay their contributions. The pensions are supplementary to the state pension to which everyone is entitled under the AOW; they are, as it were, the jam on the bread. Any holes in this safety net are filled by the government. Anyone who is no longer entitled to an unemployment benefit under the *Werkloosheidswet* (WW) – which is also based on the apportionment system – receives a supplementary benefit which is funded from tax revenues.

A DESIRE TO AVOID RISK

This all indicates a clear preference for stability and continuity, a desire to avoid risk. Dutch economist Hans van der Doel, who was very influential in the 1970s, believes that Dutch employees think keeping their jobs is more important than a salary increase, that they attach greater priority to a secure income and protection against the fickle hand of fate – including unemployment – to a better salary in the short term. The laws regulating dismissal, which have come into being since the Second World War, reflect the same fundamental belief. Employers are not free to sack employees as they see fit. They have to apply for official approval, stating their reasons. If an employer can prove that there is no longer work for the person concerned, approval is usually granted. But this must genuinely be the case, including elsewhere in the company. Many sectors of industry specify in their CAO's a specific pecking order for dismissal, usually with the younger employees being sacked first or on the principle of 'last in, first out'. The more loyal an employee is to his or her employer, the more chance there is of keeping their job. This applies particularly to civil servants and employees of non-profitmaking organizations (who have the same legal status). They can be dismissed only if their jobs are abolished, unless they fail to do their work satisfactorily for a very long period of time. Many dismissal procedures end up in court and many companies can only rid themselves of unwanted employees by paying them large sums in compensation. If it is a question of collective dismissals, trade unions frequently negotiate a favourable redundancy scheme.

For whatever reason, Dutch employees are loyal to the company. This is sometimes due to force of circumstance, because the strict laws on dismissal mean that opportunities are few. Until recently, anyone who worked for the same employer for forty years was honoured by the Queen, but this no longer occurs automatically.

The costs of this complex system of benefits and schemes are borne jointly by employers and employees. Approximately half the gross income of the average Dutch employee is deducted for taxes and social contributions. Because the system is progressive, this percentage can be much greater among those with higher incomes. This makes it very expensive to take on personnel while the employee's actual disposable income is not particularly high in international terms – although, of course, it must be remembered that it is not absolutely necessary to build up a reserve for sickness and other unexpected personal misfortunes.

This creates a large degree of personal freedom. You have to really work at it in the Netherlands to hit rock bottom. In fact, only drug addicts, alcoholics or those suffering from psychic problems ever actually get this far. Anyone who is unable to support themself will always receive a benefit from some anonymous scheme or other. No one is dependent on charity. As a result, the community has a far looser grip on the individual than it used to. In addition to the social security system, there is an extensive network of social welfare institutions which are financed from public funds and offer their services practically free.

In this way, the pillars themselves created the social conditions that allowed individuals to escape from their grip. This process developed simultaneously with the growth of the social welfare system.

Yet it was not only the actions of self-willed citizens that led to the disintegration of the pillars that has taken place since the 1960s.

Prominent figures in the pillars no longer believed in the hermetically sealed ideological/religious schools of thought that had traditionally been the guarantee of unity. This was particularly true of the Roman Catholic church, which was thrown into the spiritual fast lane by the Second Vatican Council. The Council was called by Pope John XXIII to modernize the ossified structure of the international church. The message was welcomed in the Netherlands –

which, until then, had been known for its loyalty to the Pope and to received church truths and traditions. Catholic leaders themselves called into question traditional cornerstones of the church, such as the celibacy of priests. The bishops called for a 'pastoral council' to make the church more democratic.

In the Calvinist churches, a new generation of preachers arose who subjected Protestant traditions to the same critical review. They had something in common with their Catholic colleagues – they no longer believed in a God whose authority was derived from strict laws and the threat of eternal damnation. The preached about a God of love and, as a direct consequence of this, that love should be the key word in relationships between people. The theological debate – which was publicized through the pages of *de Volkskrant* and *Trouw*, and on radio and television – centred around the idea of justice. This idea gradually acquired a more political slant. It became associated with the enormous gap between the rich industrialized countries and the Third World. At home, it was applied to Dutch society, and it was discovered that much inequality still exists. The Divine Message descended from heaven to earth, and in doing so lost much of its forceful character.

In 1993 a Calvinist supporter of this renewal, Professor H.M. Kuitert, published a bestseller entitled *Het algemeen betwijfeld christelijk geloof* – universal doubts about the Christian faith. It was these supporters of the renewal who sowed the seeds of doubt. In both Catholic and Calvinist communities, congregations began to diminish and fewer people observed their religious duties. Young people in particular had a waning interest in what the church had to offer. None of this affected the smaller, stricter church communities which held on steadfastly to their orthodox beliefs against the run of the tide. They even experienced a period of renewed growth, although – with a total of around 600,000 followers – they remained a relatively marginal group in a population of fifteen million. They did, however, retain all the paraphernalia of the old pillar system, with two daily newspapers and a new broadcasting company, the *Evangelische Omroep*. They survived because their leaders were able to resist the forces of change that were battering at the door.

Social democracy, too, went through a period of change. A new generation of politicians pushed aside – often rather ruthlessly – leaders who had helped reconstruct a country ravaged by war entirely according to the principles of the pillar system. They did this – as did the Catholics and Calvinists – under the banner of freedom. But these new socialists grasped the old symbolism of the revolutionary struggle to distinguish themselves from the post-war leaders. The latter had distanced themselves from the red flag, the singing of the 'Internationale' and the works of Karl Marx to appease their coalition partners. The new generation wanted all this back. They preferred a 'conflict model' to the harmony model that only played into the hands of the regents.

The regents. The term had returned to the centre of the political stage. The new opposition compared the current leaders with their seventeenth and eighteenth century predecessors who had kept themselves in power by co-optation, nepotism and behind the scenes wheeling and dealing. They saw current policy as once again being formed by compromises apparently agreed upon behind closed doors. In 1966 a group presented by the media as complete outsiders set up a new political party, *Democraten '66*, with a programme which went entirely against the grain of the Dutch political tradition. It advocated openness and proposed the introduction of a national referendum as a way of settling important issues. In the general elections the following year, the party won 7 of the 150 seats, an astounding result in Dutch terms.

The current leaders were part of a tradition that stretched back three centuries. Flexibility and a willingness to compromise, together with a none too flamboyant or overtly ambitious attitude, were still a prerequisite for success in politics. Mayors, ministers, state secretaries and members of parliament still had an image of being cautious. And, like their predecessors, they were wealthy. Ever since the Eighty-Years' War, the wealthy had taken themselves very seriously. They wished to be treated with honour and servility. Since pillarization had introduced 'group democracy' they had found themselves the leaders of significant parts of the population. But they by no means saw themselves as the representatives, the messengers, of the electorate. They did their best to defend the interests of their supporters, but very much in their own way.

THEY DID NOT NEED SPOKESMEN

More and more people began to question the validity of this attitude. They became *mondig*. This word, which literally means 'articulate', also embraces such qualities as self-awareness, maturity, not being afraid to speak up for oneself, making one's own decisions. Modern citizens considered themselves *mondig*. They could speak for themselves, they did not need spokesmen. They demanded a say in decisions that affected them personally. This was soon radicalized to a demand for full participation in decision-making. The new democratic party's call for a referendum was a direct result of this development. Taking their lead from developments abroad, the party's leaders also preached the end of ideology, by which they meant that the individual could now form his or her own personal political-ideological complex and therefore no longer needed those provided ready-made by the pillars.

This shift was not only illustrated by the demise of the pillarized press, it was reflected in election results. The *Katholieke Volkspartij* (KVP) in particular suffered heavy losses. The two largest Calvinist parties and the social-democratic PvdA also lost support but to a lesser extent. The trend, however, was clear – the pillars were collapsing and with them, the old model of group solidarity.

Intellectuals in particular remember the sixties as a period of germinating ideas and revolution. There were spectacular occupations at the universities. Students and lecturers demanded a say in the decisions made by their professors. These new individuals discovered that, by acting *en masse*, they could attract a great deal of attention, particularly via the television. They took part in mass demonstrations, displaying their messages on large banners, reviving a method that had long before been applied by the founders of the pillars but had fallen into disuse. The idea was that the messages on the banners would be easy to read on the television screen. These demonstrations were aimed at the regents, but usually indirectly. The latter-day regents were faithful allies of the United States, with whom the Netherlands was united in NATO, so people took to the streets in their thousands to demonstrate against US involvement in Vietnam.

In Amsterdam a group of young people rediscovered anarchism, a nineteenth century ideology based on the belief that justice can be achieved only if people are free to cooperate with each other voluntarily and without coercion.

They called themselves *provos*, a term coined by the criminologist Buikhuizen to describe those in the younger generation who rejected social norms in order to provoke a reaction. The provos in Amsterdam discovered that the regents and their power apparatus – the police in particular – were extremely easy to provoke, especially if you made them look ridiculous. In one such notorious case, a girl called Koosje Koster was convicted for handing out raisins to people on the street. The provos introduced ideas which appeared utopian but which were disarmingly practical. With their famous 'white bicycle' plan, they planned to rid the centre of Amsterdam of motorized traffic by providing bicycles that could be used by everyone free of charge. But the main focus of their activity was the weekly 'happening' in the city centre. They would gather around midnight only to be dispersed rather heavy-handedly by the police, under the watchful eyes of a crowd of spectators whose sympathies clearly lay with the provos. These happenings were centred around *Lievertje*, a statue of a street urchin donated to the city by a large tobacco company. Although many of the provos were heavy smokers, the statue was a symbol of hypocrisy – the city should not accept gifts from people who were making money from causing cancer.

An atmosphere of harassment developed in Amsterdam and the position of the mayor, Gijsbert van Hall – who was not only a social-democrat but also a descendant of a grand old regent family – became increasingly impossible. The marriage of Princess Beatrix to German diplomat Claus von Amsberg led to massive riots. The uncompromising response of the police had provoked considerable criticism in the press and on the television. The powers-that-be had lost face. After a year, the provos disbanded – the joke had gone on long enough. But they had attracted international attention with their facetious provocation of the establishment.

The success of the provos and other similar groups was partly due to the fact that sections of the media were vaguely sympathetic to their activities. Here, too, the younger generation was also pushing back the frontiers of what was acceptable. Author Jan Cremer caused an uproar with his sexual autobiography, which gave rise to a new term in the Dutch publishing world: *'onverbiddelijke bestseller'* – the relentless bestseller. Gerard Reve, a highly respected Dutch literary figure, produced a whole series of books focusing on the complete compatibility of the traditional Catholic way of life and homosexuality. His most infamous passage at the time was a description of himself having intercourse with God, in the form of a donkey. The act took place in his attic, of all places. He was taken to court for this scene but was acquitted. The authorities – not unaffected by the spirit of the times and afraid of being made to look ridiculous – no longer knew where they should draw their limits. Within a year or two, the restrictions on pornography – which had, until then, been very strict – had crumbled, as a result of which a thriving market for magazines of that genre soon grew up. There were, of course, at first regular clashes between the new entrepreneurs and the censors but they almost always resulted in the latter losing both face and authority. They were after all defenders of the standards upheld by the regents, of the tyranny of the pillars, and they were now considered to belong to what the provos – famed for their innovative use of language – described as the *'misselijk makende middenstand'* , the nauseating middle classes, and the *'klootjesvolk'*. This last term, literally the Dutch equivalent of the English phrase 'scum of the earth', was originally a derogatory term for the poor, but the provos gave it a new meaning, which soon found its way into the Van Dale, the most authoritative dictionary of the Dutch language. To the provos, the *klootjesvolk* were 'people whose interests are purely material and do not extend to the social and cultural'. It was clear for all to see that the fate of Mayor Van Hall, who should otherwise have been at the peak of his career, was sealed. Furthermore, the powers-that-be had something in their tradition that should also be applied to the current situation – the principle of sovereignty in one's own domain. Why should these new citizens not be allowed to do as they pleased as long as they were not causing trouble for others? Municipal leaders began to give the new generation more space of its own, often literally. They provided subsidies for cultural activities. And the young people themselves took advantage of this, proclaiming their right to such support. As a result, all kinds of centres grew up where they could, for example, indulge in their hippy sub-culture, in exactly the same way as the 'St. Cecilia' Roman Catholic brass band, the 'Harp of David' Reformist marching band, or the 'Art through Struggle' socialist choir had once enjoyed government support. The revolutionary youth, the new generation of critical citizens, was therefore incorporated by giving them their own space and making them dependent on the system as a whole. This pacified them and resulted in the erosion of the conflict model.

RIOTERS WRECK CARS

Not that these radical young people enjoyed the mass support of the Dutch population. On the contrary, in the second half of the sixties, *De Telegraaf*, the country's most conservative newspaper, saw its circulation increase almost fourfold to three-quarters of a million, precisely because it had taken a stand against all forms of political radicalism or anything else that threatened what was considered to be common civil decency. After a large political demonstration, when a number of parked cars had been slightly damaged during skirmishes with the police, the paper ran a famous headline: 'Rioters wreck cars'. *De Telegraaf* came out in defence of the *klootjesvolk*.

The paper was something of a cuckoo in the nest of the pillared society. It was traditionally the mouthpiece of the minority that had managed to wrest itself free of the restraints of the pillars – the remains of the liberal establishment. In Dutch terms, *De Telegraaf* was rather sensational and populist. In the fifties and sixties its editors preached law and order and vigorously opposed the expanding system of social security, which they associated with a love of interference in others' lives and considered both a waste of money and a reward for idleness. The paper also devoted great attention to the pleasures of wealth and prosperity. It embraced consumerism in a way that the concerned Calvinist – even a follower of Kuitert – would find immoral. *De Telegraaf* had a feeling for show, for the glitter of the stars and for dreams of riches and happiness. It couldn't care less for Schama's embarrassment of riches. And that was what caused the breakthrough.

The same breakthrough occurred on the television and radio. Air-time in the Netherlands was controlled by five most pillar-based broadcasting companies. These companies had a monopoly on the issue of programme information and each published their own TV and radio guide. Those who took out a subscription to the guide became members and, in this way, the broadcasting companies accumulated hundreds of thousands of members each. There were no commercials. The programmes were funded from an annual contribution from the government which was financed from a tax levied on everyone who owned a radio or television set.

Private entrepreneurs had long tried to present a united front against the broadcasting companies' monopoly. They wanted at least one commercial network alongside the existing one, that would make a profit from selling commercials. At first the political representatives of the pillars were able to prevent parliament from granting permission, but businessman Bul Verwey responded by setting up a commercial radio station on a ship outside Dutch territorial waters, beyond the reach of the Dutch authorities. The station, Radio Veronica, broadcast mainly music, with verbal link-ups being provided by a disc jockey – a new phenomenon for the Netherlands. Others imitated Verwey by broadcasting television programmes from drilling platforms in the North Sea, but the authorities soon clamped down on them – the law apparently permitted the boarding of 'artificial islands'. These measures were, however, extremely unpopular and the government was forced to change the legislation regulating broadcasting. Under the new laws, air-time would be distributed democratically, according to the number of members each broadcasting company had, and new companies would be permitted to join the system. A certain amount of advertising was also allowed.

The extent to which the pillars had disintegrated became clear when the people who had been broadcasting television programmes from the drilling platform set up the *Televisie en Radio Omroep Stichting* (TROS). Within a year, the new organization – a kind of electronic version of *De Telegraaf* – had become the country's largest broadcasting company. It later had to give up its leading position to Veronica, which also became an official broadcasting company after a change in the law made offshore radio stations illegal. Veronica now has about a million members, twice as many as the traditional companies, who have managed to survive only by abandoning many of their ideological principles in their choice of programmes. After further recent amendments to legislation, Veronica decided to leave the public broadcasting system and become a purely commercial company. The strength of TROS and Veronica is a mix of unpretentious amusement programmes, films and soap operas – the latter two largely imported from America. Such programmes had long been taboo for the other broadcasting companies. They saw television and radio as a means of educating the public, making sure they stayed on the straight and narrow, and of providing them with information presented from what they considered to be the correct viewpoint. It had been clear for a long time, however, that the new, *mondig* public no longer felt the same way. The other companies had to follow in the wake of TROS and Veronica if they did not wish to lose a lot of their members, perhaps so many that their broadcasting licences would be withdrawn. A fierce competition grew up around the recruitment of new members. From the sixties on, this was no longer fought out with arguments about the content of the programmes, but centred on the price and size of the weekly programme guide. The only exceptions to this were the conservative Calvinist *Evangelische Omroep* (EO) and the VPRO. The VPRO, short for the *Vrijzinnig Protestantse Radio Omroep*, had abandoned its Protestant principles at the end of the sixties to concentrate on experimental and innovative programmes of an intellectual nature. It could perhaps be described as *de Volkskrant* of the airwaves. In the early days of the 'renewal', the VPRO achieved notoriety with a series of provocations and scandals that mocked what others considered sacred. It was, for example, the first to show a full-frontal naked woman, an event which is still engraved on the memories of many people in their forties and fifties. Membership of the EO or the VPRO is a well-considered choice. Countless surveys have shown, however, that members of the other broadcasting companies are more likely to consider themselves subscribers to their programme guide.

Like the broadcasting companies, the network of denominational schools also managed to survive without too many problems. Modern parents, free of the constraints of the pillars, proved to be more concerned with finding a good school for their children close to their homes. The schools had also been through the process of renewal and the religious influence on education had become weaker and less exclusive. School boards frequently adopted an ecumenical approach, with various church communities working together, which had suddenly become very popular. Generally speaking, the traditional belief in the rightness of one's own particular group disappeared. This was often reflected in the names of the schools – the St. Franciscus College in Rotterdam, for example, changed its name to the City College St. Franciscus. The teachers, of course, had experienced the same process of secularization as the parents. It was exactly the same story in institutions providing social services, such as old people's homes and hospitals. The pillars remained intact, but the differences between them became increasingly obscure.

THE 'SOCIAL MIDFIELD'

The reason for this was simple enough – there was no need for the pillarized institutions, which were dependent on government grants and tax revenues, to adapt their structures. They got the money anyway. And they kept their customers, too, as long as they did not dish up an overly large helping of ideology along with whatever service they provided. As for the customers them-
selves, they did not notice that they were paying for these services. They were never presented with the bill, because they paid indirectly, through taxes or insurance schemes. In the 1980s a new term was invented for this complex of services – *het maatschappelijk middenveld*, literally the 'social midfield'. Critics claimed that, in this social midfield, all kinds of boards and committees ran influential organizations on the basis of obsolete principles, making them enormously powerful and yet accountable to no one.

And indeed, these institutions proved unassailable. Their managers and directors formed close-knit networks in which they worked together like the regents of old. And they still had their allies in the national political arena. Faced with structural election losses, the two Calvinist parties and the Katholieke Volkspartij worked more and more closely together until, in 1980, they united to form a new party, the *Christendemocratisch Appèl* (CDA). Until the early 1990s, the CDA could count on the votes of a third of the electorate. This was far less than the 50 to 55 per cent that its predecessors had always achieved in the heyday of pillarization, but it was sufficient to ensure that the Christian Democrats always dominated coalition governments. The party's leader, Ruud Lubbers, who was to lead successive governments until 1994, introduced a motto with little ideological content: 'no nonsense'. With this approach, he acquired the reputation of a careful and cautious financier, who had little patience with those who threatened to waste the taxpayers' money. His predecessors in the pillarized society would never had dominated politics with such an approach. Something had clearly changed.

The social developments of the 1960s had made quite a large dent in most individuals' traditional sense of belonging to a group. Their respect for the preacher or priest, and for authority in general, had been delivered a heavy blow, as had many other received values and norms of behaviour. Until the sixties it was considered scandalous for people to live together without being married. This was something that was only done by those Bohemians who had fled to the big city – i.e. Amsterdam – to escape the bounds of social control. Premarital sex was also severely frowned upon. If loving couples did indulge, they certainly kept it strictly to themselves. The widely available contraceptive pill – which you could get from your doctor without a great song and dance being made about it – had taken away much of the risk. In addition, the renewal in the churches had made it possible to question many

traditional rules and beliefs. Within a few years, it became acceptable for couples to live together without first having made the customary trip to the registry office and the church. Many of these relationships ended up in marriage after a time, but usually for practical reasons, often because of the desire to have children. In 1994, *Love Letters* – a television quiz programme with, as its main prize, a spectacular wedding broadcast on TV - put the spotlight on one couple in particular who, rather than living together first, really had decided to wait until their wedding day.

At the beginning of the 1970s, a feminist movement grew up which became very influential. The movement focused on the power relations within relationships. It demanded that men took on an equal share of the housework and bringing up the children, something they had – until then – always been able to escape from with the excuse that they had, after all, done a full day's work. The new feminists also claimed that women were less likely to have a higher education and that they were discriminated against in the workplace. They emphasized the fact that women were economically dependent on men, even after they were married. Women should therefore earn their own living as far as possible and develop their own careers. The feminists even suggested that perhaps, for a change, men could give up their careers to stay at home and look after their families. They demanded a wide variety of measures that would enable both partners to work, such as the large-scale introduction of crèches and an employment policy that encouraged employers to take on more women. Their lobbying was successful, particularly in the public sector and in non-profit-making organizations. The law now forbids discrimination against women when taking on employees. All job advertisements now include the qualification M/v (short for *man/vrouw*, man or woman); many also state that women are encouraged to apply or that, if more than one candidate is considered suitable for the position, preference will be given to a woman. This, however, still leaves prospective employers sufficient opportunity to appoint men, and the more radical elements among the feminists consider this practice little more than paying lip service to emancipation, while continuing to pursue a traditional policy. This apart, the movement achieved a great deal. At the universities and other institutes of higher education, formerly male strongholds, half of the students are now women. In the workplace, too, progress has been made. Yet, when the children arrive, it is still largely the women who stay at home. Women also seem to have a strong preference for courses of study that will prepare them for a career in the care sector. In spite of vigorous promotion campaigns by the government, still very few girls follow courses in the technical subjects.

[75]

Divorced women also seem to have difficulties in finding work, as a result of which they continue to be dependent on maintenance payments or social security benefits. Some feminists characterize this as the 'feminization of poverty'.

The women's movement used methods that had been made popular by the new 'mondig' citizens in the sixties. They held demonstrations; and they formed 'action committees'. Since the sixties, action committees have become a favoured form of organization for groups of individuals who devote themselves to a specific cause. This might be anything – the preservation of an old community, somewhere for young people to get together and play pop music, banning cars from a town centre or perhaps demanding greater freedom for motorists. The aim of these committees, as their name suggests, is to take action. This means, generally, undertaking activities to attract the attention of the mass media – demonstrations, occupations, petitions or refusing to pay rent. Because the media are continually looking for something out of the ordinary, it is becoming increasingly difficult to attract attention with a normal mass demonstration. All kinds of tricks are therefore used to make the event unique. Simple banners are being replaced by a wide variety of bizarre and sometimes symbolic activities. Demonstrators dress up. They present the representatives of the particular authority they are protesting against with strange gifts, such as a red card of the kind shown to offending players by referees during football matches. When the Ministry of Education wanted to close the Faculty of Social History at the University of Rotterdam in 1986, students marched through the city, dressed as mourners and carrying a coffin.

Firemen in Amsterdam once expressed their displeasure by spraying the area around the parliament buildings with foam. And in 1993, the German government received a million postcards from Dutch citizens bearing the phrase *'Ik ben woedend'* – I'm furious! – in protest at what they considered to be a revival of racism across the border.

Mayor Van Hall of Amsterdam lost so much face during his fight against the provos, that he resigned simply because he was at his wits' end. The same happened to social democratic civic leaders across the country who clashed with action committees and *mondig* citizens. They found themselves opposed within their own parties by the leaders of action committees who were trying to get their own chosen cause onto the political agenda. With its reformist nature, social democracy seemed to be the best stage for doing so.

These besieged leaders learned fast. Confrontations with *mondig* citizens, using the police to break up demonstrations and ignoring protests generally led only to scandal. So they adapted and began to treat the new opposition as their colleagues in the other pillars. In response to the conflict model of the action committees, they showed themselves prepared to enter into peaceful consultation. These days, a minister, mayor or alderman will always meet demonstrators, receive the symbolic gift with conciliatory words and show himself willing to talk. Since the sixties there has been an enormous growth in the number of PR and public information departments at every level throughout the country. Leaders declared almost from one day to the next that of course individual citizens had the right to be involved in decisionmaking. New proposals, for example in the field of physical planning, were always submitted for public enquiry. Anyone who wished to could come along to a meeting and the authorities would listen with interest – genuine or feigned – to what they had to say. This right was even laid down in legislation. The leaders of action committees soon found themselves invited to all kinds of consultations. Many of them therefore found themselves involved in reaching compromises in a way that the traditional leaders had long been accustomed to.

A good example of this approach is the government's response to student protests at universities. It introduced new legislation giving students and lecturers, via a complicated system of councils, more say in how the institutions were run. Until then, academic power had been concentrated entirely in the hands of the professors. The legislation was the work of a Catholic minister.

In this way, the consultation culture spread from the top of the pillars downwards. From then on the leaders of the new opposition were simply invited to sit around the negotiating table. They quickly learned the ropes, how to behave and how to master the compromise culture. They soon adopted the tone and style of the traditional leaders, while the latter, in their turn, just as quickly learned the language of the action committees.

In the old regent culture, formality was required in word and deed. The Dutch language has two forms for the second person: the familiar '*jij*', used between brothers, sisters and good friends, and '*U*', which is used between people who are less well acquainted, and implies a certain relationship of authority. Most children traditionally addressed their parents as '*U*', while they themselves had to be content with '*jij*'.

The two forms were also used to indicate differences in social standing. Workers, whether they wore overalls or dust coats, would always be addressed as 'jij' by the boss, but would never dream of replying in the same form. Office staff, on the other hand, who came to work in their suits, always fell into the 'U' category. In families with a working-class background, there are always anecdotes about, for example, a grandfather or great grandfather who turned up at work wearing a hat, rather than the customary workman's cap. The boss had remarked on it and they had discussed the difference between 'hats' and 'caps'. There is still a vague echo of this distinction today in that office staff often prove to be less militant during labour disputes than their blue-collar colleagues.

In relations between university students and their lecturers, the word 'jij' simply did not exist.

In the sixties, the accepted rules of behaviour rapidly became far more relaxed. 'U' was used less and less, eventually being reserved for strangers. Administrators, wishing to show that they were moving with the times, insisted on being called 'jij' and by their first names. This informality quickly took hold in the institutes of higher education. The once strict rules regarding clothing also fell prey to this revolution and jeans became the order of the day up to the higher levels of management and academia, and particularly in the non-profitmaking sector and the professions. This made it difficult to recognize the boss at a glance because he or she looked just like the rest of the staff. It all gave a very democratic impression. After centuries in the driving seat, the high and mighty seemed to have disappeared from the scene.

Had they really disappeared or had they simply hidden their high-and-mightiness from view? It is arguable whether relations in the country had become as democratic as they seemed. A secretary was still in a subordinate position, even if she did call her boss 'Jan' or 'Piet' and could afford to complain now and then without fear of reprisal. The country's managers quickly learned to explain their decisions in great detail. Keen observers realized, however, that – after all the consultations and 'joint decisionmaking' were out of the way – the original proposals usually remained essentially the same. And, in spite of all the jolly 'Jan'-ing and 'Piet'-ing, it continues to be inadvisable to take a radical stand against the decisions of superiors. Not only can it damage your career, it is incredibly difficult to keep it up in the face of so much reasonableness and willingness to listen from above. In the sixties, the work of the American Marxist Herbert Marcuse, and particularly his theory of 're-pressive tolerance', enjoyed great popularity for a while among left-wing intellectuals.

[78]

De Telegraaf was scornful of all this. Part of the new, *mondig* public wanted nothing to do with the consultation culture which, in their opinion, led only to inert bureaucracy. Their inspiration was the free entrepreneur, whose livelihood depended on his ability to respond alertly to the free market. They saw the state as a dangerous and interfering body that – with all its subsidies and social security provisions – took away people's sense of responsibility for their own lives and was therefore ultimately a threat to their freedom. These people found their ideological home in the *Volkspartij voor Vrijheid en Democratie* (vvd), until then a relatively marginal group with its roots in the old liberal party which, since the sixties, had been granted a minority share in government by the Catholics and Calvinists.

The vvd was dominated by free entrepreneurs with a strong dislike of state intervention. The top levels of the party contained quite a large group of intellectuals. A typical example was Pieter Jacobus Oud, who was the parliamentary leader in the 1950s. Oud was a professor at the University of Rotterdam, whose reputation was largely based on his history of the Dutch state, a standard work. The vvd was a civilized and refined party. In the seventies, however, it was led by a Hans Wiegel, a young man who had flunked university and rejected the ideology of his social democratic background because he found the group mentality too claustrophobic. Wiegel adopted a popular tone, very similar to that of the editors of *De Telegraaf*. He complained about high taxes, sneered at the over-abundance of government subsidies and suggested that those on social security were lazy. The intellectual-liberal school of thought, as personified by Oud, was pushed into the background. Wiegel's favourite bogeyman was Joop den Uijl, the political leader of the PvdA, the Dutch Labour Party. Den Uijl had climbed to top of the social democratic pillar, but had absorbed the new activists into his circles of consultation. He represented an ideology with the 'redistribution of income, knowledge and power' as its main theme. Wiegel referred to this as *nivellering*, [79] levelling out, or rather levelling down, 'cutting off the heads of all the flowers that stick out above the rest'. Wiegel's model of individual freedom directly opposed that of Den Uijl, who frequently spoke of the *maakbaarheid*, the 'makability', of society. By this he meant creating a society that gave everyone the opportunity to 'develop themselves' individually. This development was more spiritual and cultural than material. Both leaders had considerable electoral success. Den Uijl managed to keep his party intact as the social democratic pillar collapsed and he was even prime minister for a four-year period in the seventies. Wiegel was the eloquent spokesman of the conservative opposition. Both gnawed away at the traditional support of the Catholic and Calvinist parties. In 1977 the PvdA won more than a third of the votes. Wiegel succeeded, however, in forming a parliamentary majority with the decimated Catholics and Calvinists, forcing the social democrats into opposition where – except for a short *intermezzo* – they would stay until 1989.

The changes in the voting behaviour of the electorate also made it clear that the pillars were disintegrating. The balance of political power in the Netherlands had always been exceptionally stable. When the Calvinist prime minister Hendrikus Colijn won two seats in 1933, it was considered a shift of great political significance and a considerable electoral success. Since the sixties, however, political parties – particularly the new democratic party D66 – have grown accustomed to far greater swings of fortune. Opinion polls show that the number of 'floating voters' – those with no fixed ideological preference, who sometimes vote for one party and sometimes for another – has grown to some 20 to 30 per cent of the electorate.

The 1994 general elections were a clear example of this development. The Christian Democrats lost 20 of their 51 seats, while the PvdA lost 12. D66 (they have since dropped the apostrophe) won 12 and the VVD, 6. And this in a parliament of 150 seats and with a system of proportional representation. The fact that this result provided the first opportunity of forming a government without a 'religious' party since the early years of the century is a clear illustration of the continuity in Dutch politics.

The negotiations that preceded the formation of the present government bore great similarity, however, to the traditional methods of the regents. The meetings between the representatives of PvdA, VVD and D66 were clothed in the greatest secrecy. After a month or so, all three party leaders announced that they would most probably have to abandon the basic principles of the manifestos on which they had won the elections. The traditions of leadership in the Netherlands have proved to be exceptionally resilient. These modern-day regents came to a satisfactory compromise and it was assumed that the 'people' would accept it without question.

This was a reasonably sound assumption. Since the 1980s, there had been a growing feeling that the people were becoming less and less interested in what the government did and how it tried to run their lives. Den Uijl, who continued to lead the social democratic opposition until the mid-'80s, had predicted this trend. He foresaw the development of a social jungle, through which each individual would have to hack their own path. He also observed the beginnings of a deep rift in society, characterized by the re-emergence of a poor and deprived class, unknown since the nineteenth century.

There are, indeed, trends in current Dutch society that point in this direction. The phenomenal growth experienced in the fifties and sixties levelled out and was interspersed with periods of severe economic depression. This pushed unemployment up to levels reminiscent of the crisis in the 1930s. This placed enormous pressure on the state, which had to provide the social security benefits to which the victims were, after all, entitled. The complex system of grants and redistribution of wealth in the Netherlands became too expensive. As a minister in the coalition government of Catholic prime minister Dries van Agt, Hans Wiegel (yes, him!) kept the wolf from the door by allowing the budget deficit to increase. But since the beginning of the 1980s it has been impossible to mobilize a political majority behind this solution. The Christian Democrats found themselves a new leader in the Catholic industrialist Ruud Lubbers, who – in typical 'no nonsense' style – placed the emphasis more on the personal responsibility of the individual for their own welfare. In this view, the government should not be overly protective in trying to shield the individual citizen from personal risk. It is up to each individual to make their own arrangements, for example by taking out personal insurance cover rather than depending on collective schemes. The state should reduce its involvement to its core administrative duties, leaving the provision of other 'services' to the private sector. This is 'privatization'. The Lubbers governments also claimed that, in trying to guarantee social justice, the state had developed a whole array of rules and regulations, many of which were perhaps superfluous. This sounded very much like the message that Wiegel had employed with such success in the seventies.

[81]

THEY OPERATED UNDER THE BANNER OF COST CONTROL

The Lubbers governments operated in practice under the banner of cost control. They aimed to reduce government expenditure because the state was simply becoming too expensive. They did this together with the vvd until 1989, when they had a dispute with the junior coalition partner and exchanged the liberals for the social democrats. The fact that the PvdA allowed Lubbers to pursue his policies in the same vein cost the party a lot of its traditional support.

Dutch society, however, proved rather unwilling to adapt. The cutbacks were an assault on what the networks of social services and interest groups – still largely organized according to the pillar system – considered to be acquired rights. They organized a very effective resistance, ensuring that the government's often radical plans were amended in countless consultations. Adopting the tactics of the action committees, they urged angry citizens to take to the streets. Never before had such large crowds gathered in front of the parliament building with such regularity to express their indignation. Lubbers proved to be an accomplished juggler of formulations and compromises and managed to protect the main outlines of his policy against this onslaught. As a result, the entire system of grants and benefit schemes survived largely intact, while the flow of funds steadily diminished. A good example of this was the policy pursued by Lubbers' minister of education, Wim Deetman. Deetman announced that the higher education sector would have to manage on a lower subsidy. To alleviate the effects of this decision, the universities would have to take a number of measures, including the prevention of 'overlap' between institutions. This was known as 'the division and concentration of tasks'. The minister left it up to the universities themselves to decide on exactly what form this division and concentration should take in practice. He thereby forced them into consultation with each other, deftly detracting their attention from joint opposition to his proposals.

It was the only possible approach, but it prevented genuinely effective action, as became clear from the confusion surrounding the *Wet Arbeidsongeschiktheid*, the Invalidity Insurance Act. This Act, known popularly as the WAO, provides employees who are unable to work due to sickness or injury with a generous benefit. It is implemented by organizations run jointly by trade unions and employers' organizations. The number of people receiving WAO benefits rapidly approached the million mark, because it was seen as a perfect way of getting rid of superfluous or difficult employees. The definition of 'sick' was very broad and could include problems of a psychological nature. Such complaints became increasingly common in sectors of industry that were no longer able to afford large numbers of staff due to economic problems. It was a public secret that the WAO was becoming more and more a place to hide the unemployed. Lubbers was unable to do anything about this until the early 1990s. And even then he did not succeed in rectifying the fundamental fault in the organization – that the WAO was implemented by a group in whose interests it was to be able to unload surplus staff in a cheap and socially acceptable manner. The eligibility requirements for a WAO benefit were tightened up and all those receiving benefits already had to be re-assessed under these new stricter rules, but neither the Act itself nor the way in which it was implemented changed radically.

During Lubbers' 'reign' the purchasing power of people on a WAO benefit fell, while the standard of living of those in work generally increased – though not significantly. Lubbers preached wage restraint as the only way to keep unemployment down and minimize the loss of jobs due to automation. In this respect, he had the support of the majority, for he was simply expressing the widely held belief that *'rijkdom niet beklijft'*, riches have wings. Wealth is the fruit of hard work, but can be swept away in a storm as easily as the leaves of autumn. A certain amount of concern and caution is never amiss. This is apparent, for example, in the Queen's speech at the annual opening of parliament. The speech, drawn up by the government, is basically a statement of its policy. The Queen reads it out at a solemn gathering of both Houses. It is always full of concern, even expressing a certain amount of fear for the future. 'The government is concerned to observe…' – it is as though they are always prepared for the worst. But, at the same time, the impression is created that the government will act in time, just before things go really wrong. This is reassuring. Ruud Lubbers was a past master at giving concerned replies to questions in his weekly television interview. He was also, fortunately, very alert.

In the 1930s, the legendary prime minister Hendrikus Colijn concluded a radio address to the nation, in which he had announced a devaluation of the guilder, with the encouraging words: *'Gaat U maar rustig slapen'* – not so much a wish that his listeners would sleep well but an assurance that they could sleep soundly in their beds. In the seventies, after the first oil crisis, premier Joop den Uijl said that the world 'would never be the same again'. This left the concerned citizen with the unspoken idea that, if we want to survive out there, we have to stick together. Only then can we be sure that the wish expressed by Sonja Barend, a famous Dutch television presenter, at the end of her show: *'En morgen gezond weer op'* – 'Let's all get up tomorrow in good health' – will be fulfilled. The Evangelische Omroep, on the other hand, remains faithful to the traditional Calvinist rule that you should never take anything in the future for granted. As the EO wishes you good night, it does not promise to return the following day, it ventures only to hope that this will be the case. Everything is in God's unpredictable hands.

For most Dutch people, however, the image of God has all but disappeared. That is why so many of them – according to researcher Ernst Zahn – sought a 'punishing hand' with more foundation in reality. They have found this in the environment, the protection of which has taken on almost religious connotations.

In spite of this, the country still has four million cars, which create enormous jams during the rush hours. More and more drivers, however, feel guilty about using their cars. It is no longer popular to be proud of having a fast, flashy and sexy 'set of wheels'. You justify your ownership of a car by claiming that you really need it, that you simply cannot get by without it. Yet car ownership continues to increase, because concern for the environment is no reason – any more than the fear of God – to change your behaviour radically in practice. The embarrassment is not sufficient to give up the riches, so to speak. Furthermore, if it is true that many Dutch people have exchanged God for the environment, it continues to be just as vague an idea as the Almighty was before He completely dissolved in their conceptual frameworks.

Since the beginning of the 1990s a new character type has entered the public debate in the Netherlands. This new individual is the exact opposite of the caring individual described above. This is the 'calculating' citizen, an amoral egoist whose only care is self-interest. The calculating citizen uses and abuses all welfare schemes and other opportunities available to him in this prosperous country. He cheats the taxman by declaring a false income. He draws unemployment benefit while also getting paid for work that goes unnoticed by the authorities. He has an equal lack of respect for the rules governing his relations with his fellow citizens as for those intended to regulate his behaviour on the roads. He is in his element in the twilight zone between legality and illegality. He is the ultimate expression of sovereignty in its own domain – where he, of course, is the domain.

The calculating citizen has become the new Devil, Beelzebub, the corrupter, the spectre just around the corner, the type of character you believe you recognize in your neighbour, the victim of much verbal abuse. This image of 'the enemy' only proves that, in spite of the ubiquitous process of individualization, much has remained the same in Dutch society. The traditional role model – moderate in all things, inclined to compromise, unlikely to shout, show off or flaunt wealth and power, honest and thrifty – has survived the storms of social change with ease.

Every Dutch man and woman knows that in their soul is a calculating citizen, who will now and then get the better of them. But then they will be troubled by a guilty conscience. At the back of their minds they will still hear the faint voice of Calvin: 'You are bad and God will find you out'. Let those who have abundance remember that they are surrounded with thorns.

Chapter 2

'And in every region the voice of the water, telling of endless
disaster, is heard and feared'

The fight against the water. Polders, windmills and pumping
stations. The need for precise coordination and cooperation.
The engineer's mentality. You can manage the water but
cannot force it. Social engineering. Society's 'water mea-
dows'. Social management, but without a master plan. The
policy of tolerance.

Het was kil op de dijk. It was bitterly cold on the dyke. To my knowledge, no novel has ever started in this way, but a more Dutch opening sentence is difficult to imagine. The word *'kil'* refers to the biting cold caused by our often unpleasant, windy climate. Dykes, embankments to keep the water – the enemy – at bay, crisscross the Dutch landscape. These days, they are crowned with a strip of tarmac, but they are no more than secondary lines of communication. The real trunk roads are the four-lane motorways that have become an equally familiar feature of the landscape – a hundred and twenty kilometres an hour, raindrops on the windscreen, grey clouds rushing in from the southwest, middle-range family saloons in front and trucks in the slow lane. And the horizon dotted with the apartment blocks of the next town. That is what I see when I think of Holland.

Holland, not the Netherlands. The area characterized by endless flat countryside, canals and dykes actually covers little more than thirty per cent of the country. It stretches out along the North Sea coast and includes roughly the provinces of Zeeland, Noord-Holland, Zuid-Holland, Friesland and

Groningen, with a few inroads into the other provinces here and there. This thirty per cent does, however, contain the large majority of the population and all the major cities. It is the heart of the country's culture and economy. The old province of Holland was the driving force of the Republic in the Golden Age and it is still the powerhouse of the country, even though this conclusion might cause a few indignantly raised eyebrows among the people of the remaining provinces. 'The Wise Men originally came from the East, but now they apparently come from the West' – this is a favourite saying of the inhabitants of Twente, a region near the German border. And the people of Limburg, who have strong emotional ties with their beautiful undulating landscape in the extreme south of the country, still have a tendency to see the 'Hollanders' as colonial masters. Outside the *Randstad* – the ring of cities in the west, dominated by Amsterdam, The Hague, Rotterdam and Utrecht – foreign visitors soon learn not to refer to the country as Holland, but as 'the Netherlands'. The image of a motorway flanked by flat, green fields is not a truly representative image. In Limburg, it snakes through river valleys and in the *Veluwe*, a nature reserve in the centre of the country, it cuts through endless woodlands.

THE WHOLE OF THE NETHERLANDS IS A DELTA

Yet all of these areas are a part of the Kingdom of the Netherlands. The name means 'low countries'. The whole of the country is actually a delta, fed mostly by the Rhine and the Maas but also, to a lesser extent, by the Scheldt and the Eems. The North Sea is never far off and is largely responsible for the windy and rainy climate.

The rivers have minds of their own. The Rhine – which has now been contained – had the tendency to change course. And the quantity of water transported by the Maas tends to vary enormously, as the people of Limburg discovered in 1993 and 1995 when unheard-of masses of water rushed into their valleys. The whole of the country is actually barely above sea level and there is no clearly defined border between the land and the water. At least, there would not be if the people of the Netherlands had not made the distinction much clearer themselves. Yet, as the floods in Limburg showed, the water is not as easily mastered as foreigners – impressed at the astounding feats of civil engineering the Dutch have achieved – might wish to believe. The foreign visitor is often heard to declare 'God made the world, but the Dutch made the Netherlands'. It is a cliché, it has probably been said for three hundred years or more, and we still like to hear it. But it should be put into context.

THE CONTEST IS, AT BEST, A DRAW

In their renowned battle against the water, it is only in this century that the Dutch have abandoned their traditional defensive strategy and gone somewhat on the offensive. And, the contest is, at best, a draw. After more than a thousand years, the water has lost none of its power, if anything it has become even more fearsome. Before the Second World War, there were no motorways or apartment blocks to spoil the view for Hendrik Marsman (1899–1945), one of the greatest Dutch poets of this century:

'Denkend aan Holland	Thinking of Holland
zie ik brede rivieren	I see wide rivers
traag door oneindig	Winding lazily through
laagland gaan,	endless low countryside,
rijen ondenkbaar ijle populieren	Rows of impossibly slim poplars
als hoge pluimen	Like feathers
aan de einder staan,	Lining the horizon,
en in de geweldige	And farmhouses, low and lost
ruimte verzonken de boerderijen	In the immense open space,
verspreid door het land,	And throughout the land
boomgroepen, dorpen,	Clusters of trees, villages,
geknotte torens, kerken en olmen	Truncated towers,
in een groots verband.	Churches and mighty elms
De lucht hangt er laag	All merging as one.
en de zon wordt er langzaam	The sky is low and the sun is slowly
in grijze veelkleurige	Smothered by mists
dampen gesmoord,	Grey and many-coloured,
en in alle gewesten	And in every region
wordt de stem van het water	The voice of the water,
met zijn eeuwige rampen	Telling of endless disaster,
gevreesd en gehoord.'	Is heard and feared.

Because the ice is melting at the North Pole, sea levels are rising. The land, on the other hand, is drying out and subsiding. This weakens Dutch defences. Debates on the possible greenhouse effect, which will accelerate the melting of the ice caps, are therefore followed attentively and with some concern. Not that the average Dutch person is afraid of getting their feet wet. They are hardly aware that they live several metres below sea level. Their concern is more of a vague worry about what will happen to their children's children. And, even now, they still tend to see the water as a threat. You can drown in water. That is the main reason why all schools organize swimming lessons. The fact that swimming is healthy is a secondary concern.

This all rests on a collective experience reaching back more than a thousand years, in which each generation learned the hard way how you can protect yourself against the *'wassende water'*, the rising waters. The Netherlands – at least the west of the country as it is today – was originally an area of marshland, similar in many ways to present-day Bangladesh. The rivers flowed into the North Sea, splitting into a number of different arms which periodically changed course, as the Ganges, Brahmaputra and Mississippi still do. Most of the water from the Rhine now enters the sea at the Hook of Holland, near Rotterdam. Its main estuary used to be sixty kilometres to the north at Katwijk, near Leiden. All that remains there is a small stream, known as the *'Oude Rijn'*, the Old Rhine.

BUT THE NORTH SEA CAN BE VERY FICKLE,
AND WASH THE DUNES AWAY

The North Sea can be very fickle. Storms whip up the water. The currents carry large quantities of sand with them, generally from the south to the north, making the coastline unstable. Shallows and, eventually, sandbanks are created. In this way, in about 5000 BC, an uninterrupted line of sand dunes was created, which were stabilized by plant growth. This row of dunes stretches out along the entire Dutch coast, broken only where the rivers empty into the sea.

But the North Sea, which created these dunes, just as easily washes them away, depositing the sand elsewhere. As the sea level continues to rise, this process becomes even more destructive. The dunes would not have lasted much longer if the Dutch had not taken measures to halt the erosion. Existing dunes can be stabilized by, for example, planting marram grass which prevents the sand from drifting in the wind. The currents can be kept at bay by constructing breakwaters covered in basalt, a very hard volcanic rock. These breakwaters, which extend a few dozen metres into the sea and break the force of the current, can be seen for example between the Hook of Holland and The Hague. Sometimes, however, the wind can whip the water up over the breakwaters and whole sections of dune will be washed away. In the north of the country, the sea continually tries to break through the line of dunes. A sea dyke was built as early as the Middle Ages near Petten, and has since regularly been enlarged and reinforced. Further to the north, the line of dunes was breached in the distant past, creating what we now know as the Frisian Islands. The most northerly point of Texel, the largest of the islands, is still being eroded in spite of all the efforts of modern technology to halt the process. Just off the southwest coast of Texel, on the other hand, a whole new island, the *Razende Bol*, is appearing above water and is already the subject of a dispute between the adjoining municipalities.

About a thousand years ago, the North Sea forced its way into the area behind Texel and formed a continually growing bay that later came to be known as the Zuider Zee. The northern region of Friesland was eventually divided into two parts, with a great expanse of water between them. The western half is now a part of the province of Noord-Holland and has largely lost its Frisian character, with the exception of its name: West-Friesland.

On the south coast of the Zuider Zee, on the edge of the Veluwe – a large area of woodland that is higher and therefore never threatened by the water – is Elburg, the oldest planned town in the Netherlands. The town is laid out entirely in a chessboard pattern. It was designed by Arent toe Boccop, who ordered the original Elburg to be evacuated at the end of the fourteenth century, because the sea could no longer be held back. The new town was founded on the higher ground further inland. Naarden, another very clearly planned town, is a good example of this retreating movement, away from the aggressive Zuider Zee, where the waters of the North Sea were not easily contained.

Behind the dunes, there was originally an area of marshland, crisscrossed with countless streams, which was still affected by the tides and where the sea water infiltrated the many arms of the river. In the present day, salt water can still be registered as far inland as Schoonhoven, a small town in Zuid-Holland on the border with the province of Utrecht. The influence of the tides can be felt even further, at Culemborg, halfway between the coast and the German border.

The area very much resembled a mangrove swamp, although the vegetation consisted, of course, of species more suited to the colder climate, such as willow trees. The organic remains of this vegetation formed a particular kind of soil, peat, in which so much of the plant structure is preserved that, after being dried, it makes an excellent fuel. Stoves have burned this peat, which can be cut loose in slices, for centuries.

In spite of its inhospitable nature, this area was populated. The Roman historian Tacitus, for example, describes in great detail the uprising of a German tribe, the Batavians, against the Emperor Vespasian in the first century AD. This caused later historians to claim the Batavians as their ancestors. After the French occupation in 1795, the country was even known as the Batavian Republic for a little more than a decade.

Archeological research has discovered that the inhabitants of the area were farmers, who mostly kept cattle. They protected themselves against the water by building artificial hills, known as *terpen*, which provided enough space for the people and their animals when the water was at its highest. Many of these hills still survive in the northern province of Friesland. They form the core of old villages and have an ancient church at their centre.

It is then a small step to enclose a larger area with an earthen embankment, a dyke. In this way, you can keep more land dry with the same amount of earth. Remains of such dykes have been found that date back to the eighth and ninth centuries. The question that arises is: why would anyone wish to enclose the land in this way?

LAND WAS PRIVATE PROPERTY

The classical cultures of the Greeks and the Romans, on which much of present European culture is still based, had the concept of land ownership. Land was private property. In many parts of Europe this eventually came to include the people living on it. They were – as is described in the statutes of the time – tied to their land.

In that other gigantic river delta where Bangladesh is now situated, there was traditionally no notion of land ownership. There were local lords to whom the farmers in the area paid tribute and taxes, but this was due to their power and the authority invested in them, not to the fact they owned the land. Land was a common resource just like the air they breathed. The people of this wet country never developed the technology to protect it against the fury of the sea and the rivers. If the Ganges changed course and the sea swept away parts of the land, the farmers would simply move to the nearest piece of dry land and put their fences up again. The region was not as densely populated as it is today. It was only when the English colonists introduced land ownership that the local lords began to protect their new property with dykes and other constructions to control the water.

The fact that the people in the Rhine/Maas delta were a thousand years ahead of the Bengalis in this respect was probably due to the fact that the land was in private hands, owned by free farmers, nobles and Catholic monasteries. If the river or the sea took a piece of your land, it was a little more difficult to move somewhere else. Anywhere you went was someone else's land.

The monasteries and nobles started to protect their land by building earthen dykes. Some of these still wind their way through the countryside. It is not always clear how it was all organized because the process started at a time when written records were hardly kept.

The first small dykes were adequate because the sea level was much lower than it is now. They also protected relatively small areas of land. A number of inventions probably also date from that time, such as the *duikertje*, which is still in use today. This is a pipe with a loose flap at one end. If the water level rises and the water attempts to flow into the pipe, the current forces the flap shut. If the water comes from the other direction, the flap opens.

THE DUTCH LANGUAGE HAS SEVERAL WORDS FOR ´CANAL´

Enclosure by a dyke has no effect on the marshy nature of the land itself. Furthermore, it forces the groundwater upwards. The construction of a dyke therefore means that the enclosed land has to be drained. This is done by digging dead straight canals, in which the water collects. The Dutch language has an enormous number of words for the English word 'canal': *sloot, gracht, vaart, vliet, tocht* and many more, all of which say something about the width, depth or function of the canal in question. But whatever kind of canal it is, drainage is always part of its function. This also applies to the ponds and streams that are so popular in the suburbs and housing estates. They are not only there because they look nice; they also keep the water out of the cellars of the houses.

Water from outside the enclosed area seeps under the dyke and is in this way connected with the groundwater inside. As sea levels rose, dykes no longer provided adequate protection. The most primitive way of getting rid of excessive water was to simply bail it out. But in the fourteenth century, a new form of energy harnessed for this purpose – the wind. The early windmills were primitive, little more than a shaft with four sails at one end and a water wheel at the other. Each generation of mill-builders, however, refined the techniques. The mills got bigger, and the sails were eventually mounted on a cap that could be turned into the wind. In the body of the mill there was a wooden mechanism that, for the time, was very energy-efficient. The mills were perfected with the introduction of the Archimedes' screw, which could raise water to a height of four metres. It is difficult to measure the power of the traditional windmill but it is estimated at between 80 and 100 horsepower. This is comparable to that of the Volvo 440, the 90-horsepower middle-range family car that is produced by Nedcar in Born, Limburg.

A piece of land enclosed by dykes and drained is called a polder. Polders require a great deal of organization, not only in their construction but also to maintain them. The water pumped out of one, ends up in another. This has proved a great problem in Bangladesh, where new polders can exacerbate the situation in neighbouring villages. This can lead to conflict and even to the dykes being destroyed. Similar conflicts occurred in Dutch history. It would seem obvious that land reclamation should be a task for a central authority. The famous delta civilizations in ancient history, notably in Egypt and Mesopotamia, were extremely authoritarian with a divine monarch and a ruling caste that played a leading role in the organization of irrigation and drainage. The counties and duchies in the Middle Ages, however, lacked the power to build up such a system. Not that they did not try. The counts of Holland charged their *baljuws* – local officials very much like the infamous Sheriff of Nottingham – with the management of the polders and dykes. They, in their turn, appointed deputies – generally known as *heemraden*, dyke reeves – from among the local farmers but, because of the limited power of the counts, they were not easy to keep under control and acquired for themselves all manner of powers and privileges, in a similar way to the civic leaders in the towns and cities, who bought off their autonomy.

Dykes were built along the river banks. The polders stood shoulder to shoulder. The many streams that crisscrossed the country were closed off with dams. Boats had to be pulled over these dams with ropes, which provided quite a lot of work. Consequently, settlements frequently sprung up around these dams. Many modern-day place names end in -dam, notably the capital, Amsterdam. The first part of the name usually refers to the stream or river that was dammed off: the Amstel in Amsterdam, the Rotte in Rotterdam and the Ee in Edam. Very often, a square or street in the centre of a town or city will also be known as the Dam. The oldest houses will be found here. The Dam in Amsterdam, where the Royal Palace and the National Monument are located, is the most famous in the Netherlands. Most of these dams were later reopened. The gap was then closed off with enormous sluice doors that could be opened to let out excess water or to allow ships and boats to pass.

The maintenance of the dykes was initially organized very simply. Farmers were responsible for the stretch of dyke adjoining their land. This resulted in some stretches being neglected. It was also unfair, because farmers in the middle of the polder, far from the dyke, escaped this obligation. From around the end of the fifteenth century, it was increasingly decided that maintenance of the dyke was the joint responsibility of all those living under its protection. Either they all worked on the upkeep of the dyke together, or they paid a kind of tax to the reeves, who would then appoint a coordinator known as the *dijkgraaf*, or dyke warden.

IT WAS NEVER COMPLETELY SAFE BEHIND THE DYKE

These wardens were very powerful. They could order people to pay taxes or to work on the dykes. They are still authorized to call on the entire population of the area under their jurisdiction to fight against the onslaught of water. It was never completely safe behind the dyke. Sea currents could erode the dyke foundation to the extent that it would suddenly collapse. Heavy storms – particularly in combination with spring tides – could throw such masses of water against the dykes that they simply could not hold out. Every generation would have to live through one or two serious floods, which would claim many victims.

Although it cannot compete with the typhoons that unleash incredible violence every year on the coast of Bangladesh, or Hong Kong or Manila, the

North Sea can still whip up a reasonably fearsome storm. Once or twice a decade, it will prodice a storm of typhoon force. This is not very often, but it was often enough. Between Gorinchem and Geertruidenberg, on the border between the provinces of Zuid-Holland and Noord-Brabant, there is an area of natural wetlands known as the *Biesbosch*, that closely resembles what the Netherlands must have been like before the dunes and the dykes. But it is not a remnant of the original 'mangrove swamp'. It used to be agricultural polder-land, but was lost to the sea during the St. Elisabeth flood of 1421 – named after the saint on whose day the water broke through. Most of the flooded land has been reclaimed over the centuries, but the Biesbosch is still as it was left when the water receded. The 'drowned land' in Saaftinge and in Zuid-Beveland is also former farmland lost in the floods. In the latter, old bricks are sometimes still found – the remains of the once thriving town of Reimerswaal, whose inhabitants gave up the fight against the water at the beginning of the seventeenth century.

WHEN THE WATER COMES, IT COMES LIKE A WALL

The effects of the floods became more serious as the sea level rose and the land subsided. When the water comes, it comes like a wall. The dyke caves in and the water rushes through, boring a deep hole into the ground immediately behind the dyke. It then spreads out, thundering and boiling, sweeping away everything in its path – trees, cattle, people... It smashes against the walls of the houses. The only way to escape its fury is to hide in the attic or – if there is still time – take refuge on a piece of dyke that can withstand the onslaught. Then it is a question of waiting, until the wind has dropped enough for boats to be sent out. During the last great floods in February 1953 – which affected large areas of Zeeland, Holland and Noord-Brabant – 1835 people were killed. More than 100,000 people had to evacuated in the days following the disaster. It was touch and go whether the dykes protecting the major cities in the west of the country would hold out. It was the most serious flood in more than a century.

But the landscape still bears the scars of earlier catastrophes. The holes bored by the screwing movement of the water as it bores into the ground behind the dyke can be twenty or thirty metres deep and fill up with ground-water. These more or less circular lakes, known in Dutch as *wielen* – are a permanent reminder of days and nights spent in fear of the water.

After the floods have subsided, the holes are usually repaired, and then begins the difficult task of pumping out the water. This takes months, even with the latest in modern technology. In the past, they had to rely on windmills. After the floods in February 1953, it was November before the last hole was repaired. Only then could the pumping start.

In olden days, everyone was therefore continually aware of the threat from the water. It has been suggested that this is why the Dutch felt such an affinity with the sombre message preached by Calvin. They did not need to be told – 'Watch and pray, for thou knowest not the day nor the hour'. The wall of water can sweep way everything that you have built up – even your life – in just a few seconds. And, indeed orthodox Calvinism is still strong in the *Alblasserwaard*, one of the lowest regions in the Netherlands, where a large number of *wielen* bear silent witness to past catastrophes.

On the other hand, this enemy – just as much as Alva and his army – was dangerous enough to force people to work together. The various bodies responsible for the upkeep of the dykes agreed on various forms of cooperation. The magnificent 17th-century *Schielandhuis* in the centre of Rotterdam is a perfect illustration of the power of these bodies. Today it houses a large historical museum.

The North Sea and the rising rivers were not the only causes of flooding. The people themselves frequently gave a helping hand. Peat-diggers, for example, dug up the fenlands in the west, leaving great ponds behind which eroded the surrounding fields. This created a threat within the dykes and behind the dunes. People must have realized the danger, but they could not live without the peat which, for many, was the only fuel they could afford. In spite of the mild climate in the Netherlands, it is not easy to survive a winter without a stove to warm the house. And particularly a few centuries ago, when temperatures dropped below freezing more frequently than they do now – as can be seen from the countless paintings from the Golden Age depicting skaters and other wintry scenes. The same process that is causing the sea level to rise, has also increased the average temperature by a few degrees.

Eventually, technology was sufficiently advanced to tackle these expanses of water. The greatest land reclaimer of all was mill-builder Jan Adriaensz Leeghwater (1575–1650). His method consisted of enclosing a lake with a dyke and a canal. He then built enough screw-mills to pump the lake dry, after which a drainage system was built. The mills were left where they were to pump away excess water. Leeghwater worked on commission from Amsterdam financiers, who saw a new polder as a good investment. They tackled the problem on a large scale. Leeghwater started with the *Beemster* lake, which covered 7,189 hectares and was continually eroding away at the surrounding land. It took two years to pump dry, after which a flood wiped out the fruits of the work in a single day. The financiers raised new capital and two years later, in 1612, the polder was once again dry. Their investment was returned many times over. The Beemster is now one of the country's most beautiful polders, with splendid historical farmhouses and elegant villages. Leeghwater repeated this magnificent feat with many other – smaller – lakes. He was, however, unable to achieve his greatest ambition – to drain the *Haarlemmermeer*, between Amsterdam and Leiden. Hundreds of mills would have been needed to tame this gigantic lake, on the site of which Schiphol Airport now stands. Leeghwater wrote a widely read and often reprinted book about the drainage of the lake, which was considered by his contemporaries to be more a work of science fiction.

NOW THEY HAD STEAM

It was not until the nineteenth century that anyone dared take up the challenge of the Haarlemmermeer. And this was because they were no longer dependent entirely on windmills. Now they had steam.

In the seventeenth and eighteenth centuries the whole of the western part of the country was covered with windmills. Because of their limited capacity, they had to be linked together in all kinds of ingenious ways. Roughly speaking, the first series of mills would pump the water into a reservoir, known as a *boezem*, a second set of mills would then pump it into another reservoir slightly higher up, and so on until the water could be emptied into a river, where it could be carried down to the sea. Only very few of these mills survived the transition to steam power, electricity and diesel engines. The best preserved system of mills is to be seen at *Kinderdijk*, in a corner of the Alblasserwaard. In spite of their great number, these mills had their work cut out to keep the Alblasserwaard dry right from the start. Some areas were often too boggy to be safe, and the average water level in the ditches was higher than now, because that was the best the mills could do. This is how the first steam engines were introduced into the Netherlands – in dribs and drabs – to help in the fight against the water. They proved their strength and reliability, however, in the draining of the massive Haarlemmermeer. Three pumping stations did the job between 1849 and 1851. One of them was named 'Leeghwater', after the seventeenth century master who thought he would need hundreds of mills.

That effectively sealed the fate of the windmills. And now, thanks to modern pumping stations operating on electricity or diesel – which have long superseded steam – it is possible to regulate the water level inside the dykes very precisely. The new pumps are also powerful enough to have solved the problem of boggy ground which had always plagued engineers in the Alblasserwaard and elsewhere. The Netherlands has never been so dry.

Water management in the Netherlands is now the responsibility of a completely separate layer of government, the *waterschappen* or *hoogheemraadschappen*, which are directly based on their medieval forerunners. They are run by elected boards, but they are not strictly democratic, because representation is biased towards land and property owners. Yet they impose taxes on the entire population, which people pay together with their gas and electricity bills. The taxes are to guarantee the quality of the water; today's water boards are also responsible for keeping the water free of chemical pollution. Their work goes largely unnoticed. The taxes are not high enough for this to cause indignation among the general public and, consequently, the boards can go about their business undisturbed by calls for greater democracy. There are, on the other hand, frequent confrontations with environmental groups, who generally resist any proposals to 'modernize' the landscape submitted by the water boards.

The steam pumping stations of the Haarlemmermeer had opened the door to modern technology. Engineers came to the conclusion that the achievements of Leeghwater and his contemporaries could be repeated on a far grander scale, that they no longer had to be content with the small land-reclamation projects that had been conducted until then, such as in Zeeland, where clay deposits formed here and there outside the dykes, or in the north, where the Wadden Sea – the stretch of sea between the coast and the Frisian Islands – was becoming increasingly shallow.

Cornelis Lely (1854–1929) was the prototype of the modern engineer who was not afraid to take on large projects. He devised a plan to put an end to the threat from the Zuider Zee. The plan had two parts. Firstly, a dyke was to be built between Noord-Holland and Friesland to cut off the Zuider Zee from the North Sea. In the newly created lake behind the dyke, Lely envisaged the drainage of a large number of polders, so that half the surface area of the lake could be reclaimed as agricultural land. What remained of the old Zuider Zee would become a freshwater lake, later to be known as the IJsselmeer. Four of the polders Lely originally planned have since been created.

Lely was the first of a generation of great engineers who had a great influence on the shape of the Netherlands as it is today. A large number of them worked for *Rijkswaterstaat*, the government department responsible for the construction and maintenance of hydraulic and other civil engineering works. Rijkswaterstaat focuses primarily on large-scale projects. It keeps the tradition of Leeghwater very much alive, restricted only by the desire of politicians to limit expenditure. Serious flooding, however, always loosens their purse strings. The *Tweede Kamer* approved Lely's 'Zuider Zee Act' two years after water from the Zuider Zee had flooded large areas of Noord-Holland.

SUCCESSFUL INVASIONS OF THE LAND BY THE HOSTILE WATER ARE NOW MORE LIKELY TO PROVOKE AN AGGRESSIVE RESPONSE

With the development of modern technology, the Dutch have largely lost their fear of, if not their respect for, the sea. Successful invasions of the land by the hostile water are now more likely to provoke an aggressive response than the traditional mumblings about the fragility of existence. The floods of 1916 cried out for decisive countermeasures, immediate action to tame the Zuider Zee, no matter what the cost. The disaster in 1953 had the same effect. All of the dykes that had been breached were in the estuaries of the Rhine/Maas delta. This was because the storm – of rare typhoon force – had pushed enormous quantities of water inland. The government appointed a commission of engineers within the first two weeks of the disaster to determine whether the delta could be sealed off, followed immediately – if necessary – by the Wadden Sea. The commission drew up a Delta Plan that would involve sealing off all exits to the sea, with the exception of one for the Scheldt and one for the Rhine, to enable continued access to the ports of Antwerp and Rotterdam. They also introduced a new concept – *deltahoogte*, delta height. All dykes and dams had to be high enough and strong enough to withstand a combination of spring tides and storms of a force that only occurred statistically once every ten thousand years.

It took approximately twenty-five years to complete the Delta Project. The enormous dykes and sluices are now a tourist attraction, which Dutch hosts proudly show visitors from abroad. Now and then there are grumblings in the papers about excessive budgets, because Rijkswaterstaat has a reputation of wanting only the biggest and the best, but the whole gigantic project appears to have given the Dutch a boost to both their national pride and their sense of security. Most people believe that disasters like that of 1953 can never happen again. This is, however, an old and dangerous misconception. Studies have shown that most authorities in areas affected by floods traditionally show not the slightest concern until the wall of water is upon them. They have had to be called from their beds, while national radio companies simply stopped broadcasting, in spite of the imminent emergency and obvious need for clear instructions and public information.

The lesson, however, finally appears to have been learned. The reinforcement of all dykes up to 'delta height' is proof of this. Yet, every Dutch heart still misses a beat when, with a storm on the way, the radio news announces 'limited dyke surveillance'.

DYKES AT DELTA HEIGHT ARE NOT ENOUGH ON THEIR OWN

Dykes at delta height may be spectacular, but they are not enough on their own. The Dutch keep their feet dry with a complex system of pumping stations and pumps, *duikertjes* and sluices, ditches and canals, across the whole country. This whole system has to be kept running by people. And that means people who know exactly what they are doing.

Water is multifunctional – ships and boats can sail on it. Until the demand for freight transport took on mass proportions, followed closely by the construction of good public highways, most freight in the Netherlands was carried by water. Even freight trains were unable to challenge this dominant position to any significant extent. You could, after all, get practically anywhere in the country by boat. The country was therefore not only crisscrossed by waterways intended for drainage, but also by a large number of canals used for freight transport. These boat canals still cut across the countryside in dead straight lines. Most date from the Golden Age and form part of a forgotten network of public transport. The canals were used by horse-drawn barges. They were slow, with a maximum speed of three or four kilometres per hour.

But they were reliable, they sailed on time, and could accommodate large numbers of passengers in their covered saloons. The only thing that could stop them plying their way up and down the canals was ice. In the time of Prince Maurits, during the Golden Age, whole armies were transported to the front by these barges. The soldiers were amazed at this wonderful and happy land, where you didn't even have to walk to the battlefield. For two centuries, the horse-drawn barges were the most reliable form of transport in the world. And the cheapest. Only in the Netherlands could you really plan a journey and be reasonably certain of the day on which – and even the time at which – you would reach your destination. These barges were an important part of the infrastructure that permitted the economic growth of the Golden Age. Today, they are the symbol of slow-moving conservatism. But they acquired that image only when the Netherlands discovered the steam train and constructed a road network, along which the post coach could race, rushing its passengers – at first only wealthy businessmen with cigars and wallets fat enough to pay the fare – to their destinations. The barges even gave rise to a whole series of political pamphlets, the authors of which had thrashed out their standpoints in discussions held in the saloon during the long, slow voyages.

GOOD ORGANIZATION AND CLOSE COOPERATION

This whole complex of 'water management' depends on good organization and close cooperation. Everything has to be carefully maintained according to fixed standards, sluices have to be opened and closed exactly at the right time, mills – and later, pumping stations – have to operate according to a clearly defined pattern. There must be detailed procedures for emergencies, such as storms or exceptionally high water, and they have to be applied in practice. This, in turn, demands a clear designation of tasks and responsibilities, so that everyone knows exactly what to do and not to do at any particular moment. And cooperation is essential, particularly in emergencies, when everything else has to be put on one side, there is no time for discussion, all disputes must be forgotten and all must pull together to avert the danger.

Perhaps this is why the desire for order and organization, in spite of a well-developed sense of individuality and in spite of 'sovereignty in one's own domain', is so strong.

In any case, there is a clear tradition of belief in the 'makability' of the landscape. In the west and north of the country there are no longer any genuine 'natural areas'. Everything is the result of human intervention – even the old lakes were created by peat digging. The landscape is the product of man's toil. This gives a completely new dimension to God's command to Adam to be Lord of creation. In olden times, the Dutch had two terms for the virgin land in the higher areas in the east and south of the country: *woeste gronden* and *onland*. These both have very negative connotations. *Woest*, meaning wild and untamed, is the very opposite of controlled and civilized; it also suggests fury, an irrational anger. The prefix *on-* is a denial, clearly suggesting badness, as in *ongeluk* (which literally means unhappiness, but is also the Dutch word for 'accident'), *onkruid* (literally 'un-plant', the weeds that strangle the corn), or *ongedierte* ('un-animals' – used to describe unwanted creatures, such as bedbugs or cockroaches). This wild 'un-land' was a threat, as hostile as the unpredictable sea. Until well into the last century it was also uncompromisingly resilient to human intervention. Agriculture in the south and the east was traditionally a combination of arable and pastoral. Farmers grew crops and kept cattle. The former was limited by the amount of natural fertilizer produced by the latter. In the impoverished province of Drenthe, the fields – with a village at their centre – lay like islands in the great expanse of heathland. On the heath grew the heather, a tough little plant with purple flowers which is excellent food for sheep. Farmers who cultivated the heath for crops, could no longer keep sheep and therefore lost their indispensable supply of manure. It was one thing or the other. *Some catch, that catch 22.* The heath of the 'wild lands' proved to have insufficient natural fertility to support crops without additional nourishment. The farmers were in a zero-sum situation that remained unchanged for centuries. It was not until the nineteenth century that cheap artificial fertilizer and specialist machinery provided them with an opportunity to break the deadlock. They allowed farmers to improve their lot on a grand scale, in the same way that their countrymen were reclaiming land from the sea at low tide in Zeeland and the North.

This also made the Dutch farmers much more active. Their representative organizations set up a whole network of agricultural education, with the Agricultural University of Wageningen as its showpiece. Within the pillars, ministers and priests set up church-based farmers' cooperatives, which included a network of banks to provide credit. These have now been incorporated – Catholic and Protestant – into the Rabobank, one of the twenty largest bank conglomerates in the world. Nowadays, the average Dutch farm is organized to produce as much as possible, and is often very specialized, mechanized and increasingly automated. The farmers have made the Netherlands one of the world's leading food exporters. This has made the average farm very capital intensive. Farmers have to know everything there is to know about their crops and livestock and have as near total control of their production processes as is possible. They have, after all, extensive commitments to the local Rabobank, which finances all this technology.

This form of agricultural exploitation depends on a continually increasing turnover. Since the end of the Second World War – even with the heavily subsidized prices guaranteed by the influential agricultural lobby in the European Community – small farmers have been increasingly squeezed out of the market. In the 1950s, the social-democratic minister Sicco Mansholt set up a system under which farmers who were unable to keep up with technological changes could be bought out by the state. Their land was then sold or leased to neighbours who did have sufficient capital. This scaling up process continues today. Since Mansholt's time, production has increased enormously, but the number of people who earn a living in agriculture – in 1900, still more than half the population – is now less than three per cent. This does not include those employed in the food processing industry.

The subsidies have led to an enormous over-production. Since the 1980s, the EC and the Dutch government have tried to do something about this. Cattle farmers have been given quotas and receive heavy fines if they exceed them.

THEY BELIEVE THAT THEY CAN REGULATE THE ENVIRONMENT

The farmers have acquired enemies among those who wish to preserve the environment. More and more Dutch people believe that our control over the environment has gone too far. What their ancestors called the *onland* is now seen as the natural environment, something crucial to the quality of life and therefore to be protected. Furthermore, we are learning from bitter experience that the earth is less manageable that we thought. Sicco Mansholt, the minister who instigated the modernization and up-scaling of Dutch agriculture, openly regretted this policy in his later days. Even the professors at Wageningen now project their esteemed institution as an 'environmental university'. They believe that they can regulate the environment. In recent years,

fields used for growing crops and grazing cattle have been 'returned to nature'. Having realized the value of the *woeste landen*, the wild and untamed lands, the Dutch have decided to 'plant' them themselves.

We are all confronted daily with the problem of the environment – the revenge of the air, the earth and water on our attempts to impose our own order upon them. Centuries of accumulated interventions by man in his natural environment are now threatening what the Dutch refer to as *leefbaarheid* – roughly equivalent to what the authors of the Limits to Growth called 'habitability'. Everyone is convinced of this. Environmental activists warn that we shall suffocate and drown in our own waste and most Dutch people believe them to a greater or lesser extent. There is a Green Party which aims to change society radically according to ecological principles. Their message is in fact that we have to start again on a completely new basis – a genuine post-industrial society. In elections, the party – under the leadership of the now grey-haired ex-provo Roel van Duijn – has had little success, winning nothing more than the odd seat on a local council. Most Dutch people believe that we can save the environment with a few practical measures. An example of this belief can be seen in an interview given by Bas van der Wal, responsible for surface waters at the Delfland water board, with the environmental journal *Milieu Aktief* about the canals in his region: 'The fish population is seriously out of balance. As a result of eutrophication, there are a lot of carp and bream. And frogs, which are not so sensitive to pesticides. And other factors are also significant, such as the structure of the canal banks. To the layman, the canals may appear to be healthy but we know that the whole ecosystem is on the point of collapse. Most of the organisms – all of which are crucial to the aquatic system – live under the water and are very small, and therefore go unnoticed by the casual observer'. Van der Wal expressed his concern about the water flea, which is under threat and is indicative of the reduction of biological diversity in the environment.

He did, however, have a number of solutions. The challenge was to create an ecosystem that resembled the 'original' natural environment as closely as possible. The only solution was therefore, in Van der Wal's opinion, to persuade the many market gardeners in Delfland to reduce their use of pesticides by 99 per cent. He had, however, little faith in this option. 'It can, of course, be very difficult to motivate the market gardeners to do this. We are therefore also looking at the possibilities for improving the quality of the water. And, of course, you can always do something to improve the natural habitat for the flora and fauna. Reservoirs can be constructed so that they do not just look like straight-sided tanks. They can be built with sloping sides and a natural bank, filled with lush aquatic vegetation. They can have deeper sections for fish to spend the winter. The presence of frogs and other amphibians, or polecats, for example, always adds to the value of the aquatic environment and makes people appreciate it more.' In this way, Van der Wal was presenting himself as the mini-Lely of the Delfland water flea.

WHAT PROFESSOR OPSCHOOR CALLS THE *MILIEUGEBRUIKSRUIMTE*

Van der Wal is typical of the kind of civil servant or public administrator that has become very common in the Netherlands over the past twenty or thirty years. These are people with a genuine interest in the quality of our living environment and who believe that it can be more or less arranged as they best see fit. Very many people share this conviction. Almost every day, the television shows 'commercials' in which the government calls on the people to be sparing in the use of what Professor J. B. Opschoor of the Free University calls the *milieugebruiksruimte*, environmental space. 'Alles heeft zijn prijs', say the Dutch. Everything has its price. Opschoor's research is intended to calculate what that price is. Environmental damage can then be counted along with investments and deducted from profit. This gives, in the professor's view, a more realistic picture of genuine costs and revenue.

The Free University was set up by Abraham Kuyper, the founder of the Calvinist pillar, and Opschoor's approach is reminiscent of the biblical message that man is God's steward and is therefore charged with the difficult task of managing the earth in a responsible manner. Yet this stewardship does give man a privileged position. After all, in Genesis, the first book of the Bible, after having created heaven and earth, God appoints Adam, the first man, the Lord of Creation. With no restrictions. This, in principle, distinguished Adam's descendants from all the other living creatures on earth. They can do as they please, subjugate the lesser animals in any way they wish. The native Indian of Guatemala feel that they are an integral part of their *milpa*, their maize field, rather than its owner or leaseholder. They have a special responsibility to the land that they share with the plants and the animals. This gives them a certain sense of caution, a recognition of their limitations, that does not exist in the biblical primacy of man. In the Bible, the only restriction on man's free reign to exploit the earth to the point of exhaustion is the stewardship imposed on him by God. This image of our relationship with the environment underlies Opschoor's work.

There are, however, here and there in the Dutch environmental movement, schools of thought that bear closer resemblance to the beliefs of the Guatemalan Indian. Yet these are restricted to a small progressive minority. The great majority believes in regulation and protection.

This desire to protect the environment rests on an older tradition. Nineteenth-century romanticism had a strong influence on the Dutch élites. They began to admire the beauty of the *woeste gronden* and imitated them in their gardens and the first municipal parks. Ornamental gardens were initially inspired by those at the French royal palace at Versailles. They represented the absolute control of man over nature. They were laid out in geometric patterns, with closely cropped lawns and clipped hedges that were often formed with great artistry into the shapes of human inventions, such as windmills. The landscape that received the greatest admiration was the reclaimed land, such as Leeghwater's polders, because it was tamed and was of use.

Romanticism meant a dramatic reversal of this view. The Versailles lookalikes were all dug up, to be replaced by wild woodlands – the wilder, the better. Dutch landscape gardeners soon learned to disguise fences and walls by the subtle planting of trees to give the impression of the edge of a large forest. Contrived-looking ponds were replaced by more 'natural' streams. The more adventurous among them even created 'ruins' and outcrops of rock. Every self-respecting town and city laid out public gardens and parks in this way. The Park on the Maas in Rotterdam and Amsterdam's Vondelpark are perfect examples. Most parks designed since that time have been largely romantic in character. There are almost no gardens left laid out in Versailles style. Gardening has become a popular hobby. Millions of people in this small, densely populated country live in flats and first-floor maisonettes, but every survey proves over and again that the greatest wish of almost every Dutch man and woman is to have a house with a front and back garden.

On the outskirts of most cities, there are complexes of *volkstuinen*. These 'people's gardens', the equivalent of what are known in English as 'allotments', date from the beginning of this century. The original idea was allow the less well-off to grow their own vegetables, since medical science had proved that they were good for your health. Today, these allotments have almost all become ornamental gardens, which their owners cherish with their hearts and souls. They probably had to spend years on the waiting list before they even got the small patch of land.

The Dutch take good care of their gardens. Those who do not mow their lawns often enough or fail to remove the weeds from their flower beds so that the seeds end up in the neighbour's garden will suffer the disapproval of the whole neighbourhood and, if he does not conform, will find himself embroiled in a genuine conflict with the other residents of the street. Weeds are unsightly. Unless, of course, they are part of a completely controlled romantic 'natural garden'. And everyone can tell the difference between this and a neglected lawn. And yet, these days, the Dutch do see their gardens as a piece of 'nature' in their own backyard, so to speak. There is general consensus that children should grow up in a 'green' environment. But green or not – and this cannot be said often enough – that environment must be as strictly controlled as possible.

At the same time there is a general romantic appreciation of what the Dutch call *de vrije natuur*, the natural, undeveloped environment. This is a very positive term, which contrasts sharply with the more traditional *woeste gronden* and *onland*. This appreciation began to take concrete form in the last quarter of the nineteenth century, simultaneously with the development of a renewed respect for the architecture of the towns and cities. Dilapidated old buildings were seen as the legacy of a great past that needed to be carefully preserved. Many people believed that their ancestors had supremely better taste than the current generations. What had previously been demolished as an obstacle to progress and a memory of an earlier, less sophisticated epoch now became eligible for protection as a national monument. The Amsterdam art critic and leading Catholic Josephus Alberdinck Thijm, for example, led a campaign against the city council's plans to fill in the *Nieuwe Zijds Voorburgwal*, a medieval canal, to make way for the building of a road. Although he lost, progressive civic leaders have since had little success in obtaining approval for the filling in of other canals – the product of the revered Golden Age – in the capital. The Nieuwe Zijds Voorburgwal built up a new reputation as the Dutch version of Fleet Street. The new road made it easy to transport the papers and the stock exchange, the source of news on the economy, was only a stone's throw away. At the same time it preserved the name of a piece of Amsterdam's glorious past that had been erased forever. It was a stab in the heart of the city, a perfect example of how not to do things. The government started to draw up a list of protected buildings, known as the 'monument list'. Their owners were not allowed to demolish or alter them without permission. A set of rules was drawn up by a group of experts whose job it was to preserve the historic character of the buildings. Subsidies were granted for 'restoration'. This expertise was provided by the *Rijksdienst Monumentenzorg*, a government department with the same status as Rijkswaterstaat. Monumentenzorg now has a complete network of branches throughout the country. It employs a large number of specialized architects, who check restoration work and ensure that owners do not change the character of their buildings by, for example, fitting plastic door or window frames.

[107]

These days, certain 'views' in towns and villages are also protected. New buildings may be constructed but they must not disturb the view, or at least not to an excessive degree. With the passage of time, the monument list has become longer and longer. In recent years, it has included an increasing number of nineteenth and twentieth century buildings, including factories from the early years of the Dutch industrial revolution. Plans to demolish exceptional old buildings always attract the attention of the specialized action committees and historical associations that are present these days in every municipality in the country.

'Woeste gronden' are seen in the same way. It is no accident that the leading organization for the protection of the natural environment in the Netherlands is the *Vereniging tot Behoud van Natuurmonumenten in Nederland,* known popularly as *Natuurmonumenten* ('monuments of nature'). It was founded in 1905 in response to Amsterdam's plans to fill in the Naardermeer – an original peat lake that had never been reclaimed – with refuse from the city. The association was set up by the liberal élite politician Gijsbert van Tienhoven and the popular biologist Jacobus Thijsse, who bought the Naardermeer and declared it a nature reserve. This was the first acquisition of many. Natuurmonumenten manages its reserves with great care, leaving nothing to chance. The members of the association have access to the reserves, as long as they remain on the specially marked out paths.

Another typical example of this approach is the release of beavers in the Biesbosch, the remains of the damage caused by the St. Elisabeth flood in 1421. The Ministry of Agriculture, Fisheries and Nature Management released the animals, imported from Eastern Europe, because historical records show that they used to be common in the area. Another example is the distinction made by Dutch biologists between 'indigenous' plants and those imported later. For a long time, it was believed that the latter detracted from the quality of the natural monuments – in the same way as later additions could ruin a historic building. This radical standpoint has lost much of its force in recent years.

MODERN ENVIRONMENTAL ACTIVISM
HAS ITS ROOTS IN THE BIG CITIES

Unlike traditional nature management, modern environmental activism has its roots in the big cities. It is in principle a separate issue, because it was originally concerned with pollution of the natural environment by human activity. This is not to say that this has traditionally been neglected. In centuries past, local administrators introduced regulations to protect the public from what we now call environmental annoyance. Foul-smelling leather tanneries, for example, or mills that beat copper – with the accompanying unavoidable racket – had to be situated well away from built-up areas. But as wealth and welfare became more normal, particularly since the 1960s, the public's expectations increased. 'Not much traffic' was the comment made by foreign minister Joseph Luns when he was allowed to look over the Wall during a visit to West Berlin in the early sixties. And indeed, streets with no cars and full of pedestrians were proof enough of the failure of communism. PvdA leader Joop den Uijl frequently expressed his opinion in public that every Dutch family should have a car. A few years later, with his fine nose for which way the wind was blowing, he held impassioned speeches about the 'quality of life' and how it was threatened by the unbridled growth of industry.

An important turning point came in 1963 when a serious fire broke out in the *Superfosfaat*, an artificial fertilizer factory in Vlaardingen, a town in Zuid-Holland, close to Rotterdam. An easterly wind blew the clouds of poison gas between the surrounding villages and out to sea. If the more normal west wind had been blowing, the gas would have drifted over the city and tens of thousands of lives might have been lost. The cabinet held an emergency meeting to prepare for a large-scale evacuation. This proved unnecessary at the last moment, but it was touch and go.

Superfosfaat was part of an enormous complex of chemical plants and refineries that had sprung up between Rotterdam and the sea. It had even been built at the expense of a cherished natural monument. Now the country had been given a clear warning of what impact a serious accident could have.

The critical generation of the 1960s embraced the environment as one of the many sins of the *misselijk makende middenstand*. Zahn's view that the environment replaced a God who was slowly dissipating into nothingness is certainly worth consideration, but the unpleasant experience of a stinking industry that sometimes went up in flames was equally as important.

Furthermore, as time went on, environmental damage became increasingly visible. Old industrial plants, such as gas works, had contaminated the ground so badly that it was a health hazard to the residents of homes built later on the same sites. This meant that the sites had to be cleaned up at great cost and, in some cases, the houses had to be demolished. Hundreds of these sites were discovered, some of which were centuries old, for example, where our industrious ancestors in the Golden Age had built white lead factories. Most were, however, more recent. It was calculated that it would cost 53 billion guilders to clean up all of these sites. This had to born by the taxpayer because the culprit was often long dead and would therefore be unlikely to pay the bill. As is customary, the environmental organizations formed a number of action committees, which mostly directed their efforts at a particular polluter or group of polluters and demanded concrete measures. At first, attention was centred on air pollution. People living near factories and other sources of air contamination were no longer prepared to breathe it in day in, day out. It was not long before surface waters and the contamination of the soil also became hot issues. After that it was the turn of capital-intensive agriculture, which used great quantities of artificial fertilizer and pesticides to increase yields as far as possible. And this, while the enormous number of livestock in the Netherlands – there are as many pigs in the country as people: 15 million – produced so much natural fertilizer that the manure mountain could no longer be used up and created another environmental problem. Political and administrative leaders treated the action committees as any other – they accepted them as partners in the debate and adopted their terminology and aims almost wholesale. The movement formed provincial and national umbrella organizations that received subsidies and started playing the role of an environmental lobby, encouraged and subsidized by the government. Most of these organizations were set up in the early seventies.

The government employed experts to regulate the environment. 'Snuffel-paaltjes', instruments for measuring the quality of the air, sprung up throughout Greater Rotterdam. They were operated by the Rijnmond En vironmental Department, who also had a telephone line available day and night to receive complaints from the public relating to the environment. The environment became the responsibility of the Ministry of Housing and Spatial Planning.

Radical critics even argued that, in the long term, there would no longer be a place in the Netherlands for intensive agriculture, which survived only because of government subsidies. Farmers, they said, should be re-educated as 'nature managers'. The subsidies could be used in far better ways than on their increasingly desperate attempts to keep their heads above water by intervening more and more in natural processes, by increasingly intensive crop cultivation and by the application of biotechnology and expensive machinery. These people are still a minority, but there are trends observable in the Netherlands that suggest a movement in that direction. It is now unlikely that the last of Lely's great polders in the IJsselmeer will be reclaimed. There is little profit to be made in the commercial exploitation of agricultural land and the Netherlands will probably have more need of the fresh water in the lake than new land. A number of municipalities in the *Oldambt*, a region in the northern province of Groningen drew up plans to flood a number of old polders, to create a lake that would attract tourists and provide more local jobs. In the heart of the province of Zuid-Holland, between Rotterdam and Gouda, a romantic 'forest' is to be planted in an old cattle farming area so that the million inhabitants of Greater Rotterdam have an extra piece of 'nature' in which to get away from it all. These days, no one in their right mind would suggest reclaiming more of the Wadden Sea, which largely falls dry at low tide. The sea is seen as a valuable nature reserve and an influential conservation association with members throughout the country aggressively resists any attempts to exploit it, such as exploratory drilling for oil and gas.

The environmental movement follows the activities of the government with a critical eye, frequently with considerable suspicion, but the two parties share the same basic conviction – that nature and the environment can ultimately be regulated and controlled.

IN A CERTAIN WAY, ENGINEERS ARE HUMBLE

Lely has become a household name in the Netherlands. He gave his name to Lelystad, the capital of the new province that is formed by his polders in the former Zuider Zee, and to the intercity railway station, Amsterdam Lelylaan. This fame is based on his vision as a hydraulic engineer. But he had many more strings to his bow. Lely was also the father of the Industrial Injuries Act, which provides compensation for people injured at work. He applied his engineer's mentality – the belief that you could regulate and control a great deal with a good set of basic assumptions, a sound knowledge of your field and practical experiments – to the problems of society. Students in Lely's time were deeply impressed by Professor Hendrik Baltus Pekelharing (1841–1922), who taught political economics at the Technical University in Delft. Pekelharing's lectures and seminars were very influential. He spoke of planning – not of the land, but of society. Many of the professor's pupils were active in politics, and frequently ended up in the *Sociaaldemocratische Arbeiderspartij*, the Social Democratic Workers' Party. Nobel Prize winner and founder of econometrics, Professor Jan Tinbergen, said in 1936 that his subject was an 'engineering science'. The development of society was equally as controllable as the course of the rivers through the flat deltalands of Holland.

There is something totalitarian about this way of thinking. Yet totalitarian ideologies, such as communism or national-socialism, never really found a solid basis in the Netherlands, not even in the technical universities. It must be admitted, however, that the Dutch mini-*führer* Anton Mussert – who founded the National Socialist Movement in the Netherlands – was an engineer. Such ideologies are, however, contrary to the engineer's creed, because they are based on a number of unshakable convictions about the way society should be organized. Whether these are founded on racial superiority, or the dictatorship of the proletariat, or collective ownership of the means of production is of no importance. What they all boil down to is that everything must be forced to conform to a predetermined pattern.

At the Delft Hydraulics Laboratory, they have a different approach. They do not attempt to subjugate the Rhine completely to their will, but to regulate the current to achieve certain restricted aims. In a certain way, engineers are humble: they sufficiently respect the laws of nature and the forces they are confronted with never to attempt to tame them completely. They know that that is the road to disaster. They also know that these laws are not purely the product of human logic. That logic has been applied to bring order to the chaos of countless empirical observations. Logic makes the laws clear to us. Socially oriented engineers have rarely come across sufficient natural order in society to be able them to establish inviolable laws – with the exception of the odd communist or Anton Mussert, but they were isolated examples. These engineers believed in regulation and control and came up with countless proposals to that effect. But these were partly based on a wide variety of beliefs with their roots in the philosophies of the pillars. They also had great faith in the results of scientific investigation. If medical researchers established that the feared disease tuberculosis was common among people who lived in dark, damp houses, they considered it their social duty to subject new buildings to statutory requirements regarding the quality of the materials used, the minimum size of doors and windows, and ventilation. This concern could sometimes take quite an extreme form. There was a department of construction engineers at Delft that spent a great deal of its time trying to design the perfect 'workers' house'. Until the early years of this century, most Dutch people still slept in a *bedstee*, a kind of cupboard set in the wall, or in the *tussenkamer*, a small, dark room between the parlour at the front of the house – where guests were received – and the back room, where the family ate and lived – except on feast days. Modern architects got rid of the *tussenkamer* and located the light points in the ceiling so that a lamp could be hung above the dining table. This would allow the workers to spend their evenings reading, as the lamp threw its clear light onto the pages.

KNOWLEDGE IS POWER

Socially oriented engineers believed strongly in the idea that knowledge is power. This was, after all, the basic tenet of their profession. Enormous publishing houses grew up within the pillars, marketing great quantities of good, cheap books which reflected the beliefs of the pillar concerned. The network of public libraries that now covers the country, complete with mobile *'bibliobussen'* to reach isolated communities, is also a concrete expression of this conviction.

Clearly this faith in the power of regulation and control is closely related to traditional Dutch paternalism, to the mentality of the regent who knows better than the people themselves what is good for them.

Foreign observers regularly remark that Dutch towns and cities are as neatly planned as the countryside. This has its roots in the same mentality. Architects like Berlage and Oud attempted to design public housing that would, as it were, invite the residents to develop themselves spiritually. And not only that, they wanted to preserve the traditional sense of community. They designed 'garden villages', in which the neat little houses – all with front and back gardens – were grouped around a sort of square. The architects of the Amsterdam School preferred to project this sense of security in castle-like complexes of stone, with gates and ornamental towers. These made the residents feel protected, as though they all lived together in a kind of citadel. Many of these complexes are now on the 'monument list'.

In a deregulated society, where everything is determined by the law of supply and demand, such public housing projects rarely get off the ground. For that reason, almost since their party was founded, the social democrats have been demanding that local authorities take responsibility for public housing. Their demands were met, but only after a very long time. Local administrators were generally prepared to support associations that wished to build good quality, cheap housing for their members by, for example, guaranteeing their loans on the capital market. Such associations sprung up everywhere and were soon an integral part of the pillar system. As a result, Catholic, Calvinist and social democratic housing developments were built shoulder-to-shoulder. These associations were largely responsible for the construction of the 'garden villages'.

The government did not take it upon itself to provide public housing on a grand scale until after the Second World War. This was actually a emergency measure demanded by the circumstances. So many houses had been destroyed during the occupation and the fighting that took place in the country, that the solution to the housing shortage could not be left to the free market. A system of distribution was set up so that the shortage could be shared as equally as possible. The rents of the houses built by the government were kept as low as possible through a system of subsidies. The wealthy, after all, had enough money to find their own houses on the free market.

The architects of the time were very enamoured of rationalism and standardized high-rise blocks in the style of Le Courbusier. The advantage of this approach was that standardization kept the price of building down. Large estates sprung up around the larger towns and cities, usually with high-rise apartment blocks surrounded by expansive playing fields and public parks. Their designs promoted a certain lifestyle. Each flat had a shower, something new for people who had been used to washing themselves once a week in a tin tub in front of the fire. To make sure the residents actually used the shower for its intended purpose, most municipalities also made them rent a small geyser at a very low price, which ensured them hot running water. In the seventies, architects once again showed a preference for low-rise, 'village garden' style housing, provoking accusations from several quarters of a 'new frumpiness'. Once again the sense of community was the motivation, but now it appeared to clash with increasing individualism and the disintegration of the pillars. Many Dutch people wanted more privacy and to be bothered as little as possible by those living around them. Countless action committees were set up to deal with problems caused by noisy or otherwise imposing neighbours.

Residents of what local councils considered to be run-down neighbourhoods set up action committees to protest against their demolition – and with some success. Since the seventies, many municipalities have pursued a policy of renovation, in which the character of the old buildings – particularly the front façades – is preserved as far as possible. Inside, the visitor finds all the fittings of a modern apartment.

The conviction that all social development can be regulated extended further than physical planning alone. It also gave rise to a comprehensive system of licences that covered an increasing range of social activities. This allowed paternalistic administrators to, for example, limit the number of bars which sold alcoholic drink, which – as everyone knows – is an obstacle to the social and individual development of the people. The government prescribed fixed opening times for shops, not only to protect their personnel from over-exploitation, but also to protect small shopkeepers from large chain stores which could easily stay open 24 hours a day by allowing their staff to work in shifts. (In the autumn of 1994, the government began to draw up plans for the far-reaching liberalization of shop opening times.)

More and more professions and commercial sectors became inaccessible to people without the required qualifications. A strict department of weights and measures ensured that consumer products met the minimum requirements for quality. A system of licences for the establishment of businesses ensured that not too many companies of the same kind were located in any one area, to avoid cut-throat competition. This administrative mentality gradually acquired a dynamic of its own, with the result that many people occasionally feel that they are suffering under a repressive and tyrannical government. For example, a licence is required to build an extra fence around your garden. Every building plan, no matter how small has to be submitted to the planning committee of the local council, whose task it is to ensure that the streets of its town or city continue to be a feast for the eye and are not spoiled by unsightly kitsch. This, in spite of the fact that, according to an old Dutch saying, 'over smaak valt niet te twisten', everyone to his own taste.

EXCESSIVE OF CARE AND GUIDANCE CAN
BE TOO MUCH OF A GOOD THING

The Netherlands has a whole group of professional 'social' engineers, who have a higher vocational education of some kind, a qualification in social studies or – since the 1960s – a degree from one of the influential social studies faculties of the universities. They are often employed as community workers.

They may be local government officials who are in charge of all kinds of community-based activities, most of which are designed to generate some sort of 'community feeling'. Others are specialists who support people in need of help in one way or another, perhaps to save their marriage or survive in society. Again it is a matter of control and regulation. This whole complex of social services is what is known as 'social work'.

But this excess of care and guidance can sometimes be too much of a good thing. Critical philosopher Hans Achterhuis caused a furore in the 1980s with his controversial book *'De markt van welzijn en geluk'*, The market for welfare and happiness, in which he takes to task this whole doctrine of guidance and control. Achterhuis, whose thought is partially rooted in nineteenth century anarchism, identifies a toxic cocktail of authoritarian paternalism and pure interference in the lives of others, which in practice does more harm than good whilst providing a living – and a good one at that – for a whole sector of 'specialists'. Achterhuis calls these people the new *vrijgestelden*. This term (which literally means 'those who are exempted') was originally used to describe activists who were paid a salary by their trade union so that they could devote themselves to the organization on a full-time basis. The government has since cut back considerably on these new 'full-time activists' and the organizations in which they work.

Yet there is much in present-day Dutch society that suggests this engineer's mentality. Many people and organizations see their tasks as largely a matter of stimulating or facilitating, promoting processes, guiding the activities of others. At some point they will usually introduce the concept of coordination, a characteristic feature of societies where there is little chance of any one individual acquiring sufficient power to become the undisputed leader. Outsiders may get the impression from the type of language used in these organizations that the complicated jargon is a cover-up for doing nothing. This is, however, rarely the case. Stimulation and guidance are very effective ways of exerting influence in a society based on consultation, whose members are accustomed to taking decisions more or less jointly and in which the main aim is a compromise acceptable to all. Stimulation and guidance mean that you are prepared to play a role in these processes, that you are not entering the arena with inflexible premises and unshakable theoretical models. Action is based on the observation and interpretation of the actual situation. A good illustration of how this works in action is the role played by the *Centraal Planbureau*, the Central Planning Office, known popularly by its Dutch abbreviation CPB.

The CPB was set up in 1945 at the government's instigation by Jan Tinbergen, the man who said that economics is an engineering science. Tinbergen, a Nobel Prize winner, devoted his life to making economic processes measurable and quantifiable. He believed that sound policy could only be based on hard facts and figures and he developed models to explain economic reality in terms of mathematical formulae. The development of the computer enabled his successors to refine these methods even further.

The CPB is, in fact, not a planning body at all. It measures the economy on the basis of a large number of indicators and makes prognoses for the future. Its most important task is to calculate the effects of policy proposals on welfare. During negotiations on new coalition governments, the partners send their compromises more and more often to the CPB so that it can 'work out' whether they will achieve the intended goals. Since the 1980s, successive governments have attempted to bring down, or at least contain, unemployment. The politicians involved in the 1994 coalition negotiations discarded many of their own compromises – often the result of hard bargaining – themselves because the CPB's computer models concluded that the effects on unemployment were too small or unfavourable. Eventually, the CPB even went so far as to make suggestions for policy itself; such recommendations have now become a feature of the CPB's regular prognoses for the Dutch economy. No matter what you think about this – some commentators, such as the well-known monetarist and publicist, Professor Eduard Bomhof, think that this veneration of computer models has gone too far – it illustrates that politicians across the spectrum by far prefer a practical, utilitarian approach to ideological assumptions.

The belief is still widespread, but no longer has the power it commanded one or two generations ago. In the 1960s, PvdA leader Joop den Uijl introduced the concept of the *'maakbare samenleving'* (literally, the 'makable' society) to describe this conviction that society can be moulded to suit some preconceived design. Today, even social democrats admit that the concept is completely outdated and has been overtaken by the facts. Too many policy measures have not achieved the intended goal, but have resulted in something entirely different or even the complete opposite. Where one lays the emphasis then depends a little on political taste. The regulations controlling dismissal, for example, may make it difficult for employers to sack their employees but, in doing so, may also render it more difficult for the jobless to find work. Or, to take another example, doubling the width of motorways; this encourages people to buy cars, thereby increasing rather than decreasing the number of vehicles on the roads – as a result of which congestion only spreads to the urban road networks within the cities.

Yet only a very few of those involved in the debate genuinely wish to return to what they refer to as the 'caretaker state', where the government protects only the life and property of its citizens, and everything else is left to the free play of social forces. The debate is not about regulation or no regulation but about what form it should take. This, again, is related to the respect for the power of the water which Dutch hydraulic engineers retain in spite of their knowledge and experience. You can redirect the course of a river but you cannot stop it from flowing. Anyone who has been up on the top of a river dyke in the Netherlands will have noticed that they are built quite a way back from the actual banks of the river. The stretches of land between the dyke and the river are known as *uiterwaarden*. These are usually water meadows used by farmers to graze their cattle. Some may be protected by low dykes, but they are largely left to the whims of the water. When the water level is exceptionally high – which is always predicted in time to allow the farmers to remove the cattle – the *uiterwaarden* are generally flooded. If the dykes were built along the river banks, it would be impossible – even with today's technology – to contain the water. The rivers – and the sea, for that matter – must be given room to breathe or they will turn into wild beasts, bursting out of their cages and destroy everything in their way. The moral is that much can be regulated and controlled, but if you go too far, you will call down unheard-of powers upon yourself. A practical and logical approach will always produce usable results, but you always have to work with, not against, the situation as you find it. And, often enough, in spite of your wishes, intentions and principles, you will find that you have to leave some breathing space, in just the same way as the dykes must never be built too close to the river banks.

SOCIETY, TOO, HAS ITS ´UITERWAARDEN´

Society, too, has its '*uiterwaarden*', water meadows outside the dykes where administrators find it impossible to impose any clear order. This belief is deeply entrenched in the Dutch way of thinking. Those who attempt to steer social processes frequently discover that they are uncontrollable and the most they can hope for is to contain them, to prevent them from getting any worse. And the tradition of enforced tolerance, which the regents of the old Republic had to adopt to survive, makes the idea of restricted control more acceptable, even attractive. In addition to respect for individuality and the recognition of another's sovereignty in their own domain, this mentality is closely related to what foreign observers often see as an exaggerated liberality and lawlessness in the Netherlands.

Rotterdam is by far the largest port in the world. Schiphol is one of Europe's leading airports. The transport of goods to and from other countries is one of the mainstays of the Dutch economy. The slow but unstoppable process of federalization in Europe is leading to the gradual phasing out of border controls across the continent. This makes the Netherlands a very open society, and not only in a positive sense. It is not difficult for drugs smugglers to conceal a consignment of hashish – or worse – in amongst the enormous quantity of goods that pass through the country legally. The use of drugs – no matter whether they are hard or soft – is illegal in the Netherlands. In the past, this never caused any serious problems. A small Chinese minority, which had made its way to Amsterdam and Rotterdam usually via the Dutch East Indies, used opium. The police never succeeded in infiltrating this very closed group. The government, however, believed that there was little harm in opium use as long as it was kept under control and continued to be nothing more than a way of passing the time for old men who had become accustomed to using the drug in their home country. The police therefore tolerated opium dens as long as the owners restricted their clientele to members of the Chinese community.

A GREY AREA DEVELOPED BETWEEN THE WORD AND DEED OF THE LAW

In 1911 a Christian-dominated government had imposed restrictions on prostitution. Women were not forbidden to sell sexual favours, but all activities relating to it, such as pimping, renting hotel rooms by the hour or running brothels, were illegal. It was clear from the start that this law was impossible to enforce. It was therefore applied only partially. In areas where prostitution traditionally flourished, such as the world-famous *Wallen* in the centre of Amsterdam or *Katendrecht* in Rotterdam, the practitioners of the world's oldest profession were more or less allowed to go about their business. The police were, however, very active in removing young girls below the minimum age from the streets and, where possible, returning them to their parents or finding them places in children's homes.

Prostitution was, however, banned from other neighbourhoods. The authorities believed that, in this way, the evil was concentrated in an isolated area – Katendrecht was actually a peninsula with only one road connecting it to the outside world. In this way a grey area developed between the word of the law and how it is practised. The authorities defended this approach with the argument that, if the worst came to the worst, they had the situation under control and could stop it getting out of hand. This was true of prostitution and of the opium trade.

In the 1960s, hashish and marijuana suddenly became very popular among young people, because the use of illegal substances was a perfect expression of the growing culture of protest. The drugs were of an excellent quality and came into the country through a variety of channels. At first the government's response was very aggressive, as the well-known experimental poet Simon Vinkenoog – the prophet of the young revolution – discovered. He was imprisoned for a few months for the possession of a small quantity of hashish, the use of which he successfully propagated as mind-expanding and inspirational.

Making an example of Vinkenoog had no effect. The use of soft drugs increased sharply. A number of experts declared in the media, without receiving too much criticism, that marijuana and its derivatives were not addictive, or at least less so than alcohol or nicotine. This resulted in a certain amount of tolerance in practice. Some youth centres even appointed their own dealers so that their visitors could be guaranteed a good quality supply of drugs and not run the risk of ending up with a doctored product that often contained dangerous chemicals. Gradually this policy led to the tolerance of 'coffee shops' where unsuspecting customers who actually ordered coffee were met with surprise and amusement. The Dutch are great coffee drinkers, but the many cafés and other establishments where they can indulge themselves have not been referred to as coffee shops for twenty years or more. Here, too, the argument is that this allows a practice that cannot be stamped out to be controlled. The authorities, however, act decisively if they discover that hard drugs are also being sold in a coffee shop or if marijuana is sold openly.

An illustration of a hemp leaf on the package is permitted, but no more.

On the other hand, the government continues to fight the suppliers. Every now and then there are reports in the papers that the customs have intercepted fishing boats full of hashish or have discovered hundreds of kilos stashed away somewhere. Everyone is aware of the paradox inherent in this policy of tolerance and it has many critics.

One of the arguments for permitting the use of soft drugs was to maintain a clear distinction between the 'hash scene' and the users of heroin and cocaine.

The use of hard drugs – in spite of claims to the contrary, particularly from abroad – is not tolerated by the Dutch government and the police devote a great deal of time and manpower to combatting it. Nevertheless, since the sixties, a hard drugs scene has developed in the towns and cities.

Heroin and cocaine are not only extremely addictive but also expensive. Once addicted you need thousands of guilders a month to 'score', several times higher than an average salary. Very few people can earn that much from honest work. Hard drug addiction is therefore the cause of a large percentage of the burglaries, muggings, and car and bicycle thefts in the Netherlands. It has also led to an increase in street prostitution. Addicts who earn their shots this way are usually very young women, but not always. And it is a heyday for the pimps, who now use the hypodermic needle to exercise their power. The majority of people in prison in the Netherlands are addicts and the expansion of drugs-related crimes in recent years has necessitated a considerable increase in the number of prison cells. In the hard drugs scene, a certain amount of use is tolerated, but the reasoning behind it is slightly different. The authorities concentrate on tracking down the big dealers, the incredibly wealthy leaders of the heroin and cocaine cartels, so that they can 'strangle the evil at its source'. The addict on the street and the small-time dealer generally have little to fear, unless they cause a public nuisance, i.e. if there are complaints from the neighbours.

At the same time, the police allow all kinds of bodies that provide assistance to addicts all the room they need to operate. Since Aids has become common among addicts – passed on by the use of dirty needles – there are places where they can get clean hypodermics. An addict without Aids is always better than one with it. Other organizations help addicts to beat their habit by providing them with methadon, a chemical which removes the withdrawal symptoms but – in typical Calvinist style – does not give the feelings of happiness and contentment that make heroin so tempting. Some of the organizations even have areas where addicts – who are usually on the street and completely down and out – can find shelter for a while and are even allowed to indulge use drugs.

Most of the larger cities, and Amsterdam and Rotterdam in particular, have special zones where the police tolerate street prostitutes, most of whom are addicts. Few people live in the designated areas so that no opposition can be expected from local residents.

More and more high-ranking police officers and officials of the Public Prosecutor's Office are publicly advocating the legalization of hard drugs. Their argument is, why should heroin and cocaine be banned when nicotine and alcohol (more than half a million Dutch people have serious drink problems) are socially accepted? Legalization would remove hard drugs from the criminal circuit overnight. The government could then market the drugs at an acceptable price – comparable, for example, with the price of strong liquor – so that the habit would be less expensive and addicts would no longer have to steal. This would make it easier to help addicts and remove most of the related social problems. The opponents of legalization are by far in the majority. Their main argument is that the Netherlands would stand alone in introducing such a policy and be considered a pariah among civilized countries.

Current practice, however, with its mixture of tolerance and strict measures has already provoked strong criticism from neighbouring countries. The Netherlands defends itself with the argument that the use of hard drugs in the country is no worse than elsewhere and certainly less of a problem than in large metropolises like New York or Los Angeles. The latter is certainly true. The Netherlands – with a population of almost 16 million – has between twenty-two and twenty-three thousand hard drug addicts, which is not a particularly high percentage. The government, however, is sensitive to the criticism. In 1994, the police started a campaign against foreign addicts who come to the

Netherlands by car to buy hard drugs. They are frequently met at the border by drugs runners, guides who take them to a place where they can buy what they need. Both dealers and runners are regularly picked up in large-scale raids in which Dutch police work together with colleagues from neighbouring countries. They also exchange computerized information, which has proved invaluable in tracking down suspects.

In spite of this relatively tolerant approach, hard drugs use and the crime that accompanies it are considered serious problems in the Netherlands in the 1990s. They have certainly become a visible part of the street life in the major cities. Experience in other countries has shown that a hard line, based on repressive laws and criminal prosecution, produces few results. Yet there is equally little evidence to prove that the twin Dutch dykes of help and tolerance have successfully contained the problem to the extent that the people of the Netherlands can feel safe in their social polder.

WHERE LIFE AND DEATH MEET

A policy of tolerance, making the best of the situation, regulating the level of the steam as it were, is also pursued in the Netherlands in a much more dangerous area, where life and death meet. In the past twenty years this has led to two fierce debates in the country, first about abortion, and then about euthanasia.

'*Baas in eigen buik*', 'Be the boss in your own belly', was the lighthearted motto of the feminist movement that had grown out of the revolutionary ideals of the sixties. It was a direct pointer to the possibility of abortion. Another common slogan on their banners was '*Vrouw, beslis*', 'Woman, decide for yourself'.

The law was clear – abortion was the equivalent of murder. Yet as early as the fifties and sixties it was possible to find doctors who were prepared to terminate pregnancies. They justified this by saying that, if they did not do it, it would be done by backstreet abortionists who only too often put their clients' lives in danger. As long as these doctors did not publicize their activities too much, they were left relatively alone. In the sixties, however, the *Nederlandse Vereniging voor Sexuele Hervorming* (NVSH) – the Dutch Association for Sexual Reform – gathered a great deal of support. The association advocated sexual freedom and placed the right to abortion on the agenda. This provoked a great deal of opposition, especially from religious groups, who spoke of the rights of the unborn child and considered the foetus as the 'weakest of the weak' in society, thereby deserving of protection. Non-Christian parties, including the vibrant new D66, pressed for the legalization of abortion, arguing that – particularly in the first few weeks of the pregnancy – the foetus could not be considered a human being. At the same time, clinics started to appear – often set up under the auspices of the NVSH – where abortions could be obtained without problem. Eventually a compromise was reached in the form of a law that allowed abortion up to the third month, subject to a large number of conditions. These were, however, defined in such vague terms that any woman who wishes to can obtain an abortion without problem. This possibility is frequently taken advantage of by women from neighbouring countries, who sometimes arrive in groups in hired buses.

There is still strong opposition to this form of tolerance, but it has little effect. The argument that enforcing the letter of the law would lead to greater problems and the return of the backstreet abortionist has greater public support than the idea that the unborn child is the 'weakest of the weak'.

The *Vereniging voor Vrijwillige Euthanasie*, the Association for Voluntary Euthanasia, defends the right of individuals to put an end themselves to what it calls unbearable suffering. It says that doctors should be able to help patients whose situation offers no hope of recovery to end their lives. This goes against the Hippocratic oath which all medical practitioners in the Netherlands feel bound by. It is their duty to prolong life, not to shorten it. On the other hand, advances in medical science now offer the possibility of prolonging patients' lives even when there is no prospect of successfully treating their illnesses. The most tragic examples are coma patients, who are frequently kept alive for decades, barely more than vegetables, while machines regulate their vital functions.

People who are seriously ill often end up in a situation where only a heart-lung machine, for example, keeps them on this side of the border between life and death. This places doctors and other medical staff in a terrible dilemma – should they leave the machine on or is it more humane to switch it off? The latter is a form of euthanasia, the 'good death'. And, if a cancer patient, suffering indescribably and deteriorating in front of your eyes, says that he or she wishes to die with dignity, who is to refuse? In practice, the machine is disconnected. Many doctors will respect their patients' wishes to die with dignity.

Many Dutch people – including myself – know of this happening in their own immediate circle. In my case, it was a married woman under forty who was dying of lung cancer. She had a long talk about it to her Catholic doctor, who gave her enough pills to enable her to end her misery when she thought that the time had come. She did this one afternoon, after giving herself time to take leave of her husband and child. The pills first made her sleepy and, after an hour or so, she died without pain.

This had, and still has, a great effect on me. For everyone who was close to her, including myself, it was a great comfort that a humane doctor had given her the choice. We were grateful for this form of tolerance. The same doctor who had given her the pills certified that she had died a natural death, so there was no need for an autopsy. Otherwise the pathologist would almost certainly have established death by poisoning and the doctor would have been prosecuted. But no one saw any reason to request an autopsy, including the specialists at the Roman Catholic Hospital that had discharged the woman a few weeks before her death in the conviction that, with radiation and chemotherapy, she could live another year. In her case, tolerance allowed her suffering to come to an end.

The activities of the Association for Voluntary Euthanasia were therefore not valued too highly in many medical circles. They focused attention on a practice that in which well considered and responsible decisions were made on a case-by-case basis, but which became more difficult when exposed to the light of day. After all, no matter what euphemism you used, the doctors were intentionally terminating a life. In the eyes of the law, it was murder, manslaughter or negligent homicide. Moreover, the word itself, euthanasia, has negative connotations. It was used by Hitler and the Nazis to describe the extermination of what they considered 'inferior forms of life'. In the 1940s this led to the killing of thousands of mentally and physically handicapped Germans. The opponents of euthanasia compare disconnecting a heart-lung machine to this type of genocide. In their eyes, tolerating euthanasia for incurable patients, which they consider nothing short of murder, is the top of a long and slippery slope.

And, of course, who is to determine at what point suffering becomes 'unbearable'? Sometimes the patient is able to make that decision himself or herself. But what if the decision has to be taken by others – the family, for example? This is a common criticism from opponents in the church. In the

1980s, the husband of a woman who had been in a coma for several years asked the hospital for permission to switch off the life-support machine. The doctors at the hospital, which was a Christian institution, refused to do it and forbade the husband to do so himself. He then sought publicity for his case, hoping in this way to be able to end his wife's suffering. After a heated public debate, his wife was disconnected from the machine and allowed to die. Another aspect of the problem is that of new-born babies who are so severely handicapped that they have little chance of survival and no prospects at all of leading a valuable existence. But who decides what constitutes a 'valuable existence'? Who defines 'little chance of survival'? Does it mean a few months? A few years, perhaps? Never reaching adulthood?

In the view of many Dutch people, such questions should never even be asked. That is the top of the slippery slope. Once you start to slide down and you end up thinking like Hitler.

This whole impassioned debate has resulted in a law which obliges doctors who perform euthanasia to inform the Public Prosecutor, who then decides whether criminal proceedings should be instigated against them. The debate on euthanasia shows up the weak spot in the tolerance approach. It is not so much the room it leaves for subjective judgement, but the fact that the limits tend to be pushed back; or rather – to use a cynical, but in this case justified, analogy – the 'zone of tolerance' gradually spreads, organically, like a spot of black ink on the blotting paper of society.

If only the dykes hold out and our feet stay dry. Marsman's warning is equally applicable to the sometimes stormy waters of social and ethical issues:

'And in every region
the voice of the water,
telling of endless disaster,
is heard and feared'

Chapter 3

'How I love those gentlemen in black'

The need to be on time. A life regulated by diaries. Appointments for everything. Consultation and the search for consensus. The meeting culture. A feasible compromise as the ultimate aim. Confidence in the government. The primacy of policy.

At every bus and tram stop in the country there is a timetable posted which gives the departure times to the minute – 19.37, 08.57, etc. The timetables in the booklets published by the various transport companies, however, inform passengers that they should allow five minutes either way when planning a trip. They also state categorically that no rights can be derived from the information given. This aside, the aim is clear – the buses should run exactly on time. The same applies to the railways. If a train is delayed, passengers are informed via the public address system and on the departure boards exactly how long the delay will be. They wait on the platforms, embittered, because they wish that the public transport system would live up to its promises. In practice, it hardly ever does. Buses and trams get stuck in traffic, the rail network continues to be over-burdened – at least until the completion of a large-scale project aimed at doubling many stretches of track from two to four. This leads to critical questions in parliament and discontented commentaries in the newspapers. Arriving late is associated with failure and unreliability.

This is evident, too, in the making and keeping of appointments. Anyone who turns up at a company or other organization without first making an appointment, will be greeted with confusion and, more often than not, irritation. The daily activities of the staff are strictly planned from hour to hour and unexpected visitors interrupt this schedule. They will be treated rather brusquely and shown the door within ten minutes. And they will be lucky if they get this far. More likely they will find themselves confronted with a secretary who will scour the diary of the person they wish to see for a time when he or she is free. This will often be a week or so later and the appointment will be specified to the nearest quarter of an hour. It is then crucial to get there on time, or the whole procedure will start again. The person concerned will, after all, already be busy with their next appointment. They cannot interrupt their schedule or they will also be thought unreliable.

There are exceptions to this rule. Government departments in particular often have information desks where you can ask questions without first making an appointment. You just take a number and wait your turn. But even these departments tend to fall back on the appointment system, especially if you have a question that cannot be answered in a minute or two. Even most hairdressers have adopted the system. Barbers where you can still just walk in and have your hair cut are an exception these days and usually announce this added service with a large sign outside.

The appointment system has penetrated deeply into everyday life in the Netherlands. Practically everyone has a diary on them, which is produced immediately someone wants to contact them. Even for a lunch or dinner date, presumably a pleasurable occasion, they will look at their dairies with knitted brow until they can find a time when they have no business or family commitments.

Particularly people whose jobs include considerable organizational responsibilities, or who have to attend a lot of meetings – and that is not uncommon in a society held together by consultation and consensus – tend to have overfull diaries. For several years I was the secretary of an editorial advisory board. It was often a problem getting the whole group together, even if the next meeting was not for three months. Most Dutch people are used to this ritual. You can count on it taking a good ten or fifteen minutes at the end of a meeting to set a date for a following one. Some secretaries try to save time by suggesting a list of dates be sent around. After a few days, everyone receives a list with ten or so possible dates and times, together with a request to mark the dates that they are free and send the list back without delay. The secretary then hopes that everyone will do just this and that one date will be acceptable to all of them. In practice, however, this rarely works, because others are competing for the participants' time and their diaries are getting fuller and fuller. That is why most professional secretaries prefer to prolong a meeting for 15 minutes or even half an hour to set a new date rather than choose the more difficult method of sending out lists.

DUTCH CHILDREN RECEIVE THEIR FIRST DIARIES AT PRIMARY SCHOOL

Foreigners sometimes complain about the horror of a life controlled by a diary and Dutch people – before taking their leave because they have an appointment somewhere else a quarter of an hour later – eagerly agree with them. The diary culture is very deeply entrenched. Dutch children receive their first diaries at primary school when, after the first few years of playing around, things get serious and they are given their first homework. The teachers dictate the exercises and make sure that they are noted down. A school diary is therefore an indispensable attribute for any self-respecting school child. Competition for a share in the market is fierce, reaching a peak towards the end of the summer holidays, just before the start of the new academic year. In the past decade, school diaries have become something of a status symbol. There are very businesslike diaries for the keen student, which provide space only for writing down homework and appointments. Others offer a great deal more, providing clues about the subculture to which its owner belongs and becoming part of his or her identity. They may have a romantic design or even a political content. Or they may be full of pictures of pop idols. They might contain interviews with sports heroes or pious tracts on the problems of the Third World.

Once they have passed their final exams and gone out into the world, school children and students can no longer live without their diaries. Almost all Dutch people have more than one, not so much because the burden of appointments makes this necessary, but rather because a new diary is a favourite gift for clients and other business contacts. Shops, banks, companies and government departments start distributing pocket diaries on a grand scale from the middle of November, their name discreetly printed in silver letters on the front cover.

This explains the irritation that arises if the train or bus is too late, or if the traffic going into the city is at a standstill. The system works only if everyone keeps their appointments. Surprises and exceptional circumstances demand improvisation and the subservience to the dictates of the diary have destroyed the ability to find a spontaneous solution to an unexpected situation. Hence the irritation. Anyone who arrives late knows that they will be accused of the kind of *mañana* mentality considered typical of Spaniards and Latin Americans. They cannot keep their appointments and – as a well-known Dutch saying goes – they don't do today what they can do tomorrow. The cause of the problem is often the overburdened infrastructure, but most Dutch people still blame themselves.

As in other parts of the world, the diary culture grew out of the industrial revolution, which started in the Netherlands about a hundred and twenty years ago and, as it were, created the practical preconditions for the culture to develop. Farmers traditionally live by the rhythm of the seasons. They have few obligations that need to be fulfilled at certain times of the day. The same applies to towns dominated by trade and craft workshops. Most church towers have had clocks since the Middle Ages, but they were largely symbols of prestige. They became reliable only when Christiaan Huygens, a physicist from The Hague, discovered the secrets of the pendulum and used his new knowledge to build an accurate timepiece. This remained the basic principle of all clocks until electronics offered a digital alternative.

The people rarely looked at the clocks in the church towers. They knew the time of day from the sound of the church bells. They were originally intended to call the faithful to prayer. They made a different sound for various occasions. For a Mass, they played long, loud notes; for a wedding they were joyful and for a funeral, mournful. Softer tones were used to call people to the Angelus every morning and Vespers in the evenings. Local authorities also used the bells to inform the populace of more worldly events. They were rung, for example, a quarter of an hour before the city gates were closed for the night. In many cities, a special bell was rung to inform craft masters that their apprentices had to go home for their evening meal. Every community had a number of signals of this kind to inform the people that it was time for a certain activity to be performed. The different sounds were achieved by using bells of different sizes. As the range of bells grew, they automatically evolved into a musical instrument. Examples of this instrument, known as a carillon, can still be found in practically every town and city. They have been status symbols for many centuries.

Carillon bells are not tolled in the way that conventional bells are. They are struck on the outside by hammers operated by a kind of keyboard, which the carillonneur plays by striking the 'keys' with his fists.

This is why, in many Dutch towns, you can still hear the bells ringing at unusual times of the day. They may be calling long-dead apprentices for their dinner or warning the people that the city gates, dismantled long before, are about to close. These traditions are frequently continued without local residents – with the exception of a small group of initiates – knowing why the bells are ringing. It may even simply be because their ancestors had built the signal into the Huygens clock mechanism two or three centuries previously.

The carillon music that tinkles across many a market square is often mechanical. The hammers are activated by a gigantic – often very old – music box. Most churches with a carillon do, however, have a carillonneur, who they share with the other churches in the area, and who is called in to give a concert at certain times, perhaps on market day or on feast days. This is their chance to really show what they can do. Bent over the keyboard, they alternate traditional Dutch tunes and Bach with ragtime, the latest hits from the pop charts or songs about the merits of the national football team. It is background music for the people on the street, but most concerts are announced in the local press, sometimes with a list of the numbers to be played.

These are sweet memories of distant, less hectic times. Most towns also have relics dating from the era when the foundations of modern society, with its obsession with time, were laid. These are the street clocks, mounted on poles for all to see. Many of them are still there, but there used to be far more. They enabled people without watches to arrive where they were going on time. They were a public service in the same vein as street lighting. This is because the rhythm to which the Dutch live, according to their diaries, is the rhythm of the machine and mass production.

A craftsman works at his own pace and with his own tools. He takes the raw material and turns it into an end product. That is no longer possible once production is organized differently. If you take the work of the craftsman, divide it up into separate tasks and ensure that every worker contributes a small part of the end product, then all those involved have to work at the same speed, starting and stopping at exactly the same moment. Production proceeds far more quickly and efficiently, as Adam Smith, the prophet of capitalism, illustrated in the 'Wealth of Nations' with his example of a pin factory. If one link in this chain fails, however, none of the others can produce anything. That is why assembly line production demands greater control and discipline.

This becomes even more important when the pace of the work is no longer determined by the people themselves but by machines. Once a steam engine has worked up enough pressure to set all the wheels turning, everyone has to be ready. And then there is no mercy – you have to adapt to the tempo of the machine. There is a strong dose of wishful thinking in the old socialist adage 'heel het raderwerk staat stil, als Uw machtige arm het wil', roughly translated 'You have the power in your arm to bring the whole machine to a standstill'. The dictatorship of the machine means that you cannot arrive at about seven o'clock to start work. You have to be there dead on seven, because that is when the machine is switched on.

THE DUTCH ARE SURROUNDED BY CLOCKS

This same modern industry produced the instruments that allowed people to fulfil this requirement, and mass production made them affordable. Alarm clocks started appearing in the shops during the last twenty-five years of the last century. It was, however, well into the twentieth century before the average worker could afford one. Until then, they were woken up in the mornings by a *porder* – a 'prodder' – a pitiful soul who was paid a pittance to tap on the windows of his clients with a long stick until they heard him and shouted out that they were getting up. Nowadays, alarm clocks are consumer articles with absolutely no prestige value. Even a Rolex, the most prestigious watch in the world, is considered to prove only that the wearer is a show-off.

The Dutch are surrounded by clocks. There is an alarm clock next to the bed. There is a clock in the living room, primarily for decoration. Most kitchens have one, as do most places of work. They are so common that the radio no longer gives the exact time, except for the six beeps of the atomic clock just before the hourly news bulletin.

This situation was not reached without a certain amount of resistance. Some historians describe the recent history of the Netherlands as a disciplinary process, with order and regularity being imposed on the masses, where necessary with a heavy hand. And there were indeed examples of industrial calamities in the last quarter of the nineteenth century caused by the fact that the local population were unable to adapt to a completely different rhythm overnight. They bear more than a passing resemblance to the failed 'development projects' of our own time.

Yet the climate for such a change was most likely far more favourable in the Netherlands than in many other parts of the world. The hard-fought struggle against the water, the eternal threat from the sea, had forced the Dutch to organize and work closely together, and to divide tasks down to the last detail. Secondly there was an élite that 'understood' the demands of this new age. They were used to organizing their lives.

Foreigners will soon notice that the 'holy' diary of Dutch friends and colleagues is full of appointments, meetings and what they call *'overleg'*. *Overleg* literally means 'consultation' but this is an inadequate translation of what has become an entire concept to the Dutch. It is closer to the English 'in conference', an equally vague and discouraging phrase. Generally, you can get through to the person you are calling without encountering too many problems, even if you only succeed in making an appointment for a later date. But if you are confronted with a colleague or a department secretary who informs you that the person you wish to speak to is 'in a meeting' or 'in *overleg*', you may as well give up.

[134]

A MEETING IS A SUCCESS ONLY IF A CONSENSUS IS REACHED

Anyone in a meeting or in *overleg* can be disturbed only in a real emergency, such as a death in the family. Meetings are completely shut off from the outside world. If you do persist long enough to get someone out of a meeting, you will almost always hear a hurried, nervous and irritated voice at the other end of the line, hardly prepared to listen to anything you say. This response – noncommittal and verging on the allergic – is a product of the compromise culture. A meeting is a success only if a consensus is reached. This requires that everyone follows the entire discussion and participates if possible, even if only with an approving smile now and then. The whole process is disrupted if someone has to leave the meeting and frequently the discussion is held up until they return. For the same reasons, it is simply 'not done' to arrive late or leave early. If it is unavoidable, then good reasons have to be given. Many people who are unable to attend meetings – even if their presence is not compulsory – send a notification of their absence to the chairman, who reads it out at the beginning of the proceedings. Arriving late, cancelling or simply not turning up implies that you do not consider the issues to be discussed or – even worse – the others present at the meeting, sufficiently important to warrant your attention. Their revenge is not to take you seriously in the future. Moreover, if you are not there, you no longer have a voice, a vote to influence the outcome. In a compromise culture, it is crucial to take an active part in the collective creation of thoughts and ideas.

The old regents of the Republic, who could only achieve anything by exercising the greatest caution and finally reaching a consensus, learned this fundamental lesson. If you wanted to have a say, you had to be there. Because it was a matter of voluntary cooperation, decisions made by only a few were ineffective. Towns, regions and provinces imposed no sanctions on those who refused to abide by the decision of the majority. A good chairman or secretary therefore always ensured that as many people as possible were present when decisions were made.

And then a consensus has to be reached. This is not always easy. Politicians have always devoted great attention to informal *overleg* outside the official conference room to prepare the ground for the compromise they hope to achieve. This is still an important feature of Dutch politics at all levels. Ruud Lubbers, who stepped down in 1994 after the longest period as prime minister in the country's history, was a past master at 'massaging the souls' of his opponents and then formulating a compromise acceptable to all. Tributes to his character always refer to this as his greatest talent. The Dutch have an expression for these informal discussions, which frequently take place in private. They say that issues have been talked about in the *'wandelgangen'*, the name given to the corridors that run through the *Binnenhof*, the traditional home of Dutch parliament.

BOUND BY NEITHER MANDATE NOR INSTRUCTION

In spite of all this, reaching a compromise has always been and still is a difficult process. This was particularly true in the days of the Republic, because the representatives of a town, region or province frequently claimed to have no mandate to go along with a certain proposal. They first had to consult with the people they represented and then act on their instructions. During the days of horse-drawn barges, this could sometimes take weeks. Although a threat to national security would normally result in the agreement of all concerned, most decisions became bogged down in endless argument. The central authorities in the Republic succeeded only twice in drawing up a declaration of war before the enemy – no doubt tired of waiting – sent their own declaration to the Binnenhof. The law now specifies very clearly that the representatives of the people – from local councils up to parliament – can make decisions *'zonder last of ruggespraak'*, 'bound by neither mandate nor instruction'.

This method of working requires that every step of the decisionmaking process be recorded accurately and the decision itself be laid down in writing as unambiguously as possible. Appointments have to be committed to paper, otherwise there is the risk that they will be interpreted in different ways at a later date. There will then be no higher authority to put an end to the new round of bickering this produces. To this day, the Dutch commit almost everything to paper – the written word is sacred. There is a certain distrust of oral agreements. If an oral agreement is made, and it is to a certain extent official, the parties prefer to follow it up with a written confirmation, which often concludes with the qualification that the agreement is valid unless statement is made to contrary. The written word is law.

The regents of the Republic, with their endless processes of decisionmaking, were part of a self-appointed aristocracy which became increasingly corrupt as time went on. Yet the system had been in existence for more than two hundred years when the country was invaded by the French in 1795. The invaders were supported by opposition groups within the country which advocated a variety of alternative forms of effective government. The French controlled the country for 18 years, until 1813. From 1810, the Netherlands even belonged to the Napoleonic empire. During that time, the entire administrative structure of the country was reorganized. The loose confederation was replaced by a single state, in which the relations between the central government, the provinces and the municipalities were clearly defined. There was a single body of legislation and all citizens were equal before the law. And all the obstacles that had made it so difficult to maintain unity in the Republic were removed.

Once Napoleon had been driven out, these new structures were preserved and built upon. The final century of the Republic acquired the reputation of a dark period in Dutch history, which it retains to this day. Since then, corruption has been considered a cardinal sin. It is important that political leaders and captains of industry are seen as having integrity. Men or women of integrity are able to resist the temptation of riches. They scrupulously keep to their agreements and to the rules, and do not try to interpret them to their own advantage. They work according to fixed procedures which are familiar to everybody. They make decisions without thought of personal gain. In short, they are the very antithesis of the regents of their accursed ancestors.

CONSCIENTIOUS, ACCURATE AND PUNCTUAL

Against this background, the written registration of decisionmaking processes and the decisions they resulted in acquired an even greater importance.

Anyone reading through modern job advertisements or descriptions will often encounter terms such as 'conscientious', 'accurate' and 'punctual'. Carelessness, not keeping records up to date and similar traits are considered undesirable. They may be acceptable, even endearing in artists or romantics, but such people are never more than marginal. They may receive enthusiastic applause and even, in time, be honoured by the Queen but they are rarely have any genuine impact on 'what really matters'.

Accuracy and precision is crucial. This is no surprise. The Dutch élite has always had close connections with trade. And in trade, you always have to have the latest figures to hand. If the book-keeping is faulty, the business will founder. The education system that has grown up since the beginning of the nineteenth century, with its quality controlled by the government, has always devoted great attention to arithmetic and clear handwriting. Until the arrival of the typewriter – and later the word processor – the ability to write in clearly legible, standard handwriting was an important qualification for getting a job. Many Dutch people still submit their job applications with a handwritten letter. Until about twenty years ago, this was a basic requirement for being asked for an interview.

The Napoleonic bureaucracy is based on clearly defined tasks and powers and a hierarchic structure of authority. Activities are performed according to fixed procedures. There is a complex system of reporting from the higher to the lower regions. All correspondence is stored in filing systems that enable it to be retrieved quickly, even after many years. Large quantities of information are gathered and filed away. Research is carried out.

It was the French emperor who first made all Dutch people choose a surname which was passed down from father to son. This enabled a register to be drawn up of births, deaths and marriages, primarily to conscript men of fighting age for the massive armies Napoleon sent to their deaths in the battlefields of Europe. This register has now become an important bureaucratic instrument. It tells the authorities exactly where everyone lives, how old they are and the composition of their families. It also contains one other very important piece of information. It lists everyone's chosen faith under the heading 'Religion'.

Some Dutch people have very strange surnames. They may be called 'Niemandsverdriet' ('No man's sorrow'), 'Naaktgeboren' ('Born naked') or 'Klootjes' ('Balls'). These names were adopted by their ancestors in an early attempt to 'dodge the draft' or simply to make the French occupiers look ridiculous.

After the fall of Napoleon, the Netherlands regained its independence. There was no longer any reason to mistrust the authorities as representatives of a foreign power. Since then, most Dutch people have trusted the government as something that belongs to them. They are loyal and convinced that it has good intentions, even though its actions may not have the desired effect in practice. This applies even to governments that do not reflect their own political convictions. They mean well, they simply have the wrong idea about how to go about it.

This same approach is found in the private sector. The Netherlands has a strong labour movement, but there has never been much support for groups who see industry and 'the management' as their natural enemies. It is generally assumed that directors and managers also have good intentions.

As more and more people acquired the right to vote, this whole structure of trust gained in legitimacy. The effects of democracy were also felt outside politics. Managers had a tendency to consult with what was known as the *'bedrijfskern'*, a kind of committee in which the trade unions took part. This eventually led to the Works Councils Act, which specifies that every company with more than fifty employees had to have a kind of 'parliament' elected directly by the personnel. In practice, Works Councils have only an advisory function, but the management is obliged to discuss certain important matters – mostly those that may affect the number of jobs in the organization – with the Council before making a decision. Experience has shown that a Works Council whose members are able to argue convincingly can have a considerable influence on how the company is run. This has also proved to contribute to the commercial success of the company as a whole.

YOU HAVE TO EXERCISE SELF-CONTROL

You do, however, have to exercise self-control. This applies *mutatis mutandis* to decisionmaking in whatever form in the Netherlands. There is no room for strong emotions. The meetings of the regents in the days of the Republic were models of polite detachment. If you want to ensure that the final compromise contains as many of your own ideas as possible, you must not allow yourself to lapse into magnificent oratory and theatrical performances. On the contrary, you mistrust such behaviour. You should be cautious in expressing support or opposition. Any suggestion of prima donna tendencies should be ruthlessly nipped in the bud. Not by the forceful presentation your own argument, but by calmly ignoring the guilty party. Rhetoric is not a highly developed art in the Netherlands. Most members of parliament speak in a monotonous tone, often reading from a piece of paper. Only the most capable speakers are not thrown into confusion by interruptions, which are permitted only under certain circumstances. The entire proceedings take place in an air of extreme detachment. It is the argument itself that matters, not the manner in which it is presented. If a speaker puts his case too elegantly, it may even be counter-productive.

Meetings in the Netherlands follow a set pattern. It is not done to challenge the leadership of the chairman. It is their job to give everyone the chance to say their piece and they are allergic to anything that threatens to interrupt the orderly progress of the meeting. Everyone tries to make it clear that it is the issue under discussion that is at stake and not the persons involved, because – as explained earlier – this has led to bad experiences in the past. It can take a long time to reach agreement. The average chairman will try to reach a general consensus so that, at the end of the meeting, he can safely ask if anyone is in disagreement.

Although this may appear to contradict the above description of the consensus culture of the meeting, there is almost always at least one person in disagreement. If someone strongly opposes what has been agreed by the meeting, he or she will ask that this be recorded in the minutes. It will have no effect on the implementation of the decision and, in many cases, those who opposed the motion will contribute loyally to carrying it out. After all, they lost democratically and everyone knows how they stand.

The regents in the Republic represented a city or region; and in the days of pillarization you were a member of a social group, i.e. you had a Calvinist, a Catholic, a liberal or a social-democratic background. This made it more difficult to reach a general consensus. Each pillar rested on a set of general principles that were not up for negotiation. The decisionmaking process would reach stalemate if people with different sets of beliefs were not prepared to work together. Yet very few chose this extreme, because it meant relinquishing all influence. Well into the 1950s, the Calvinist pillar objected to funfairs as a source of decadent pleasures, spangled palaces of temptation, where Satan kept house. Calvinist political leaders therefore always voted against the issue of permits to fairs and advocated the introduction of an official ban. They had a similarly uncompromising opposition to lotteries, always opposing them in the full knowledge that their proposals would never be passed. Their counterparts in the other pillars respected their position. They, too, had certain issues on which they were not prepared to negotiate. Such issues were always immaterial, with little or no money at stake. After losing the vote, they could always say that they had done their best. In some cases, of course, principles may outweigh one's willingness to compromise. Most Dutch people will not go to this extreme, but there are exceptions. Assuming, however, for the sake of simplicity, that election results reflect the distribution of social beliefs, this is no more than 10 per cent of the electorate. Of the 150 members of the *Tweede Kamer*, perhaps ten to fifteen will always take a position on principle. They represent the very small parties, who are often at loggerheads with each other. In the 1994 parliament, there were seven strict Calvinist members divided among three parties, the differences between which are clear only to real insiders. Seven extreme-left members were divided among two parties. Five of these belong to Groen Links, an uneasy alliance of pacifist socialists, communists and Christian radicals, who have difficulty agreeing among themselves. The larger political parties have a tendency to tolerate these principled colleagues as a quaint part of national folklore, but their roles are never more than marginal. Such marginal opposition is found wherever people cooperate in the Netherlands. They stand outside the main process of compromise. Some may be valued for their intellectual knowledge and the contribution they make, but more often they are seen as fools who are not to be taken seriously. The distinction between the two types can be very vague.

Yet they do fulfil a function. You can scarcely reproach the seven Calvinist members for regularly reminding their colleagues of God's punishing hand. Activists in the extreme-left parties often claim that they first proposed ideas that later become common property. Where the environment is concerned, this is certainly true. Isolated radicals who are not amenable to reasonable argument sometimes prove to be trendsetters. But they are the exception.

In 1934 Jan Gresshof, poet and chief editor of the *Nieuwe Arnhemse Courant*, had a space left over on the front page. Thinking of the nearby *Velperplein*, which was often frequented by the élite of Arnhem, the dignified capital of the province of Gelderland, he wrote the following:

'Liefdesverklaring

Ik houd zo van die donkre burgerheren
Die langzaam wandlen over 't Velperplein
In deze koele winterzonneschijn:
De dominee, de dokter, de notaris
En 't klerkje dat vandaag wat vroeger klaar is.
Maar 't kan verkeren.

Zo onmiskenbaar ziet men aan hun kleren
Dat zij rechtvaardig zijn, terwijl de plicht
Die eedle lijnen groefde in hun gezicht:
De dominee, de dokter, de notaris,
Drievuldig beeld van al wat wijs en waar is.
Maar 't kan verkeren.

Op aarde valt voor hen niets meer te leren,
Zij zijn volkomen gaaf en afgerond,
Oud-liberaal, wantrouwend en gezond:
De dominee, de dokter, de notaris,
Voor wie de liefde zelfs zonder gevaar is.
Maar 't kan verkeren.

Zij gaan zich nu voorzichtig laten scheren,
Om daarna, met ervaring en verstand,
Een glas te drinken op het heil van 't land:
De dominee, de dokter, de notaris.
'k Weet geen probleem dat hun na zes te zwaar is.
Maar 't kan verkeren.

Ik hou zo van die zindelijke heren,
Levende monumenten op het plein
In deze veel te heldre winterschijn:
De dominee, de dokter, de notaris,
Die denken uw dichter niet goed gaar is.
Maar 't kan verkeren'.

'Declaration of love

How I love those gentlemen in black
Who slowly walk across the Velperplein
In the cool winter sunshine:
The minister, the doctor, the lawyer
And the clerk who has finished a little earlier today.
But the tide can change.

[142]

Their clothing leaves no doubt
Of their integrity, while duty has etched
The noble lines in their faces:
The minister, the doctor, the lawyer
A threefold image of wisdom and truth.
But the tide can change.

There is nothing left on earth for them to learn,
They are perfect and complete,
Old liberals[1], distrustful and healthy:
The minister, the doctor, the lawyer,
For whom even love presents no threat.
But the tide can change.

After having their faces carefully shaved,
With experience and good sense,
They shall raise a glass to the country:
The minister, the doctor, the lawyer.
After six, no problem is beyond them.
But the tide can change.

How I love these cleancut gentlemen
Living monuments on the square
In this much too clear winter's sun:
The minister, the doctor, the lawyer,
Who think this poet not quite sane.
But the tide can change.'

---

1 This was frequently used to describe liberals of a stately and conservative
persuasion.

They did indeed consider the poet 'not quite sane'. Greshoff was fired on the spot. Too many gentlemanly subscribers had recognized themselves in his words. They considered the light-hearted satire an attack on their persons and saw to it that its author was removed from their midst – the same author they had allowed a place in their company as chief editor. He had overstepped the mark. The discomfort felt by the gentlemen of Arnhem led to much cheerful indignation in the rest of the country. But this did not get Greshoff his job back. He moved abroad, and his *'Liefdesverklaring'* became one of the best-known poems in the history of Dutch literature.

[143]

PLAYING THE INJURED INNOCENT

Such sensitivity may at first seem surprising in a country that is proud of its tolerance. Personal conflicts are, however, more difficult to gloss over than disputes of a more businesslike or practical nature. For anyone who believes in the culture of the compromise, a direct attack on the personality is difficult to accept. It is considered a blow below the belt. Indignation is then directed at the attacker, while the victims can lick their wounds in public and 'play the injured innocent'. If Greshoff had made old-liberal ideology the subject of his irony instead of persons clearly recognisable to those in the know, nothing would probably have happened to him.

Nowadays, the limits are a little less restrictive, but personal remarks – positive as well as negative – can still cause general resentment. After the spectacular loss of the Christian Democrats in the 1994 general elections, many people put it down to the party's strategy, which had focused too much on the persona of the party leader and not enough on the Christian democratic background. An enquiry concluded that the party had not projected enough 'warmth'; what it meant was that it did not radiate the warmth of the group, inviting people with similar beliefs and ideas to come together.

THE NETHERLANDS SUFFERS FROM A CERTAIN PREDICTABILITY

All in all, this leads to effective cooperation, but never to spectacular change. The chances of a radical about-turn, no matter the area concerned, are very small. It does, however, allow all concerned to set out a course which – although it may never be adventurous – is clear for all to see. The Netherlands suffers from a certain predictability. Every agreement, each appointment, leads to another and this produces a certain continuity. You could almost say that society has its own diary, which is already full quite a way into the future.

The real solidity of the whole system becomes clear only in a crisis. In this century, this has happened once only, during the German occupation between 1940 and 1945.

On 10 May 1940, as part of the *Blitzkrieg*, motorized German troops invaded the Netherlands from the western front. Five days later, the Dutch armed forces capitulated. The Queen and the cabinet had fled to London several days earlier, where they set up a government in exile.

Hitler's national socialism was based on racism. The German people were superior to all others. The Nazis, however, held the Dutch in high esteem. Some of them even considered their neighbours, whose language was closely related to their own, as Germans who had lost their way through a quirk of history. This injustice could now be rectified. Berlin ordered that, if food was scarce, rations for the Dutch people had to be 90 per cent of those for the German occupiers.

Hitler appointed the Austrian Nazi Arthur Seyss-Inquart as *Reichskommissar* in the Netherlands, to run the country now that the government had fled to England. His primary task was to reorganize the Dutch economy as far as possible to serve the war effort. But he had a secondary, more idealistic mission – to convert the people of the Netherlands to Hitler's sacred doctrine. Until then, national socialism had not acquired much support in the country. Anton Mussert, leader of the National-Socialist Movement (NSB) headed a four-man faction in parliament and, as such, belonged to the marginal figures referred to above. Seyss-Inquart was confident, however, that – if he adopted the right approach – he would quickly cure the Dutch of their misgivings.

German social traditions are radically different than those of the Dutch. While the regents in the Netherlands were governing by consensus, across their eastern borders dictatorial princes were ruling with an iron hand. In Germany, there was a tendency to equate the common interest with the interest of the State. Social groups were therefore expected to serve the State, not to effectively take part in it through a complex of consultation and compromise. The sense of hierarchy was very strong.

Seyss-Inquart found that the Netherlands was a very organized society. With the exception of the government, practically everyone had remained at their posts. This had been ordered in a National War Directive that had been issued prior to the German invasion, to protect the interests of the Dutch people. It was, at the same time, forbidden to help the enemy to wage war. There were no exact guidelines. The document was very vague. Seyss-Inquart left the entire administrative structure intact. He placed his own observers in strategic posts within the apparatus to ensure that everything went as it should and to take action if it did not.

BECAUSE THEY WERE 'BAD'

The time of the German occupation continues to be the cause of heated controversy to this day. The main question is whether, when faced with the test, the Dutch people failed or not. Did we resist to a man, or were we simply cowardly collaborators who changed our loyalties according to the course of the war? The occupation was considered of such importance that, a few months after the German capitulation, the government set up the Netherlands State Institute for War Documentation to keep a record of what had happened. The Institute's director, historian Lou de Jong, acquired a very independent position. The first volume of his monumental history appeared in the sixties. It was a bestseller, as were each of the subsequent volumes as soon as they were published. De Jong's work provoked fierce debate and destroyed reputations. What he unearthed did not always make for enjoyable reading. He shattered the myth of an intransigent people standing up to the terror of the occupier. Many prominent figures proved to have done things during the occupation – particularly in the early years, when the prospects of an allied victory were still very slight – which, with hindsight, were of a highly dubious character. Were these people 'good' or 'bad'? It was a question, said Jaap Burger, the minister of justice just before the liberation in 1945, of dealing not with people who had done bad things, but with those who were 'bad'. This disturbed memories of the entire period. It was no longer a matter of what happened, but of deciding how 'good' or 'bad' the people involved had been. There was, of course, no doubt about Mussert and his collaborators. Mussert had already been executed as a traitor to his country. Nor was there much of a problem condemning the thousands of Dutch people (rather too many) who joined the 'Westland' ss unit voluntarily. Outside of these obvious cases, however, it was by no means as clear cut.

There is almost complete agreement among historians today that most Dutch people adopted a kind of tactic of accommodation during the occupation. They tried to continue their everyday lives as far as possible and adapted to the changing circumstances where possible. Only a minority chose either active resistance or full collaboration. The majority just let it happen.

Another question is, however, more interesting. Was Seyss-Inquart successful in carrying out the orders of his *Führer*? The answer is yes and no. Every time he manoeuvred Dutch individuals and organizations into positions where they had to profess their allegiance, the result was a fiasco. When he announced that students could attend university only after they had signed a declaration of loyalty, 90 per cent of them stayed away. When he placed Nazis in leading positions in the traditional pillar organizations, their members left in droves. Trade unions, for example, simply folded. With a few exceptions, new organizations set up along national-socialist lines remained little more than empty shells. Collectors for a Nazi-based charity known as *Winterhulp*, 'Winter Aid', were simply ignored. The radio in London encouraged this with a famous motto: *'Nog niet het knoopje van mijn gulp gaat er naar de Winterhulp'* – 'I'll give not even the button from my trouser fly to the Winterhulp'. The radio and press, controlled by the Nazis, rapidly lost credibility as the war progressed.

That is one side of the coin. But as long as the measures imposed by the occupying Nazis did not demand any show of loyalty, people cooperated with little trouble, sometimes even willingly. This was particularly true in the early years of the occupation. It is clearly illustrated by an excerpt from the illegal newspaper *Het Parool* from 21 August 1942, headed 'The Gestapo and distribution in the Netherlands': 'Every distribution office in the Netherlands has to keep a record of all missing or false ration vouchers or vouchers stuck on the wrong ration cards. The list has to be sent to the Central Distribution Office in The Hague. On 30 June 1942, the heads of all local distribution offices in the country received a confidential letter from the central office that, as of 1 July, a copy of this list has to be sent to the *Deutsche Sicherheits Polizei*, at the Binnenhof in The Hague. In this way, our distribution offices can help to prevent the sending of completely innocent people to the concentration camp for distribution offenders in Ommen. Distribution officials, do not follow these orders. Check less thoroughly or do not send in the lists'.

The illegal press was full of such appeals, together with sad conclusions that these were often ignored out of a misguided sense of duty. The Netherlands had a tradition of trust in the government. Incorruptible and efficient civil servants rarely considered sabotage. They were not only afraid of reprisals – a legitimate fear, considering the lengths to which the Germans were prepared to go – they simply asked themselves each time whether the limit had yet been reached. And, accustomed to making practical compromises, they quickly tended to think that, this time, the demands of the occupier were acceptable. Furthermore, Seyss-Inquart tended to fill vacancies with members of the NSB. The party even had to set up a correspondence course for aspiring mayors. Many public officials defended their decision to stay put with the claim that anything was better than giving up their job to someone from the NSB.

During the occupation, local authorities erupted into feverish activity. Free of parliamentary control, they introduced a flood of new rules and regulations which no longer had to run the gauntlet of public debate. In 1941, they introduced new regulations for road traffic. These were followed by a new, less complex system of income tax. It is estimated that 90 per cent of these new directives were left intact after the country was liberated. In between times, measures imposed by Seyss-Inquart to increase the power of Hitler's totalitarian hand over the people of the Netherlands slipped through the net. Consequently, the Nazis succeeded completely in sucking the economy of the country dry. The authorities generally cooperated in the selection of young men for forced labour in Germany, including – later in the occupation – those who already had jobs. Eventually, all men under forty had to register. The whole system worked very smoothly.

THE HISTORY OF A MURDER

It was due to this attitude that the Nazis were largely able to carry out the most criminal part of their programme in the Netherlands – the extermination of the Jews. 'This book portrays the history of a murder' says Professor Jaques Presser at the beginning of his book *'Ondergang'*, a masterful description of the Final Solution in the Netherlands. The book, which he wrote at the request of the Netherlands State Institute for War Documentation, had a devastating effect. Presser proved conclusively that the Germans were able to isolate, transport and eventually eliminate the Dutch Jews without too many problems because of the cooperation of the organizations involved and the fact that resistance was generally too late and never more than fragmentary. In spite of this, however, the first measures against the Jews were greeted with a mass expression of protest throughout Amsterdam.

THERE IS AN ATMOSPHERE OF RESOLUTE DEFIANCE AMID THE GRIEF

In a square near the seventeenth century Ashkenazi and Sephardi synagogues in the centre of Amsterdam, there is a statue of a dock worker. The man is standing, his muscular body tense, his fists clenched, staring defiantly out at the windswept square in front of him. Every year, on 25 February, a crowd gathers around the statue. Wreaths are laid by representatives of the city council and many others who are clearly members of some committee or other organization. They are often old people, but the crowd comprises a wide range of age groups. Often, the more elderly visitors are accompanied by their grandchildren, who they have brought along in the hope that something of the significance of the occasion will remain with them. There is an atmosphere of resolute defiance amid the grief. They are there to commemorate the February Strike. The docker represents all of the city's workers, who downed tools *en masse* on 25 February 1941 in protest at the persecution of their Jewish colleagues. The whole of Amsterdam took part, and even the stock exchange closed for trading as its staff joined in the strike..

The Jews had been persecuted on the streets. A sort of militia of Dutch national-socialists had incited anti-Semitic riots, and the people of the city had come out in support of their Jewish neighbours. The Germans responded by openly intensifying their terror campaign against the Jews. The small underground Communist Party called for a strike. On 25 and 26 February, there was a general strike in Amsterdam and a number of neighbouring towns. On the second day, the occupier came out in force to end the protest.

The statue of the dock worker keeps the memory of the strike and the solidarity of the city's workers alive. The annual commemoration not only recalls the heroic deeds of those days but is also a manifestation of defiance against continuing terror and racism. It is of great psychological value to the people of Amsterdam. After the liberation, the Queen granted the city permission to include in its coat of arms the following motto: '*Heldhaftig, vastberaden, barmhartig*', 'Valiant, resolute, merciful'.

The square itself is now bare and empty, a place where you would seldom go from choice. The magnificent synagogues show, however, that it must once have been the centre of a busy Jewish community. All that is gone. There is a song that describes this loss, written by Kees Manders and sung by Rika Jansen:

'*Als vader weer bladert in zijn fotoboek*
dan sta je versteld als hij weer vertelt
Van de Weesperstraat en de Jodenhoek.
Als hij dan verhaalt hoe het leven begon
bij het ontwaken, handel en zaken
Humor en gein, dat was de levensbron
en had je een dag eens geen mazzel gehad
Dan 's-avonds naar de Tip Top
waar je je sores vergat.
Soms riep d'r nog één in 't late uur:
'*Ik heb mooie olijven en uitjes in 't zuur'.*
Amsterdam huilt, waar het eens heeft gelachen.
Amsterdam huilt, nog voelt het de pijn'.

[149]

'When father looks through his photographs
We are amazed at the stories he tells
Of the Weesperstraat and the Jodenhoek.
He tells of how the day started,
The trade and the business, the humour and
The wit that was the source of life.
And if one day you didn't have much luck
You could go the Tip Top in the evening
And forget all your troubles.
Sometimes, late at night, you could still hear
The call: 'Lovely olives, pickled onions!'
Amsterdam weeps,
Where once it laughed.
Amsterdam weeps, it still feels the pain.

In '*Ondergang*', Jaques Presser explains how this happened. The Nazis learned their lesson from the strike and, instead of terrorizing the Jews on the streets, they adopted a more administrative approach. They introduced a whole series of small-scale measures to put increasing pressure on their victims.

The register of births, marriages and deaths introduced by Napoleon now proved its worth. Since it recorded not only name, address and age, but also religion, it was simple to weed out the Jews. Some local officials hit upon the idea of spiriting away the incriminating cards, but this often occurred too late and only on a very small scale. Moreover, in the first few months of the occupation, everyone in the country had received a form to fill in, declaring whether they had Jewish parents or grandparents. Practically everyone had faithfully returned the form, as one should do with forms issued by the government. This, in spite of the ominous title of the document: *Ariërverklaring*, Declaration of Aryan Descent. A conscientious civil servant in The Hague by the name of Lentz saw an opportunity to introduce one of his pet plans, which the Dutch government had always left on the shelf for reasons of economy. Under this plan, every Dutch citizen would have to carry an identity document. Lentz had designed one which was almost impossible to forge with the methods available at the time. Seyss-Inquart gave him all the cooperation and support he required. Lentz spent the entire occupation diligently perfecting his system of identification. He never understood why he was so unpopular after the liberation.

When war broke out, the Jewish community in the Netherlands amounted to about 140,000 people. Most were descended from refugees who had fled to the Republic to escape persecution in less tolerant countries. Their special status had officially been abolished in 1795. The Dutch Jews knew that they belonged in the Netherlands. The pillarized society allowed them to retain their own identity where and whenever they wanted without fear of repercussion. Many words with Hebrew or Yiddish origins had become a part of the Dutch language. Amsterdammers proudly refer to their city to this day as 'Mokum', which is derived from the Hebrew word for 'town'. Everyone knows where the word comes from. The unofficial anthem of the capital starts with the sentence *'In Mokum ben ik rijk en gelukkig tegelijk, geef mij maar Amsterdam'*, 'In Mokum I am rich and happy at the same time, just give me Amsterdam'.

Jews never felt any reason to mistrust the government or its representatives. Not even when it issued the *Ariërverklaring*. Not when it fired all Jewish civil servants – at first, on full salary. Nor when it dismissed all Jewish teachers and gave them new jobs at special Jewish schools.

Most Dutch people responded to these measures with some resentment, but considered them at least 'recognizable'. After the February Strike, the Germans set up a Jewish Council for Amsterdam. It was headed by two leading figures from the Jewish community and had a wide range of administrative powers. This, too, seemed acceptable. It was probably a good thing that there was a representative body that could mediate with the occupier. The leaders of the Council soon discovered, however, that they had not been appointed to talk to the Germans. They simply had to carry out their orders. These orders were largely a matter of selecting people for transportation to Germany or even further east. The criteria for selection continually changed. There were of course all kinds of procedures for appeal against selection, or even to be added to the list if one so desired. It was all set up very correctly, right down to the medical examinations. In this way, the Germans were able to increasingly isolate the Jews from their fellow citizens. They devised a way of acquiring the Jews' property without too many problems by forcing them to transfer it to a special Jewish bank. With the cooperation of local authorities throughout the country and under the supervision of the Dutch police, they concentrated the country's entire Jewish community in the area where the statue of the dock worker now stands.

The pace of these measures was determined by the rate at which the death camps in Poland were able to 'process' those who were sent there. Transportation took place in two phases. The selected groups were picked up and taken to Amsterdam Central Station in extra city trams. They were then taken by train to the Westerbork transit camp near the German border. A freight train packed full of deportees left Westerbork every week bound for the gas chambers in Auschwitz-Birkenau.

The trams were driven by employees of the City Public Transport Company. After the liberation, Presser noted with some bitterness that the Dutch rail network had not only survived the war almost intact, it had been extended – with a new stretch of line between Hooghalen and Westerbork. Of the 140,000 Dutch Jews – men, women and children – 110,000 were murdered. This is 79 per cent. In France and Belgium, both of which were occupied during the war, the percentages were 40 and 38 respectively. This is not because the Dutch are more anti-Semitic, it is just that in the other two countries, the people were able to sabotage the Nazi extermination machine more quickly and more effectively. There were protests enough against the persecution of the Jews in

the Netherlands – the churches in particular responded very vociferously –
but there was too little practical, 'silent resistance'. When the resistance movement, both in and outside the Jewish community, began to set up escape networks, it was already too late.

The longer the occupation lasted, the more the resistance movement,
which was made up of a wide variety of groups and individuals, grew and the
more it could count on the sympathy of the population. Active cooperation
was, however, a different matter. Throughout the war, the entire structure of
government and bureaucracy, with the occasional exception, followed the
orders of Seyss-Inquart and his officials. The civil servants involved could not
comprehend that this was not just another party with whom they had to
negotiate, but a totally unscrupulous enemy who was not prepared to talk,
who would always demand complete and unconditional compliance. Even
when he appeared prepared to adapt, to be – for a brief moment – open to
reason, it was never anything more than a strategic marking of time, a pause
before clamping down even harder than before.

This does not detract from the heroic deeds of thousands of Dutch men
and women who risked their lives or of the undaunted members of the resistance who helped those pursued by the Nazis to escape and sometimes made a
significant contribution to the eventual allied victory. In one area, the Dutch
resistance was far better organized than its fellow movements in other countries – the publication of illegal leaflets, pamphlets, books and even, newspapers. Towards the end of the occupation, circulation of illegal papers reached
about a million a day, all of which were composed, printed and distributed in
secret. The catalogue of illegal publications issued by the Institute for War
Documentation comprises hundreds of pages. In spite of the fact that most
Dutch people adopted a tactic of accommodation during the occupation, they
still wished to express their opinions – which had not changed – without them
being censored. And they were prepared to run a considerable risk do so. The
punishment for the possession of illegal publications was imprisonment and
internment in a concentration camp; for writing, distribution and printing, it
was death.

The memory of the Second World War still plays a significant role in many
public debates and this is increasing rather than decreasing. Articles related to
the war appear in the newspapers on a regular basis. The Netherlands State
Institute for War Documentation still exists, even now that De Jong's massive

historical work has been completed. Books appear every year on the occupation and the war continues to be a favourite topic for writers of fiction. The occupation has even acquired a certain mythical character. It is deeply entrenched in the collective memory of the nation, providing a backdrop in which good and evil fight to the death. Heroes defy the ss with the verve of Luke Skywalker in his struggle against Darth Vader.

Yet, at the same time, there is a realization that it was not a particularly illustrious period in our history. The mistakes made during the occupation will not be made again. The obligation to carry some form of identification is now completely normal in all our neighbouring countries. Any Dutch government that considers introducing a similar obligation immediately finds itself at the centre of a heated debate in which the hated term 'identity card' plays a central role. It was not until 1994, after a long and difficult process, that the government succeeded in introducing at least some form of ID obligation. Dutch citizens now have to be able to prove their identity in certain situations to a number of clearly specified officials. But not with identity cards. They must produce their passport, driving licence or an ID pass issued by the local council. This is required, for example, at their place of work, by a number of municipal bodies and on public transport (but only if they do not have a valid ticket). It is also forbidden to take part in football riots without carrying some form of valid identification. It all sounds rather absurd, but it is explicable in the light of events.

For the same reason, Dutch people are very afraid that the information they give to different organizations will be linked up and compared. The arrival of computer networks has made this much easier and the temptation even greater. There is legislation that subjects this to very strict regulation, but experience has shown that such data can still fall into the wrong hands. It was a long time before parliament assented to the tax authorities and the social security department comparing their information – the most watertight means of finding out whether people are drawing benefits illegally. In spite of all the guarantees, there is a widespread belief that all of this information is secretly stored together in one place.

Presser's lesson that the most effective response to repression is silent sabotage has not been learned. When the government of Saudi Arabia, an important business partner for the Netherlands, demanded that visa applications be accompanied by a declaration that the applicant was not Jewish, there was a public debate on whether this new version of the *Ariërverklaring* should be accepted and whether the Christian churches should provide copies from their parish records as additional evidence. The churches refused. No one suggested neutralizing this anti-Semitic measure by providing as much background information as possible (especially created for the occasion) to accompany the declaration, particularly for people of Jewish descent. Most Dutch people who had to go to Arab countries on business did their best – without feeling overly embarrassed or thinking too much about it – to prove their 'Aryan' background when asked to do so. They thought it a reasonable request, considering the conflict with Israel. They did not see anything sinister behind it. And they certainly did not feel that they were effectively going against the grain of public opinion, which was – and still is – almost entirely on the side of the Israelis.

MANY DUTCH PEOPLE ARE VERY SENSITIVE TO REPRESSION IN OTHER COUNTRIES

The Dutch are very opinionated but they also have a great respect for rules and agreements. After all, they are used to rules being agreed 'democratically' and in consultation. In many parts of the world, of course, the law is imposed on the populace by a government whose position effectively rests on power and repression. In spite of this deeply ingrained respect for authority, however, many Dutch people are very sensitive to this repression in other countries. The media devote much attention to it. There are countless committees expressing solidarity with repressed countries and peoples in far-flung parts of the world, which tend to adopt the traditional tactics of the action committees. In the Netherlands, Amnesty International is practically a mass organization. And anyone, no matter where they may be, who dares undertake a *coup d'état* – especially a military one – can count on a protest demonstration in front of his Embassy in the Netherlands. Such protest is, however, limited to verbal condemnation. It rarely extends to concrete action. Calls for trade boycotts or other punitive measures are generally rejected by a majority in parliament or by the government, unless they represent a consensus of international Western (and since the collapse of the Soviet empire, even global) opinion. Amnesty International explains its success in the Netherlands by the fact that it gives people the idea that they are at least doing something to prove that they are 'good' and not 'bad' like those who betrayed their country in the war, and perhaps many others. Yet this gives no reason to assume that, if the country is ever occupied again, the Dutch will prove themselves any more able to resist than they did during the Nazi occupation.

One explanation is the fact that the Dutch have little experience of foreign domination. They have been accustomed to having a structure of government manned by their own people for centuries and they do not consider their rulers dangerous outsiders. The people of the area known historically as Flanders, which now constitutes the northern part of Belgium, have succeeded in freeing themselves from foreign domination only in the past fifty years. Here, 'silent resistance' has developed into a fine art. The Flemish have become past masters not only of tax evasion but also at quietly dismantling dictatorial structures. During the Second World War, they were far more successful at deceiving the Nazis than their fellow Dutch-speakers just across the border. The Dutch artist and resistance fighter Eduard Veterman, who was a master forger of false documents, wrote in his war memoirs *'Keizersgracht 763'*: 'It was of course comical that the police of a Brussels suburb became 'bulk buyers'. Belgian government officials were far more active in this respect than their Dutch colleagues'.

After the liberation, both the organization and the staff of the Dutch bureaucratic apparatus remained largely intact. Only those who were overt supporters of the Nazis, such as the members of the NSB, were actually removed from their positions. The situation was not examined with a more critical eye until much later. In 1958, Professor Jan de Quay – who set up a short-lived 'Netherlands Union' shortly after the occupation which accepted Hitler's vision of Europe – became the prime minister without provoking an outcry. His deputies all had successful careers. That would no longer be possible today – especially since the publication of De Jong's work.

Belief in the good intentions of the powers-that-be had also survived the war intact and, to a large extent, is still strong today. The Dutch have a number of objective reasons for this belief. They know that even the largest organizations take account of the individual. They can count on agreements and promises being kept within the agreed period of time. If this does not happen, there are always procedures for appeal. No one has to simply accept a tax demand, an order from the local council or any other manifestation of power from above. They can object, their appeal will be taken seriously and there is a good chance that they will win. If one or the other party refuses to budge, there are specialized independent courts. This can lead to long-drawn-out procedures which, in many cases, have a deterrent effect. The threat of being taken to court is often used as a weapon. Not because the Dutch are particularly fond of dragging their compatriots up in front of a judge, but because the threat itself generally leads to a new round of negotiations and, eventually, to a compromise that is acceptable to all concerned. It is all a matter of give and take.

THEY ALWAYS HAVE A LITTLE ´LOOSE CHANGE´ IN THEIR POCKETS

Anyone who sits down with a sigh to fill in their tax forms, knows from the outset that the officials at the tax department will most likely not accept all of the deductions they have claimed. They tend to accept this, together with the fact that they will at least get something back. They include a few less probable items, in the hope that the tax people will focus on these and let the others slip through. In the same way, trade unions, employers' organizations and interest groups submit proposals in the knowledge that a large part of what they have presented will have to be surrendered during negotiations. They always have, as it were, a little 'loose change' in their pockets.

You don't come far in the Netherlands without this loose change. This applies as much to the public at large as to sports clubs, school boards and university departments. Everyone is used to having their say and being able to recognize at least a part of it in the final decision.

Anyone who needs the approval of others to realize a plan of some kind, will first conduct an informal survey in the immediate environment to ascertain how feasible it is. In this way, you get some kind of indication of what will be acceptable to everyone. You then draw up a plan which includes a certain amount of loose change. This should consist of items which are not essential to the success of the plan, but which are certain to provoke objections from various quarters. After this, there is a round of consultation with all parties concerned, during which – as expected – objections of all kinds are raised.

ANY EXPRESSION OF ONE´S OWN TALENT IS COUNTERPRODUCTIVE

Outright rejections are very rare. Comments are usually presented as suggestions for improvement, marginal rather than challenging anything essential.

The person submitting the proposals is open to such suggestions and lays his loose change on the table, one coin at a time. This requires skill and experience. The quicker he shows his loose change, the more the others will demand from him. It is a slow and, for outsiders, sometimes irritating process – particularly as it is so difficult to intervene while the process runs its course. Any expression of one's own talent or excellence tends to be counterproductive. As does any defence of the proposals based on their inherent superiority. Anyone who uses arguments like 'This is the solution we are looking for', 'All our troubles are over' or 'Don't mess around with this, it's already perfect' will only succeed in uniting the opposition against them. Criticisms will then be [157] directed at the essentials of the proposal and the whole thing rejected because the proposer has made it clear that he is not prepared to negotiate but wishes to impose his will on the others. They feel that their opinions are not being taken into consideration and that they have made no contribution to the issue under discussion. As far as they are concerned, there is nothing more to discuss. Once this happens, the only alternative is the exercise of power. Those in a position of authority, who are higher in the hierarchy, can impose their will, steer the discussion in a certain direction and set limits. But even then it is not advisable to leave no room at all for those in a subordinate position to make their contribution. They will then use the most powerful weapon at their disposal – complete disinterest. They will lose their motivation. They will, as it were, withdraw their creativity. They continue to do everything by the rules, but make it clear to their friends and acquaintances that they no longer really give a damn what happens. Lack of motivation among the staff is a common problem in almost all organizations and companies in the Netherlands, particularly because the law makes it very difficult to dismiss employees simply because they 'don't care'. Managers should be aware of this. Although they might wish to give job applicants an impression of themselves as resolute and vigorous leaders, the socially responsible thing to do is to assure prospective employees that they are always 'prepared to listen' and believe very strongly in the indispensability of genuine *overleg*.

IT IS MORE A WAY EXCHANGING INFORMATION

As I mentioned above, it is impossible to translate the word *'overleg'*. The literal translation 'consultation' does not embrace the full meaning of the term in

Dutch. It is a form of group communication which aims not so much at reaching a decision as giving the parties involved the opportunity to exchange information. The Dutch spend many of their working hours in 'overleg'. This means that they are discussing the state of affairs with their colleagues. They describe in detail the activities they are engaged in and the rest of the group are, in principle, entitled to make comments or ask questions. Superiors will explain their plans to those below them in the hierarchy in detail and inform them of their consultations with colleagues elsewhere in the organization. Everyone, and superiors in particular, gives their reasons for doing or not doing something. They are not afraid of questions, no matter how critical they may be, and take the time to answer them. Tempers very rarely rise during these consultations. If they do, something is wrong.

At the end of the *overleg*, everyone has an idea of what the other wishes to achieve. This is very important if the system is to function correctly. After all the questions, comments and reactions, the limits of a generally acceptable consensus have become more or less clear. Often the chairman will conclude with satisfaction that *'de neuzen weer in dezelfde richting wijzen'*, all noses are pointing in the same direction, or – in typically Dutch fashion – *'de klokken zijn gelijk gezet'*, the clocks are all showing the same time. Such *overleg* may lead to practical decisions being made, but more often than not results in little more than an exchange of information. Afterwards the participants can be seen, diaries at the ready, making appointments with each other.

Yet it is considered normal to complain about all this *overleg* and the endless meetings. You soon get the feeling that they make little contribution to efficiency. Most meetings are therefore characterized by a certain degree of dullness and apathy. Boredom is never far away and can strike at any minute, particularly because the Dutch rarely use their unquestioned, but underdeveloped, talent for rhetoric. Everyone must, in principle, have their say. This requires a strict and manipulative chairman. Most chairmen restrict themselves to keeping interruptions to a minimum, on the principle that people have the right to finish what they are saying. This may be fair, but does little to make the discussion more lively.

The whole process of *overleg* ensures that the complaints do not lead to this form of communication being employed less frequently. Everyone complains very vociferously, but anyone who does not take it sufficiently seriously does so only to their own detriment. Especially if the other participants are their subordinates.

There is a serious risk inherent in the whole business. The original aim may be lost in endless rounds of consultation and meetings. Compromises pile up until the final result is so watered down that it would have been better not to have done anything at all. This kind of net result is familiar from history lessons on the Republic.

EVERY ORGANISATION HAS A *BELEID*

There is, of course, an instrument to prevent this happening – '*het beleid*'.

'*Beleid*' is usually translated as 'policy'. Although this is sometimes adequate, in most cases, like *overleg*, it cannot be translated by any one English term. The word originally indicated a kind of precise and cautious way of working. Anyone who sets about repairing a microscope should not go at it like a bull at a gate, but should be patient and tackle the problem with *beleid*. Typically, a synonym for *beleid* used in this way is *overleg*. Every organisation has a policy, from the government down the smallest local club. Philips and Shell have a *beleid*, and so does the printers at the end of the street, with its workforce of four. And, of course, it is all down on paper. The *beleid* describes the aims of the organization and the kinds of activities it undertakes. It also sets limits for these aims and activities. Everything may be very clearly formulated, but more often than not it is rather vague. The partners involved in discussion of a proposal can determine from the *beleid* whether it falls within the specified limits. Compromises that fall outside these limits can be rejected as not being a part of the *beleid*. On the other hand, elements may often be added to existing activities because they are considered to fall within the bounds of the *beleid*. If, for example, it is the *beleid* of the government to employ more women – as is indeed the case – the personnel departments of the various ministries must direct their recruitment campaigns to take this into account. There can be no debate about this. Anyone who questions it is immediately put in his place. *Beleid* is *beleid*.

Beleid, of course, comes into being through the process of *overleg*, in which everyone concerned takes part. But once it is in place, it rapidly becomes immutable. Everyone knows that they have to act within the limits of the *beleid* –

or else. That is why it is accorded such great importance. Those with ambition do their best to be as closely involved in the process of making *beleid* as possible. When talking to friends and colleagues or having a drink in the pub, they will boast of the contribution they have made. In job applications, they will make as much of it as they can, because it demands respect. It is no surprise that the one of the highest jobs in the civil service is that of *'beleids-adviseur'.*

IF PEOPLE ARE NOT SATISFIED, THEY BLAME IT ON *BELEID*

All this leads to the conclusion, especially in government circles, that problems are caused by a lack of *beleid.* Interest groups, professional associations and action committees adopt this idea and continually make demands for *beleid* on this and *beleid* on that. Politicians pacify the public with pledges to formulate new *beleid* to deal with their complaints. And if this takes too long, they will soon be pilloried by the media. They can, on the other hand, evade difficult issues by saying that, fortunately, there is a *beleid* that deals with that very problem. There is a good chance that no one will ask what this *beleid* actually entails.

If people are not satisfied, they will tell their friends in the café that there is something wrong with the *beleid.* It is stupid. It is out of date. Or it does not take account of the facts. If it is not changed – and changed quickly and radically – then we shall all (and this is where they stare despairingly into their glass or point accusingly with their index fingers) go to the dogs. There is no other way out.

Beleid is a serious business. It is far too easily seen as a solution in itself, and not always out of a desire for an easy life. It is largely due to the fact that most Dutch people – when it comes down to it – believe that most things can be controlled. All it takes is good organization (and if that fails there is always the *gedoogbeleid,* the policy of 'tolerance'). This belief has been reinforced by the process of modernization that began in the last twenty-five years of the nineteenth century and the boundless prosperity that has developed since the end of the Second World War. Modern society is a success story and it leads people to believe that if you take the right measures at the right place and at the right time you will always achieve the desired result.

Beleid is often then a matter of regulating existing processes. The government initially started doing this when circumstances left it with no other choice. Although the Netherlands managed to keep out of the First World War (1914–1918), its economy suffered severely and there were serious food shortages. The complete collapse of the commercial sector was prevented only by a large number of radical government measures. Others were introduced to ensure a reasonably fair distribution of what little food was available. The acute economic depression caused by the Wall Street crash of 1929 also provoked a wave of government regulations and measures aimed at keeping the impact in the Netherlands to a minimum. And it was *beleid* that held all of these measures together in some form of cohesive whole. Consequently, government intervention in economy and society became normal, although there were critics who spoke of 'St. Bureaucratius' and many others who complained that the government certainly seemed to appoint a large number of commissions to investigate a whole range of problems and come up with solutions. Yet this criticism was to no avail. The intention behind all the commissions was to remove the ideological content from the process of formulating *beleid* as much as possible. The whole exercise is, after all, only worthwhile if the result enjoys sufficiently broad support. The parties in the consensus always have to recognize some of their own contribution in the final result, or at least not see too many elements of the opposing parties' viewpoints which – after all – they vigorously opposed during the *overleg*. It is therefore always better if *beleid* appears to be based on facts or scientific research. The commissions are made up of academics or representatives of interest groups, plus a number of 'independent experts'. Everyone hopes that, if the various 'interested' members are unable to find a consensus, the experts – with their knowledge of the facts – will be come up with a solution to suit everyone.

[161]

A new group of specialists has developed in the civil service, in interest groups and in some sectors of industry – the *beleidsmedewerkers*, 'policy officials'. These people frequently have departments of their own and their jobs carry a high status. Civil servants always try to include the word *beleid* in their job descriptions, because it gives them good grounds for demanding promotion to a higher salary scale. In the Netherlands, there is nothing political about working on *beleid*. Government specialists are proud of the fact that they can operate efficiently under any kind of political leadership. As good civil servants, they are always 'loyal' to their superiors, whether they be ministers, members of the provincial executive or local aldermen. The minister's ideological views will therefore be difficult to recognize in the documents in which his or her *beleid* is laid out. An efficient *beleidsafdeling*, the department responsible for drawing up the documents, is at the centre of a whole web of contacts throughout society. Its work is supported not only by all kinds of special committees, but also by representatives of interest groups and organizations which continually submit detailed recommendations on the content of the *beleid*, frequently in the form of fully worked out draft reports and documents. Countless permanent advisory bodies have grown up around the various ministries which concern themselves with a wide range of issues, from the most general to the extremely specific. The Advisory Council on Government Policy (known in Dutch as the WRR) can concern itself with practically any area it chooses. The Advisory Council on Development-Related Research, on the other hand, is concerned with a narrow area of research. Both have a professional staff. The WRR has its own office and is large enough for people to make a successful career for themselves. Most of these advisory councils are entitled to submit advice, whether it is requested or not – and they take full advantage of this right.

The more independent the members of a council or an ad hoc advisory committee, the greater the chance that they submit recommendations that are not considered feasible because they have insufficient '*maatschappelijk draagvlak*'. This is another Dutch term that defies translation. It roughly means 'support in society', but implies more than simply obtaining the agreement of the general public for a proposed course of action. It is a question of whether the proposals will have a reasonable chance of success when exposed to the network of committees, interest groups and public enquiries that they will have to pass through before the necessary consensus is reached. Recommendations with insufficient *draagvlak* are usually discussed in the media, often after being presented at a press conference, but then disappear into a drawer. *Beleidsafdelingen* are very good at filing away vast quantities of information which only resurfaces decades later when some aspiring historian digs it out while researching a PhD. *Beleid* can cover a very limited area, but can sometimes get out of hand. A perfect example of this is '*Een Wereld van Verschil*', 'A World of Difference', a document published by Jan Pronk, the social democratic Minister for Development Cooperation, shortly after the start of his second term of office in 1993. This *beleidsnota*, or policy document, runs to 385 pages – which is a lot of reading material but not untypical for such publications. Its subtitle, 'A new framework for development cooperation in the 1990s', indicates the purpose of the document. It will clearly set out the direction which development policy is to take and, at the same time, specify its limitations.

Pronk has become something of a 'Mr. Development Cooperation' in the Netherlands. He is known for wearing his heart on his sleeve and for his outspoken views. A pupil of Nobel prizewinner Jan Tinbergen, Pronk believes that the world is wrongly organized. Anyone who tries to solve the problem of poverty is continually obstructed by a system that protects the haves and leaves the have-nots to their sad fate. This calls for supranational action. During his second term of office the minister emerged as a keen supporter of military intervention in conflict areas, as long as it takes the form of a peace-keeping force under the auspices of the United Nations (i.e. he sought to solve the conflict by persuading the warring parties to accept a compromise – Pronk, for all his internationalism, is still Dutch). This conviction is not expressed in 'A World of Difference', at least not explicitly. A third of the document outlines recent historical developments, with the emphasis on social and economic processes. It therefore does not provide a clear theoretical framework, but rather describes a multifaceted process. This historical review is followed by detailed analyses of the situation in the various continents. The chapter entitled 'The quality of policy implementation', laying out exactly what the Netherlands should do, is only thirty pages long, a meagre ten per cent of the entire document. The proposals contained in this chapter are based on the analysis of the processes described and the largely undisputed principle that funds should be allocated as efficiently as possible. The emphasis (and note the broad definition) should lie on the alleviation of poverty. This is because 'despite important advances, for example in reducing infant and child mortality, increasing literacy and raising life expectancy, one billion people live below the poverty line. They have little hope of an improvement in their living conditions'.

This observation alone is sufficient to justify the broad framework. The idea that poverty is unavoidable enjoys little credibility in a country where no one is, in principle, left to fend for themselves. When the document was debated in parliament, no one questioned the priority assigned to poverty alleviation.

A World of Difference also describes in detail the various categories of poverty and of poor people. This is necessary because it proposes a specific *beleid* for each category. Poverty is seen as a reversible process, a problem that can be solved by intervening at the right time and place with the right measures. The result will be a form of global organization that gives everyone the prospect of a reasonable standard of living. Let there be no confusion about this – the document does not identify the structural causes of poverty and propose new structures to replace them. It advocates intervention on a grand scale in existing processes. It fails to mention that the Dutch development effort – the equivalent of about one guilder per member of the world's population per year – is a drop in the ocean in terms of global processes. It does specify with reasonable precision the conditions under which projects can be funded from the Dutch development budget. A *beleidsnota* for the further reclamation of land from the North Sea could have been written along the same lines.

[164]

Jan Pronk is a notorious workaholic who largely writes his policy documents himself. This does not make him popular with everyone. Ministers should not interfere too enthusiastically in the draft documents that their staff have drawn up after so much *overleg* and advice. They may return them with a few comments in the margin, which will then be incorporated into the text by the *beleidsafdeling* concerned, until the minister has nothing more to add. Most policy documents are the joint efforts of several authors and you often come across people who proudly tell you that they are responsible for a certain chapter or paragraph, or that they had a say in how it was put together. This means that they were involved in the *overleg* in which the embryonic document was discussed.

BELEID TENDS TO BE RATHER SHORT-LIVED

The problem is that *beleid* tends to be rather short-lived. Circumstances change rapidly and with them the foundation, or at least part of it, on which the policy is built. Three years after the publication of his magnum opus, Pronk had to produce a kind of supplement to take account of recent developments, particularly the almost entirely unexpected explosion of ethnic violence in Eastern Europe. This time the document was only 123 pages long. But again, its title spoke volumes: *'Een Wereld van Geschil. De grenzen van de ontwikkelingssamenwerking verkend'*, 'A World of Dispute: a survey of the frontiers of development cooperation'. At the request of parliament, Pronk also produced a number of documents on various aspects of his policy, which will, in their turn, have to be modified at some time in the future. In this way, the wheels of the machinery of *beleid* – both large and small – keep turning throughout the country.

SOCIETY, TOO, HAS A DIARY FOR KEEPING TRACK OF APPOINTMENTS

Beleid is aimed at the future. The Dutch take it for granted that society, too, has a kind of diary for keeping track of appointments. They can leaf back [165] through the planning for the past six months or so, which ensures continuity. Continuity is a 'Good Thing'. Companies and organizations proudly state the year in which they were founded if it is long enough ago to give them an air of respectability. In their view, there is nothing coincidental about this great age. It is an indication of the foresight of their founding fathers, a characteristic which the current generation of leaders has no difficulty in believing they have inherited.

Many Dutch people strongly believe in the predictability of events. Pro-posals are frequently dismissed because they affect only the short term. Good *beleid* aims at the long term, or at least, the medium-long term. In practice, this results in a great deal of analysis and brainstorming which is frequently overtaken by developments. There is then a tendency to hang on to the existing *beleid* and to see the new circumstances as incidental rather than structural. Experience has shown that companies and organizations that feel sure of their position are the first to adapt their *beleid* to changing circumstances.

When asked about his vision of the year 2000 in the daily newspaper, the *Haagsche Courant,* on 9 July 1994, futurologist Professor L.J. Schoonenboom replied: 'In terms of *beleid*, the year 2000 has absolutely no significance at all'.

Beleid is a growing sector and the number of people working in it is still rising. They are even benefiting from the policy of cutbacks that the government has been pursuing since the 1980s, because *beleid* is of course necessary to implement the cuts. It is striking that many *beleidsafdelingen* spare them-selves while other departments have to shape up and trim down. This has pro-voked much criticism in recent years, but the *beleidsmakers* – the policy-ma-kers – have been relatively successful in preserving their position, even now that the value of 'middle management' – as elsewhere in the industrialized world – is being critically re-evaluated in the Netherlands. Policy officials, with their special status, fall a little outside this category. After all, without *beleid* the social processes of negotiation would become uncontrollable.

Yet some people still wonder about the value of all this effort. Does *beleid* ever actually help to solve problems? This is a difficult question to answer, because the documents in which *beleid* is laid out are rarely unequivocal and seldom have a single aim. They generally have a number of parallel objectives, or the main aim is divided into components. In Pronk's fight against poverty, a number of other elements also play an important role, notably protection of the environment and the emancipation of women. This multiplicity of aims is related to the character of compromise that such documents always have; their authors try to put as much as possible into them to satisfy as many interest groups as possible. And it does not stop there. In the search for greater effectiveness and workability, secondary policies are devised to suit a whole range of smaller target groups. After all, there are no such things as all-embracing models which you can simply impose on reality, even if you have to break a few corners off here and there. There are always exceptions and specific circumstances which demand special treatment. This ultimately makes *beleid* very complex and its results difficult to measure. It also means that the system of rules and regulations it gives rise to are extremely complicated and difficult to unravel. For example, the level of social security benefits depends on the family situation of the applicant. Two individuals receive more than a married couple, but applicants whose partner is in paid employment are not entitled to a benefit. There are now more than twenty different ways of categorizing people who live together. Social security officials also have difficulties in distinguishing between the categories and complain about their colleagues in the *beleidsafdeling* who are responsible for making the rules which they have to implement as best they can. Reports of ridiculous situations that have arisen as the result of different forms of *beleid* clashing with each other also appear regularly in the media..

Every now and then, politicians attempt to put an end to such undesirable situations. The matter then gets bogged down in parliament, where the representatives of the people speak earnestly of injustice and 'extreme emergencies'. The ministers – or, lower down the ladder, councillors – then fall over themselves to pledge that they will draw up a special *beleid* to address these urgent situations. This led in one notorious case to the failure of an attempt to simplify tax legislation. The original proposal from a committee of experts was amended to such an extent that the new system of rules and regulations was no less complicated than the original one. It was also considered unfair. Too many people fell *'tussen de wal en de schip'*, between the ship and the quayside, where – as we all know – you can all too easily get crushed to a pulp.

WE PASSED THAT STATION LONG AGO

The consequences of *beleid* are often the opposite of what was intended. When the government attempted to prevent companies from dismissing employees who were no longer able to do their jobs for medical reasons by introducing fines, the companies simply paid the fines and imposed far stricter requirements on the health of new employees. Applicants whose health was questionable, or which might prove to be so at some time in the future found it almost impossible to get a job. This made it very difficult for disabled or older people to find paid employment.

It is always possible to change *beleid* eventually, but it cannot be achieved overnight. Every single measure has, after all, been discussed at great length. 'That discussion has already been closed' or 'we passed that station long ago' are common and often effective responses to suggestions that existing policy should be reviewed. It is possible to get the discussion reopened only if it can be proved that circumstances have changed to such an extent that the *beleid* is 'hanging in the air', i.e. that it no longer has sufficient *maatschappelijk draagvlak*. This makes the decision-making process in the Netherlands somewhat slow. The Dutch have a word for this: *'stroperig'*, from *stroop*, the thick syrup they like to pour over their pancakes. Although this implies a certain self-criticism, it has resulted in little more than good intentions. There is a well-known Dutch expression: *'waar gehakt wordt, vallen spaanders'*. Roughly translated, it means 'if you chop down trees, watch out for flying splinters'. The message is clear – just leave the trees where they are.

Anyone who is likely to be affected by some form of *beleid* or another would therefore be well-advised to follow the process closely and, where possible, become directly involved in it. The usual way to do this is to join in the *overleg*. In their attempts to involve as many people and interested bodies as possible in their activities, *beleidsmakers* promote such participation themselves. It is, after all, a prerequisite for the ultimate legitimacy of their product.

The action committees of the sixties helped them in this endeavour by fighting for the introduction of public enquiries on as many issues as possible. These enquiries are public meetings to which people who are affected by the proposed *beleid* are invited. They may be the representatives of certain sectors, the residents of a particular street or employees in a certain branch of industry. The meetings are in effect a form of *overleg*. The body organizing the meeting outlines its plans, often presenting a number of alternatives. Afterwards, everyone is invited to ask questions and give their comments. This frequently leads to some of those present volunteering to sit on a working group to examine the issues further and present recommendations, which offers them an opportunity to share in the decisionmaking process.

Again, it is not advisable to swim too enthusiastically against the current, because this is inconsistent with the search for a consensus and the general tendency not to see things in black-and-white terms. Yet there is often an undercurrent of suspicion at these meetings. Many of those present believe that there is something they are not being told, a 'hidden agenda'. There is only one course of action open if you are suspected of having a hidden agenda – complete openness. No one will actually say anything, but you will notice that your partners in the discussion are increasingly cool and reserved. It is not advisable to bring it up yourself; you should never ask outright: 'So you think I have a hidden agenda?'. The only effective antidote is transparency, putting your cards on the table, providing as much information in as much detail as you can. This is, however, easier said than done. Bureaucracies and similar organizations have a tendency to keep quiet about things that are still being discussed internally. These are sensitive issues. It is very rare that they will come out and say 'We haven't reached agreement on that yet' or 'That is a very sensitive issue and any comment might have repercussions for everyone involved'. It is in this fertile soil of silence that suspicions of a hidden agenda germinate and grow.

During the Republic, the regents held all their *overleg* behind closed doors. The phenomenon of representative bodies meeting in public dates back only to the nineteenth century. Openness was one of the main demands of the action committees that grew up in the sixties. This initially led to a great proliferation of public galleries. Parties represented on local councils across the country were more or less forced to hold their internal preparatory consultations in public. The openness did not, however, last for long. The more experienced party members simply transferred the real business of reaching a consensus to the *wandelgangen* or to all kinds of informal meetings. Consequently, traditional *overleg* behind closed doors has undergone something of a revival since the 1980s. The negotiations on the formation of the new coalition government in 1994 were more secretive than ever. This development was actually very predictable – you do not create an atmosphere conducive to consensus by inviting a whole crowd of outsiders to listen to every word that is exchanged.

This form of confidentiality provides ample opportunity to influence the process of making *beleid* by mobilizing external factors. The Netherlands has a free press with relatively little respect for the powers-that-be. Politicians and others who wish to manipulate the process in some way or another regularly take advantage of this. They leak information to the press and good journalists are always very pleased with themselves when they find confidential documents in their post. The media devote considerable attention to the information. Journalists will always protect their sources at any price, even though – unlike doctors, for example – they have not sworn an oath of confidentiality. Attempts in the past to discover journalists' sources by taking them to court have always resulted in a scandal, in which the journalist emerges as a martyr for freedom. This is why those in high places who are damaged by such leaks prefer to discover who is responsible by means of an internal investigation. The culprits are very rarely fired. Their careers tend to 'take a dive' and they find themselves excluded by their superiors and colleagues. Leaking confidential information therefore always bears a certain risk. The trail should never lead back to the 'mole', at least not exclusively. The media cannot be punished for publishing 'secrets'. No one will criticize them in public, or they will restrict their comments to errors of content on which they will base their counterattack. This, too, will attract a great deal of public interest. The best and most effective way to minimize the impact of a leak – and this is what often happens in practice – is to immediately adopt an attitude of complete openness.

Furthermore, since the 1970s, there has been legislation in the Netherlands, which in principle allows everyone access to all official documents, unless they contain personal information (such as personnel files). The archives of the Internal Security Service (known in Dutch as the BVD) – the Dutch KGB or, if you prefer, CIA – are exempted from this obligation. Now that the Cold

War is over, the BVD wishes to destroy a large number of its personal files, but there is some resistance to this among the general public. There are calls for the files to be released for scientific research or, where they relate to individuals, to the persons concerned.

THE CLOAK OF CHARITY

The BVD and the government would rather see these files disappear into the shredder because, if they were opened up to all and sundry, it would lead to all kinds of sordid affairs. Anyone who depends on the machinery of consensus working smoothly is a little afraid of too much mud being stirred up. It leads to conflict and open conflict goes against centuries of tradition. When it flares up, the Dutch are generally at a loss. It is, of course, a signal for conciliators to spring into action. A boss whose subordinates no longer see eye to eye will initially suggest that they all 'sit around the table and talk about it'. If that does not work, experts are called in from outside. Committees of 'wise men' – sometimes with a wise woman or two among them these days – are a popular instrument of conflict management. Judges with two opposing parties in the dock will first make an attempt at reconciliation, so that they will not have to make a judgement, and are very pleased with themselves when – as is often the case – they are successful. Many conflicts are solved in this way. But not all of them. In some cases the hostility runs very deep and can last for many years without losing any of its vehemence. The adversaries should fear isolation – it will be difficult for them to find allies in their immediate environment. Most people want the freedom to talk to who they wish. It is, however, typical of such 'feuds' that the opposing parties attempt to divide those around them into 'friends' and 'enemies'. Most Dutch people, however, do not like such clear positioning and try – usually with success – to avoid both parties. They do not want to 'burn their fingers' on such trivial matters.

If enemies wish to be reconciled, they have to be prepared to forget the past. This is encouraged by those in their direct environment. You must be prepared to cover certain things with the 'cloak of charity'. This cloak is also frequently used to avert potential conflict. No one likes to see adversaries thrashing out their differences to the very last or, as the saying goes '*vechtend over de straat rollend*', 'wrestling with each other in the street'. Those around them then try to ensure that at least one of the opposing parties 'does the honourable thing' and ceases hostilities.

It is important that the party concerned does not see this as unconditional surrender. In this way the 'arbitrators' often provide a kind of safety net to ensure that no one falls too far. Top civil servants who find themselves in trouble sometimes 'agree' to an appointment as an 'advisory councillor' to the minister. This is a perfect solution, particularly as there are many advisory councillors with genuine influence. Or it may be widely understood that a certain colleague will be devoting himself to 'special projects' in the future. One solution for politicians who can no longer be tolerated by their fellows is to accept a position as a Mayor. It is very rare that, after a conflict or a serious error, the person concerned is *'aan de dijk gezet'*. This expression, meaning literally 'set up on the dyke', dates from medieval times and refers to the practice of banishing offenders from their town, village or region. The legislation on dismissal, which makes it difficult to fire anyone without a clear reason, naturally encourages solutions of this kind, but it also has a lot to do with preserving the atmosphere needed to make decisions on the basis of consensus. When the *Partij van de Arbeid*, the Dutch Labour Party, decided to revitalize its list of candidates for the 1994 general elections, the chairman of the party set up a special office to help veteran members who were no longer up for re-election to find positions elsewhere. This is remarkable in that, in a democracy, all politicians know that their careers are dependent on the support of the grassroots in the party and on the electorate as a whole. In this way, however, the PvdA averted any potential conflict.

[171]

The same approach is used when people make genuine mistakes. In its extreme form this kind of conflict management is known as the putting the affair in the *doofpot*, literally an 'extinguisher'. It has similar connotations to the English expression 'putting a lid on it'. The best example of a scandal being effectively placed in the *doofpot* occurred in the early years of this century, when the founder of the Calvinist pillar, Abraham Kuyper, found himself in trouble. While he was a minister, two members of his pillar were honoured by the Queen. Their major achievement appeared to have been the donation of large sums of money to Kuyper's *Anti-Revolutionaire Partij* – at least this was the claim of a liberal member of parliament. A council of 'wise men' was set up, who decided that both men would have been honoured even if they had not made the donations. No one believed this. Kuyper continued to deny the allegations, but told the *Tweede Kamer* that '*Het boetekleed misstaat de man niet*'

– it was fitting for him to 'wear the hair shirt'. In the debate on the affair, his opponents stated that they had no intention of stirring up the mud any further. The affair was closed. But it was clear that, although Kuyper would continue to lead his pillar and command a great deal of respect, he would never again hold a ministerial position.

Today he would not have escaped so easily, but even now he would not have been put out on the 'social dyke'. The safety net still exists, as was shown in the greatest scandal of the 1970s, the 'Lockheed affair'. Prince Bernhard, the husband of former Queen Juliana, was also the Inspector-General of the Dutch Armed Forces and a leading ambassador of the Dutch business community. As such, he was in a position to exert considerable influence in the selection of new fighter planes. Reports in the media suggested that the Prince had allowed himself to be tempted by extensive sums of money offered to him by the American aircraft manufacturer Lockheed. Again a committee of wise men was set up, headed by one of the country's leading judges. The committee's conclusions confirmed the rumours. For Prince Bernhard, this meant in practice that he was no longer permitted to be involved in the purchase of aircraft or to wear his military uniform in public. This was a very severe punishment for the Prince. The armed forces were very dear to him and he played a leading role in the liberation of the country from the Nazis. The affair, however, did nothing to diminish the Prince's popularity and, after a few years, he started wearing his uniform now and then without raising too many eyebrows. The whole scandal had been defused by the observation of genuine openness. Conflict was prevented by the imposition of a punishment that largely left it up to the Prince to 'do the honourable thing'. And slowly but surely, the cloak of charity spread itself out across the entire affair.

In the business world, directors who do not come up to scratch are often shown the door with a 'golden handshake'; or they may be rendered harmless by transferring them to advisory positions or appointing them to the Board of Supervisory Directors. There is, however, one exception to this tolerant approach to failure: if the error has a clear ideological component, the punishment is more severe. This fate befell Willem Aantjes, the leader of the Anti-Revolutionaire Partij in the 1970s.

Like many other Dutch people, Aantjes had to do forced labour in Germany during the occupation. There was, however, one official way of being sent back to the Netherlands: to join the *Germaanse SS*, the Nazi élite corps.

Aantjes joined the ss in the last few months of the war, when the front came a little too close to the place where he was working. He used his membership purely as a ticket back home during those chaotic final months of the conflict. Thirty years later, however, he was still not forgiven. Stigmatized, he resigned all his political positions. There was no question of him becoming a Mayor. After a year or so, he became the chairman of the Dutch Caravaning and Camping Council, hardly a prominent body.

Aantjes had been 'bad' in the war. His ploy to escape from the danger zone entailed him swearing an oath of loyalty to the Nazi cause. As the occupation became increasingly a thing of the past and the struggle between good and evil took on mythological proportions in the collective memory, there was less and less understanding for those, like Aantjes, who had 'weakened'. Anyone who tried to spread the cloak of charity over affairs of this nature soon found it to be full of holes. You might imagine that someone with a Communist background would suffer a similar fate, but until now there has been little evidence of this. During the Cold War, of course, the small group of Communists in the Netherlands were marginalized and they sought sanctuary in an extreme Stalinist party. They were isolated and treated with suspicion and had little chance of building successful careers. The Communist Party has now been wound up but former activists appear to suffer little from their past. A number of the editors of the once notorious party newspaper *De Waarheid* – The Truth – now hold prominent positions in the media. And the *Tweede Kamer* has a conference room named after Marcus Bakker, the legendary parliamentary leader of the party during the heyday of Communism in the Netherlands.

There are two reasons for this. Firstly, the Communists played a leading role in the resistance during the occupation. This has never been forgotten and certainly not been denigrated in any way. Secondly, Communist doctrine – as opposed to Communist practice – is emotionally acceptable to the Dutch. Its ultimate aim is, after all, a just and equal society in which each individual produces and consumes according to his or her needs, thereby rendering a central state power superfluous. This is not so far removed from the Dutch consensus-based model of society. At least it sounds like a nice idea. National-socialism and fascism, on the other hand, are diametrically opposed to Dutch views on how society should be organized. They advocate the primacy of a superior people or race, who are entitled to subjugate all others to their will and, in the most extreme cases, to exterminate groups labelled as inferior. This is the complete antithesis of the centuries old Dutch tradition of consensus, compromise and sovereignty in one's own domain, which implies that all men (and women) are equal, and explains why extreme-right ideas have never really found a solid footing in the Netherlands.

This may simply be a fortunate coincidence, or it may be that living one's life according to a diary full of *overleg* and discussions on *beleid* has a moderating – No, permit me, as a Dutchman, to say it, a civilizing – effect.

As Gresshof said: 'How I love those gentlemen in black.

But, let us not forget his reminder, that 'the tide can change'.

Chapter 4

'Holland has stayed Holland because our old folk attended to their business'

[175]

From fishermen to merchants and transporters. The Netherlands as a trading nation. Continuity as a basic principle of business. Competition, but not to the death. Cost control. Know your neighbours, for they are all potential customers. International orientation.

Around the end of May and the beginning of June, many Dutch people emerge as lovers of raw fish. Announcements in the media have already set their mouths watering – the new herring catch has arrived. The first batches are usually bought up for thousands of guilders by restaurants sporting a row of Michelin stars. After that, the price drops to a few guilders and queues form at the fish stalls on the nation's markets. The Dutch like to eat their herring in the street. In Amsterdam, they use a small fork to pick up small pieces of fillet from a cardboard 'plate', but in the rest of the country, the fish is grasped by the tail and devoured with relish. The stall will often have a large bowl of chopped raw onions through which the herring is first 'passed' to make it even more delicious. In the interests of hygiene, many fish stalls therefore have a notice asking customers to do this only once, before starting to enjoy this traditional delicacy.

THE FISH HAS NOT BEEN SALTED IN THE TRADITIONAL WAY

People born and bred in the Zuid-Holland town of Vlaardingen are also partial to their 'new herring', but many of them eat it with mixed feelings. They point to the red streak near the bones – a telltale sign that the fish has not been gutted and salted in the traditional way. It has been frozen. They insist that these little traces of blood detract from the real taste. Then they lament the decline of the Dutch herring industry. The posters in the fishmongers' windows announce the arrival of the *'Hollandse Nieuwe'*, but in Vlaardingen, they know better – the fish are all imported from Denmark.

The last survivors of the Dutch herring fleet hung up their nets about twenty years ago, because they could no longer earn a living. This marked the end of a proud tradition that stretched back over six centuries. Every school-child still learns that, in 1385, in the village of Biervliet in Zeeland, Willem Beu-kelszoon invented *haringkaken*. This is a method of removing the intestines of the fish with a single cut of a knife. If the herring are then stored in vats be-tween layers of salt they can be kept almost indefinitely. The only disadvantage of this method is that the longer the fish are stored, the saltier the taste and, af-ter a year or so, they are no longer fit for consumption. This is why the arrival of the new catch was such an event – the taste had not yet been contaminated by the salt.

The herring appear in the North Sea at the beginning of May. In the old days, on the first day of the season, the fishermen would decorate their boats with colourful flags and there would be celebrations in towns like Vlaar-dingen, Scheveningen and Ijmuiden, and in the many smaller fishing villages. The fleet would set sail that same day, heralding the start of the annual herring race. The first vats to be brought back to shore would fetch enormous sums at the *afslag*, a kind of fish auction. Since all crew members received a share of the proceeds, everyone did their utmost to win the race. This explains the nostal-gia of the people of Vlaardingen. Today, the harbour is practically empty, al-though the town itself is thriving. It is home to a large branch of Royal Dutch / Shell and Unilever chose it as a site for one of its most important research laboratories. People in the street will point out the creators of Becel low-fat margarine or Mona desserts, products from Vlaardingen that can be found in every supermarket in Europe and far beyond. In terms of volume, washing powder – from Unilever and other manufacturers – is probably the town's big-gest export. The old town centre, where once run-down fishermen's cottages stood together in rows, is now dominated by shopping malls.

The decline of the fishing industry did not bring poverty – on the contrary.

People in their thirties and forties remember how, at the end of the 1950s, their fathers – embittered and to no avail – went on strike for a fixed wage instead of the meagre share of the catch granted them by the shipowners. They are aware that it was because their parents had to scrimp and save that the herring industry survived for so long, with its endless toil and obedience to the shipowners in their mansions at the head of the harbour. They themselves have been to college and can afford their own homes because they have a well-paid job at the Unilever Research Laboratory, or at Shell, or at one of the other chemical companies on the other side of the river that stand shoulder to shoulder right down to the coast, thirty kilometres away. Yet they still often feel that they live in a completely new town, one that has banished old Vlaardingen to the local Fishery Museum. They no longer hear the rattle of the steam-powered winches or the thumping of a ship's engine. The only sound of work being done in the town now – if it is warm and the office windows are open – is the occasional beep from a personal computer.

Yet there is a connection between the computers and the fish. The enormous schools of herring that used to swim down into the North Sea towards the English Channel made the people living on the Dutch coast into fishermen. And this, in turn, made them into traders. The industrial complexes on the other side of the river belong to the port of Rotterdam, the second largest city in the Netherlands, which projects itself as a 'Mainport' and which handles a greater tonnage of goods annually than any other seaport in the world. This all started in the Middle Ages with small vats of salted herring for the international market. Anyone who studies the history of the towns and cities in the west of the country will discover that, originally, their economies were frequently dependent on fishing. Even as late as the Golden Age, which the Dutch themselves are more likely to associate with international trade, the fishing industry was essential to the preservation of what was the highest level of prosperity in Europe at the time.

AN UNEXPECTED STORM WILL DRIVE SHIPS UP ONTO THE BEACHES

The traditional herring therefore has more to do with present-day Vlaardingen than most people realize. The port of Rotterdam, the international airport at Schiphol, the Amsterdam Stock Exchange, the trucks that carry freight to Iran and beyond, the international branches of the ABN AMRO bank from New

York to Hong Kong – they all have their roots in the fish that tempted the Dutch to man their boats centuries ago. It was through this that they discovered that the sea was not only an enemy, but also a friend which gave them access to faraway lands. But it takes courage to go to sea – even these days, when beams of light from lighthouses penetrate deep into the night, each with its own rhythm, and with computers on the bridge and satellite communications to aid navigation. The North Sea sometimes outwits even the most accurate of weather forecasts and an unexpected storm will drive ships up onto the beaches. A number of seamen still perish every year and, in spite of advanced technology and the port traffic control, ships are still required to take a pilot on board who has a long experience of navigating in the treacherous waters.

The medieval sailors depended entirely on their experience to navigate their wooden-hulled ships. Most of them did not even have a compass. They were at the mercy of unpredictable winds that changed direction suddenly and regularly. Once at sea, they had no conmmunication with the shore. Raging storms and pirates were a continual and immediate threat. Modern-day fisherman, who are usually based in Katwijk or Urk and who fish not for herring but cod or delicious sole, use boats with powerful engines. They search for their catch with sounding equipment. Their ship's radio ensures a permanent contact with their home port. If anyone is seriously injured or sick, a helicopter appears to take them to a hospital. Their forefathers were left to fend for themselves and to the fickle hand of fate – fishing was a risky business.

THIS MADE THE FISHERMEN INTO TOUGH SURVIVORS

This made the fishermen into tough survivors. The crew of a fishing boat knew that they depended on each other and that, in principle, everything outside the boat was a threat. 'And the spirit of God moved upon the face of the waters', says the book of Genesis. This was all they had to believe in. Dutch fishermen still tend to be very religious, generally preferring a strict form of Calvinism, with its belief in a vengeful God who will save only a few and who sends raging storms to punish man for his wickedness. They are also extremely independent characters who will allow nothing to stand in their way when there are fish to be caught. When the Ministry of Agriculture, Nature Management and Fisheries imposed quotas as a result of agreements made in the European Community to prevent the sea being over-fished, an enormous illegal trade developed outside the official auctions. Even the strict Calvinists among the fishermen showed unprecedented creativity in evading the watchful eyes of the inspectors. The affair grew into a scandal that cost the agriculture minister his job and his political career.

Fishing taught the seamen how to survive the dangers of being at sea and they ventured further and further from their home ports. Gradually they accumulated the knowledge necessary for merchant shipping to develop, initially in the seas of northern Europe, later as far as the coasts of Turkey and, by the end of the sixteenth century, throughout the world. Dutch cities became emporia where products from the far corners of the earth were bought and sold. It was not simply a matter of import and export. Transit was perhaps even more important, and a tour through the port of Rotterdam will show that this is still the case today. Gigantic containers are hoisted from ships' holds and mounted straight onto the back of trucks. Dutch truck drivers are known throughout Europe and they have that same resilience, independence and stubbornness that kept their ancestors alive on the open sea.

'Zie ik Hollands vlag op verre kust, dan juicht mijn hart 'victorie', 'When I see the flag of Holland on a far coast, my heart cries 'victory''. This line comes from an old song that children used to learn at school. It has now been filed away as a dubious example of obsolete imperialism, but the emotions it describes are genuine. The average Dutch man or woman will feel a swell of pride when they see the imposing building of the ING Bank, complete with its Dutch lion, on the Avenida Paulista in Sao Paulo; or when they discover that the Alaska milk powder for sale all over Manila was produced in Noord-Brabant; or when they go for a drink in a bar in Hong Kong and run into a group of rough-talking compatriots from a dredging company in Sliedrecht (who are there to build an artificial island for the new international airport that the city is to take with it as a dowry when it is returned to China). 'Not bad going

for such a small country', they think to themselves. When you belong to a population of only fifteen million, there is a certain prestige in seeing companies from your homeland playing a leading role in faraway countries.

IF YOU ENCOUNTER THEM AT SEA, THEY WILL ROB YOU

'A pirate state lies on the sea, Between the Scheldt and Eastern Friesland!'. Even the Dutch sometimes find themselves believing this, not without a certain secret pride. It is a quotation from 'Max Havelaar or the Coffee Auctions of the Dutch Trading Company', a nineteenth century novel in which the author, Eduard Douwes Dekker (known to his readers by his pseudonym, Multatuli), revitalized Dutch literature all on his own. The book is a devastating indictment of criminal colonial and trading practices with the kind of power usually associated with Joseph Conrad. It unearthed a collective guilty conscience that now causes many a shiver at the sight of a Dutch flag flying in a foreign land. There is an ancient Chinese text that, after praising the Dutch for their seamanship, says: 'But if you encounter them at sea, they will rob you'. Most Dutch people know this quotation, but are unsure what to make of it. And the image of the Dutch merchant with a Bible under one arm and his cash book under the other has long been a cliché in the business world. 'Go and sell what thou hast, and give it to the poor … and come and follow me' said Jesus to the rich young man. The man chose to keep his riches and 'went away sorrowful'. This story from the Bible is well-known to both Calvinists and Catholics and most Dutch people have to admit to themselves that, like the young man, they 'go away sorrowful'.

Christendom, as such, has little in common with the business world. Business practice has traditionally been more closely related to sin. Catholics considered it against the will of God to charge interest for lending money right up to the end of the Middle Ages – a belief that is being revived by modern-day Islam. The first Calvinists were a little less strict about this, but they too had their doubts about the pursuit of riches. It was wrong to accumulate money for its own sake. *'Geld maakt niet gelukkig'*. 'Money can't buy happiness'. It is an old saying and mass culture – with its popular fiction and, more recently, home-grown television soap operas – is living proof of its wisdom. The enormous popularity of successful series like Dallas, Dynasty and Santa Barbara can also be attributed to this conviction. The message is clear – the rich and famous may have everything their hearts desire, but they are certainly not happy.

This has, however, never been a reason for the Dutch to neglect their bank accounts. A seventeenth century sea captain was supposed to have said that he would 'sail to hell and back if it would earn him a couple of farthings'. Yet the ambivalence of this position remains. The effect it has on the lives of the rich needs no repeating here, but it also has an impact on the way the Dutch do business and on the way in which they calculate their opportunities and risks. There is another saying: '*Zo gewonnen, zo geronnen*', roughly equivalent to the English expression 'ready money will away'. You will not find many people in the Netherlands who believe in 'getting rich quick'. Wealth is the result of a long and continual process. This is not to say that a swindler with a get-rich-quick scheme will not find a sympathetic ear in the Netherlands, but he will have to have a very convincing line of argument. Once the whole affair is exposed, the media are more likely to express delight at the misfortune of the victims than indignation at the criminal practices to which they fell prey. There is no pleasure as great as that caused by the sufferings of others and no one will show an ounce of sympathy for those who have lost their savings. They should have known better.

In the entire history of the Netherlands, there is only one recorded example of widespread speculation fever. For a short time in the seventeenth century, the price of tulip bulbs began to approach that of houses. The Dutch word for speculation, *windhandel*, dates from this time. Since then, every boom has been greeted with suspicion. In contrast to serious investors, speculators have a very bad reputation. Dealers in options, who appeared in the financial world at the end of the 1980s, are largely seen as the players in a very dangerous game. This, in spite of the fact that the options market has become an indispensable instrument in the financial world – even for sound financiers, who claim that they use it to cover themselves against risk.

Many people think that the dealers on the options markets lack what previous generations called 'solidity'. Before you do business with someone you should make sure that they are solid. That is to say, not too impetuous, careful with their money and, if possible, with many years of experience in the same area of activity. There is little respect for anyone who moves from one thing to another. An obituary to Benk Moret, one of the founders of the renowned firm of accountants Moret, Ernst & Young stated his credentials very clearly in the second paragraph: 'Moret came from a family of accountants'. It added: 'He was an administrator and an entrepreneur with great vision, daring, energy and decisiveness, determined when it came to important matters, flexible and prepared to compromise about things that he did not consider essential'. And of course, all kinds of evidence is proffered to support these claims. Under Moret's leadership, the firm expanded steadily, frequently through mergers with competitors. He had a vision that resulted in a process of continual growth. The obituary made no mention of spectacular coups or commercial *tours de force*, even though they doubtlessly occurred.

Similarly, on the 40th anniversary of the tugboat king Murk Lels of Smit Internationale, an employee wrote the following ode to his widely respected boss:

'Mastermind in towing business
undisputed salvage king
Ruler of the world's best tugboats,
knowing prizeman in the ring
Let your houseflag in the future
eager wanted colours be
Let there always be employ for
Smit's towing company'.

Lel's major talents are clear: he never gave up and he assured continuity and – at least this is what the amateur poet hopes – this would remain the case in the future. Lel's obituary closed with this poem, in spite of the fact that he was the director of a very adventurous company. Smit Internationale goes to the help of ships in distress and salvages wrecks. This is often on a 'no cure, no pay' basis. Or it may be a race against other companies, with the first to fix a line winning the contract or – if the vessel has been abandoned – claiming ownership. Yet the poet does not recall any of the undisputed salvage king's more exciting ventures. For him it is important that the company flag keeps flying. For him, that was Murk Lel's great achievement.

A good businessman does not put all his eggs in one basket. He is prepared to take risks, even big ones at times, but all-or-nothing situations have to be avoided at all costs. This mentality was already in place in the late Middle Ages. Merchants preferred to take out shares in a ship or several ships rather than have a vessel or fleet of their own. If a ship then fell prey to the whimsical North Sea or to the ever-present pirates, they did not lose everything because the risk was sufficiently spread. This arrangement also meant that other merchants were seen not only as competitors but also as colleagues with whom you might cooperate in certain circumstances. Anyone who aimed at continuity was not afraid of the fight, but would think twice before allowing it to become a matter of life and death. This attitude survives today. The Dutch business community has a large number of sector organizations which have all kinds of agreements with each other. The Royal Federation of Printers, for example, has developed a set of standard contracts which contain no agreements on prices but do cover a lot of other matters, like the minimum period of notice that has to be given to cancel the graphic preparation of a magazine. When times are hard, it may be possible to negotiate these conditions with hard-pressed printing companies, but in normal circumstances no one would think of undercutting their competitors by offering more lenient terms.

[183]

Price agreements are not unusual in the Dutch business community. Newspapers, for instance, have coordinated their subscription rates for many years, and a price war at the kiosks is inconceivable. In such a climate, it is a small step for company directors to consider merging with their competitors. This can lead to monopolies. The formation of monopolies was forbidden a century ago in the United States. A similar debate took place at the same time in the Netherlands. Politicians, with the liberals at their forefront, hit upon a different solution. They decided that monopoly companies – and they were thinking primarily of companies that provided public services, such as the gas supply or the telephone and, later, public transport – should be owned by the government. This would enable the representatives of the people to ensure that the monopoly was not abused. As a result, municipal councils, provincial authorities and the central government became entrepreneurs. This ideology held sway until the 1980s, when it was replaced by a new wave of privatization, the reasons for which will be examined later.

Government regulation of the private sector represents the continuation of a tradition that stretches back centuries in Dutch and European history. In the Middle Ages, practically every trade or craft was organized into guilds aimed at protecting the interests of their members. Rules with the power of law ensured that competition did not get out of hand and that individual members could not expand to an extent that could threaten the survival of others. In some cases, technological developments were forbidden, because they would provide their perpetrators with an unfair advantage. The training of new members was tightly controlled and the guilds tended to impose increasingly difficult requirements to deny access to newcomers as much as possible. The rule of the guilds lasted until the French invaded in 1795 and brought with them freedom of entrepreneurship.

In 1596, the first Dutch ships reached what is now Indonesia and broke the monopoly that Portuguese seafarers had enjoyed for over a century. The large number of expeditions that followed the safe return of these first explorers led the government to intervene. It encouraged all the new investors to work together in the *Verenigde Oost-Indische Compagnie*, the United East India Company. The bait was an undisputed monopoly on trade in goods from Asia. The officially sanctioned piracy in the Caribbean – aimed at ships from hostile Spain – was later organized in the same way under the auspices of the West India Company, which also acquired a monopoly on the transport of slaves from Africa to North and South America.

Both companies were among the first to issue shares that were traded on the Amsterdam Stock Exchange. They were run by a form of Governing Board but operated on a fairly decentralized basis. The two companies also wished to secure a monopoly on purchasing. They tried to get their suppliers to agree to a kind of contract for an unlimited period which would not permit them to do business with other companies – from France or England, for example. This was frequently a question of who had the greatest firepower at their disposal. The companies had to 'conquer' strategic points, where they also held the political power and could, if necessary, finance entire armies to keep the place under their control. This eventually proved too expensive for the West India Company, but its counterpart in the Orient was in a far better financial position. It became the largest company in the world, a position which it maintained for at least one hundred and fifty years, making it the first genuine multinational. Throughout most of its existence, it paid out reasonably high dividends to its shareholders. The company finally failed as a result of the high cost of preserving its purchasing monopoly and because it became bogged down in its own vast bureaucracy. But two hundred years is still a respectable age for any company to reach.

THE PATRONESS RECEIVED GOODS FROM ALL OVER THE WORLD

The façade of the seventeenth century City Hall in Amsterdam is decorated with a relief showing, in the eyes of its civic leaders, the basis of the city's prosperity – it depicts the patroness of the city receiving goods from all over the world. The message is clear – Amsterdam was one of the world's leading ports and its success – as I have already said – lay not in import or export but in the transhipment of goods on Dutch ships. Certain goods, such as tobacco or sugar, were also processed during this process of transport from supplier to market. The descendants of the North Sea fishermen had become carriers of cargo and they completely dominated the European merchant shipping industry. Practically all the grain exported from northwest Europe was shipped from Dutch ports and it was a long time before other countries – particularly England and, to a lesser extent, France – were able to catch up. They succeeded only by pursuing protectionist policies that eventually broke the dominant position of the Dutch traders.

The leading merchants in the Netherlands came from the ruling regent families and their ideas had a considerable impact on the country's foreign policy. This was consequently based on a single immutable principle – the Netherlands was in favour of an international system in which there were as few obstacles to trade as possible. Most wars during the illustrious Golden Age were fought with that aim in mind. But wars are expensive and merchants tend to assess their costs with a critical eye, especially if they do not produce the desired effect quickly enough – and, as time went by, this was more and more often the case. As a result, they adopted a policy of neutrality which was increasingly presented as a matter of principle. The Netherlands tried to stay on good terms with as many foreign powers as possible to ensure that business could go on without being disrupted. This continued to be the basic *raison d'être* for the neutral position maintained by the country right up until the German invasion of 1940. It closely resembled the traditional Swiss policy of neutrality. At times, there was even a tendency to don the pure white cloak of pacifism and civilization to disguise the real reason for its neutrality.

The German occupation put a stop to this policy for good. The Netherlands joined the Western alliance and became a faithful member of NATO. At the same time it emerged as a champion of supranational cooperation. It was one of the founding members of the European Community and is always at the forefront of discussions on greater federalization. After all, federalization means the creation of larger economic areas in which the obstacles to free trade are removed. The means may have changed, but the end is the same – to create a system where the international movement of goods is restricted as little as possible.

Today, as in the past, the Netherlands assigns great importance to international law. In front of the City Hall in Rotterdam, the world's largest port, there is a statue of the seventeenth century regent/scholar Hugo de Groot, the founding father of this belief in the need for supranational regulation. His major work, the *mare libero*, argued that the seas should be open to all and that the sovereignty of coastal states should not extend further than three miles from the shore. The three-mile distance was not arbitrary – it was the maximum range of the largest cannons of the time. De Groot's ideas became generally accepted and survived almost up to the present day. The principle of the open seas has, however, been considerably eroded by the exploitation of natural resources under the seabed. The belief that these resources should not be the sole property of the coastal states but should be shared by all mankind and, therefore, controlled by the United Nations is popular in the Netherlands. This is no surprise – for a small country with such a short coastline, this would be the best deal.

Anyone from outside the European Union who tries to find a market for their products in the Netherlands is in for a surprise. The doors of the EU are wide open for most raw materials, unless they are freely available in the continent itself. Those who offer manufactured or semi-manufactured products, however, will find that, the more complex processing their products have undergone, the higher the import duties they will have to pay. The EU has even imposed quotas on the import of certain products, such as textiles and tapioca. This is, to say the least, not entirely compatible with the lofty principle of free access to international markets. It is therefore not uncommon to hear the word 'hypocrisy' used in this respect around directors' tables and at ministries of economic affairs in developing countries. The Netherlands defends its approach officially by claiming that a small country cannot follow its own course without suffering the consequences and that it always makes a plea for free trade in discussions with the other members of the Union and in international fora. And, indeed, diplomats and ambassadors always have evidence to hand to support this claim. Yet critics at home frequently suggest that Dutch companies could perhaps be a little less compliant in toeing the official line. They are accused of giving priority to the cash book above the Bible. Whatever the reason, the Netherlands has come little further than good intentions. And if outsiders complain of fine talk, weakness and hypocrisy, the response is that, after all, everyone is entitled to their opinion.

YOU SHOULD NOT STEAL FROM YOUR OWN PURSE

The Dutch have an expression: *'Je moet geen dief zijn van je eigen portemonnee'*. Literally, it means 'You should not steal from your own purse'. This attitude – 'If we don't do it, someone else will' – is deeply embedded in the Dutch way of thinking and most people are prepared to accept it for what it is – cynicism. They would rather be seen as cynical than naïve.

And besides, what is all this talk of free trade? The Netherlands has a centuries-old tradition of government intervention in the economy. Real free trade existed only during the period of liberal domination in the nineteenth century and that lasted only a few decades. The State's tendency to take over companies with a monopoly has already been mentioned. But it went further than that. In 1902, the government set up state-run coal mines because the privately operated mining sector was – in the eyes of public opinion – too chaotic. The crisis caused by the First World War led to much more direct economic intervention, to which everyone soon became accustomed. A new wave of intervention followed the 1929 Wall Street Crash. The driving force behind this was the former managing director of Shell, the antirevolutionary Hendrikus Colijn. The government naturally had the tendency to surround this increased involvement in the economy with all kinds of *overleg*, accustomed as it was to making decisions on a consensus basis. The business world not only got used to this intervention, but actually began to request it. Company directors request help from the government if their organization or the entire sector is in some kind of difficulty. The State has, for example, stepped in several times to save Fokker, the Netherlands' only aircraft manufacturer. It also intervened to prevent Daf, the truck builders, from going bankrupt. Such measures sometimes involve hundreds of millions and, in the case of the dying shipbuilding industry, billions of guilders. The State always provides support only on the condition that the company involved carries out a reorganization. This form of intervention has not always been successful. The Dutch shipbuilding industry, once a world leader, still failed to compete with new and cheaper shipyards in South-East Asia even after the government pumped billions of guilders into it. Fokker's directors were unable to get the company out of the red and it is now a part of the German DASA concern.

Daf's private car sector was taken over by the Swedish company Volvo in the 1970s, an operation which required a large injection of funds from the government. The cars that roll off the production line today are the result of a joint venture between the company itself, the Japanese manufacturers Mitsubishi and the State.

THE STATE REPEATEDLY KNOCKS AWAY THE INVISIBLE HAND

This policy is generally defended with the argument that it fights unemployment. But equally important is the underlying belief that the Netherlands cannot afford to lose the technological know-how that is contained in these large companies. This was the reason for supporting the DSM shipyard in Rotterdam, which builds highly advanced submarines. It was considered crucial that this know-how and capacity stayed in Dutch hands.

Another effective argument in favour of bailing out large companies on the verge of collapse is that, if they go down, they will take a large number of suppliers and other companies with them. In this way, the State repeatedly knocks away the invisible hand that Adam Smith projected as the best regulator of the economy. Smith's hand, however, is resilient and always bounces back. The fiasco in the shipbuilding industry led to a scandal and a parliamentary enquiry. Ever since, the government has been a little more careful about where it spends its cash and the critics of such policies have grown in number. They consider government intervention too defensive, aimed only at preserving economic sectors which an advanced industrialized country can better leave to others. Intervention, if at all, should be directed towards new, more promising areas of activity.

Many people may agree with this view in their hearts, but it does not rise to the surface too easily. In a society based on consensus, vested interests can exert considerable influence. This makes it very difficult to leave a particular economic sector to its fate. The entire Dutch agricultural sector would collapse immediately if the government and the EU abolished the extensive system of grants and protectionist measures. The agricultural lobby is, however, far too powerful and influential to allow anything of this kind to happen. Furthermore, a country may have military-strategic reasons for wishing to pro-

duce a large proportion of its food supply itself. Left to its own devices, the invisible hand would cause a great deal of disruption, particularly in the short and medium term. There is a gigantic food-processing industry closely related to the agricultural sector which is essential to the Dutch export market. Farmers in Zeeland and Noord-Brabant produce their traditional sugar beet which is sent to large refineries, while cane sugar from the tropics is often cheaper and of better quality. No one dares to take

steps to remedy this situation, since it would involve destroying the livelihood of an entire region.

In the 1980s, the large Dutch multinational electronics company Philips repeatedly demanded that the European Community take protectionist measures against Japanese and Korean competitors who it claimed were guilty of dumping practices. The Dutch government has a rich tradition of price control. The main reason for this is to keep inflation under control, but it is a good example of calculated intervention in the daily running of the economy. Companies in certain sectors had to request permission from the Ministry of Economic Affairs before raising their prices until well into the 1980s. They had to fill in a form and give their reasons for the proposed increase. Permission was usually granted, but not without a fight, which generally made companies think twice before they embarked on the procedure at all.

Anyone who wishes to set up a company will find themselves confronted with a maze of rules and regulations reminiscent of the old guild privileges. Many branches of trade and industry demand that people intending to start a business have some kind of diploma. In the case of the retail trade, the local authorities decide how many shops of a certain kind they want in a particular area. This is frequently based on the requirements of the sector organization itself, which wishes to subject competition to strict rules and make life difficult for *'beunhazen'*. A *beunhaas* is someone who operates a business without having the required know-how or, in the terms defined by the sector organizations, does not have the right qualifications. Because the organizations usually provide the required training themselves, the requirements are strict and candidates require a thorough knowledge of the area if they are to succeed. Anyone who does not get over this hurdle is not officially permitted to operate in the sector. In this way, the received traditions of the sector are preserved.

[190]

At first glance, such practices would appear to be more at home in the old Soviet Union. Most Dutch businessmen – there are still few women making successful careers in business – would be the first to agree, especially after the whisky bottle has been passed around. They love to complain about the jungle of laws and regulations that prevent them from earning an honest living. 'Anyone would think that profit is a dirty word', they sigh, as they have been doing regularly since the 1970s. As their mood deepens, they will start to tell the most bizarre anecdotes, which careful observers will soon notice have one thing in common – they are all concerned with what the government tells them to do and what not to do and with the violation of the rights of the hard-working entrepreneur. They will seldom complain about measures imposed to restrict the competition. These stories will never be drawn from their own personal experience, but will be based on hearsay and specific details will be vague. It is then very simple to prick their balloon of doom by agreeing that they are indeed at the mercy of an overpowering State that has them in a stranglehold, giving them no hope at all for the future. They will then generally run up the red, white and blue flag and state defensively that things are not that bad after all.

In the early 1980s, I took a delegation of Tanzanians to visit the headquarters of the *Vereniging van Nederlandse Ondernemingen* (vno), the leading employers' organization in the Netherlands. Our hosts complained bitterly about wage costs and government regulation, which were making life so difficult for them. One of the Tanzanian visitors asked politely, if the situation was so bad, how had they managed to pay for this luxurious office? The silence with which this question was greeted spoke volumes.

Admittedly, this anecdote has a demagogic component. It does, however, put the whole culture of complaint about over-regulation into perspective. A stroll through any town centre or a glance in the newspapers, with their countless advertisements in which companies try to outdo their competitors in praising their products and services, shows that the Netherlands is, above all, a free-market economy where a company's success depends in the first instance on it finding the right combination of quality and price.

QUALITY IS THE MAIN PRIORITY – AND WITH GOOD REASON

Quality is the main priority – and with good reason. The strength of the economy has never been its competitive prices. The Netherlands is not a cheap country. Its companies have to survive by providing service, reliability and good quality. The country is simply not cut out for the bottom end of the market. And, if that ever was the case, that position has now been amply filled by low-salary countries. In the 1970s, with the exception of a few specialized companies, all the country's textile manufacturers folded. The same fate befell the shipbuilding industry. At Philips, the consumer electronics division has long been the weak link in the chain. Philips has never pursued a policy of price cutting. A Philips television may have been a little more expensive, but you knew that you had bought a quality product and that an extensive service network was available to repair any faults that may occur.

This alone, however, is not enough for a company to survive against international competition – particularly from Asia. Philips' directors can take small solace in the fact that they are not alone in this. Generally speaking, Dutch producers of technologically simple articles and semi-manufactured products do not have an easy time, except in sectors where the Netherlands has a traditional lead, such as cheese, flowers and fresh vegetables. And even in these sectors, competition is increasing steadily.

The same applies to services. The Dutch merchant fleet – one of the top ten in the world in the fifties – is of little importance today. Shipowners now sail largely under the Panamanian or Liberian flags. But in areas where the Netherlands has undisputed know-how – such as dredging or a wide variety of other civil engineering activities relating to water or water management – business is thriving.

There is an observable shift from industrial production to the provision of services. This is a common trend in all highly developed economies, but in the Netherlands, it has an added dimension in that it is entirely in keeping with the country's historical traditions. The Netherlands was, after all, the home of the great trading houses and the banks they needed in order to operate. It possessed no natural raw materials on which to build up an industrial base. At least, that was the general belief until the 1960s, when it was discovered that the country was sitting on a gold mine in the form of a natural gas bubble of OPEC proportions.

In Germany, the Netherlands' neighbour and by far largest trading partner, it was a different story. Since the last quarter of the nineteenth century the German government had promoted the build up of an enormous industrial apparatus, which is still the basis of the country's phenomenal prosperity today. Such a policy has never existed in the Netherlands. Industrial development did occur, but was largely the work of visionary entrepreneurs rather than the result of any concerted effort by the government. And, of course, there was undoubtedly a knock-on effect from Germany. This lack of a genuine industrial policy has been the subject of regular public debate right up to the present day.

This may be the reason why industrialists and entrepreneurs rarely achieve national prominence. The reputation of Ruud Lubbers, who – as prime minister – dominated Dutch politics from 1983 to 1994, was based on many things but not on the fact that he came from an extremely successful family of industrialists. Lubbers also did his best to keep this in the background, as did his predecessor in the thirties, Hendrikus Colijn. Colijn enjoyed great trust as a principled Calvinist. His career at Shell had nothing to do with his electoral successes.

There are no industrialists in the Pantheon of the average Dutch person, with perhaps two exceptions – Albert Plesman and Anthonie Fokker. The first founded KLM and the second the renowned aircraft building company. Their work closely resembled that of the great explorers of the seventeenth century to whom they were frequently compared by their contemporaries. It is, however, their pioneer spirit that is so admired, not their abilities as entrepreneurs. If you dig a little deeper, you may come across the name of Anton Philips, the founder of the electronics concern, but few others. Someone like Henry Deterding is little known, except to historians. Yet he was the man behind Shell, the only person who could pose a serious threat to the mighty Esso, owned by the Rockefellers.

[193]

FREE ENTREPRENEURSHIP CARRIES A HIGH SOCIAL STATUS

How would average Dutch parents react if their daughter came home with a businessman? Or – in the new age of emancipation – their son, with a business woman? It is very unlikely that they would be shocked, because free entrepreneurship carries a high social status. People will proudly tell you if they have their own business. A traditional mother might still prefer to see her daughter turn up with a doctor (preferably a surgeon) or a professor on her arm, because these professions are held in even higher esteem. Nevertheless, the business sector enjoys a great deal of respect. Another illustration of this is the confidence that Dutch employees tend to show in their employers. In most cases, they believe in the company and its products and will become very defensive in the face of outside criticism. This pride, however, is always in the product first and the boss second.

Dutch employers therefore have little difficulty in exercising their authority, as long as they follow the traditional Dutch pattern of *overleg* and justifying their decisions. Shipbuilder Bartel Wilton, one of the most respected directors in Rotterdam in the fifties and sixties, once declared: 'You have to make the most of the circumstances, cooperate with the people you work with and ensure that errors do not occur as a result of misunderstandings'. On the issue of the statutory requirement for a Works Council, he said: 'In a cold climate, you put on warm clothes. You don't change the climate that way, but you do make it easer to live with. It is the same in business. You still have employers and employees, but they have to find a way to get along'. Wilton was known to some as 'Red Bart'. This suggestion of socialist leanings has been attributed to a surprising number of Dutch entrepreneurs – most of whom have been upstanding liberals or Christian democrats. It simply means that they are the kind of person you can talk to, someone with whom you can make a good, practical deal to suit the demands of the situation.

ENTREPRENEURSHIP BASED ON A SOUND KNOWLEDGE OF THE MARKET

This, too, may have its roots in the Dutch merchant tradition. The commercial spirit in the Netherlands is concerned not so much with building up industrial emporia as with delivering a specific quantity of goods to a certain place at an agreed price. This is entrepreneurship based on a sound knowledge of the market. It means making the right offer at the right time so that the customer takes the bait. You can only succeed in this if you have a thorough ground knowledge of the sector you are working in and of the circumstances of your potential customer, and can make a good estimate of how much they would be prepared to pay and what they are worth. There is an old Dutch saying: *'Je moet weten wat er in de wereld te koop is'*, literally 'You must know what's on sale out in the world'. For the Dutch, success in business demands a keen interest in what is going on in the outside world. This attitude is reflected in society at large. Until well into this century, the newspapers printed the foreign news on the front page, before the national and local news. And in that order of priority – from international down to local. During the Golden Age, Amsterdam, the merchant city, was arguably the most important information centre in the world. Large companies like the United East India Company had enormous networks, which enabled them to gather information on their competitors and which were therefore significant instruments of industrial sabotage. If you wanted to know the latest news about everything and everyone, you had to go to Amsterdam. Resourceful businessmen turned this into an export product. In 1620, for example, printer Broer Jansz started publishing an English version of his weekly newspaper and shipping it to London. The first English daily paper, the Daily News, which appeared in 1702, printed proudly under its name that it contained all reports from the *Opregte Haarlemse Courant*. The *Gazette de Leyde*, a French-language paper published twice weekly in Leiden, had a wide European readership and was the most reliable source of news across the continent for more than a century. The Netherlands long ago lost its leading position as a collector and distributor of news to other centres like London, Paris and New York, but the interest is still there.

FOREIGN BOOKS CAN BE BOUGHT EVEN IN THE SMALLEST PLACES

The Dutch have believed since the Golden Age that knowledge of more than one – and preferably more – foreign languages is an indispensable component of a good education. Every child that progresses further than the primary school – and, since the mid-twentieth century, this means all children – obtain a basic knowledge of English and, in most cases, French and German. Until the 1960s, it was compulsory for further education students to take all three foreign languages in their final examinations, except those following lower and intermediate technical courses. Since then, they may drop two of the three, but by then they have had two hours of lessons a week in the language for a period of two years.

[195]

The Netherlands is the leading importer of books from Anglo-Saxon countries in the non-English-speaking world. Foreign books can be bought even in the smallest provincial towns, as can newspapers and magazines.

Until the Second World War, France and Germany competed fiercely for the first place in this market, with Britain consistently in third place. After the liberation, English took over the first place. You only have to look in any bookshop or station kiosk, with their wide assortment of paperbacks from the larger British and American publishers, for proof of this. They are not there for the tourists. You can buy the Times Literary Supplement, *Die Zeit*, the New York Review of Books or the *Nouvelles Literaires* at most railway stations. Or, if you prefer, *Barron's*, the *Financial Times*, the European edition of the *Wall Street Journal*, the *Handelsblatt*, *Fortune* or *24 Ore*.

Foreigners who wish to practice their Dutch complain that they get little chance to do so. The Dutch tend to switch immediately to English, or even to the native language of the person they are talking to, if they can speak it. This is also a throwback to the old merchant tradition. It is always better to speak the language of your business partner than for him to speak yours. That is also why little effort has been made to increase the influence of the Dutch language in the world, particularly in comparison with the concerted campaigns of the British or French, or even of a relatively small country like Sweden. There is no coordinated system for teaching Dutch to newcomers to the Netherlands. The Dutch always express their admiration when a foreigner proves to have mastered their language, after which they will often switch directly to English, so that the listener's only option is to claim not to speak it. The same applies to educational institutions. The Netherlands has a whole system of English graduate courses, largely designed to save foreigners the trouble of learning Dutch. Universities who wish to attract foreign students tend to give their courses in the English language rather than set up facilities for them to learn Dutch quickly. During the colonial period, the Dutch rulers in Indonesia preferred to speak Malay – or what passed for Malay in their view – than their own language, and they were not at all pleased if a 'native' proved to speak Dutch.

Many Dutch people are convinced that they can speak foreign languages, particularly English, rather well. This can be very irritating, particularly for immigrants of Anglo-Saxon origin. They find themselves faced with countless mistakes and minor errors and receive answers to their questions, posed in carefully perfected Dutch, in a highly personalized interpretation of Shakespeare's idiom. Dutch people can often be heard to claim that they 'speak English far better than they write it'. In the words of an American with 20 years' experience of the Netherlands: 'This is a typical example of their over-confidence. But, in comparison with many other nationalities, the Dutch do speak surprisingly good English'. In spite of this, she concluded that many Dutch people over-estimate their mastery of the language.

This is a matter of argument. For the Dutch, a foreign language is an instrument. They learn it to enable them to communicate. They start communicating when they have learned only a few words and are not ashamed of making grammatical errors. Educational television offers courses in a variety of languages, with Indonesian and Mandarin Chinese being surprisingly popular choices. The courses are designed to enable people to conduct a simple conversation, and also provide considerable background information on the customs and practices of the country where the language is spoken.

'*s-Lands wijs, 's-lands eer*'. This Dutch expression, meaning literally 'a country's wisdom is a country's honour', is roughly equivalent to the English expression 'When in Rome, do as the Romans do'. Another Dutch saying '*De klant is koning'*, the customer is king, reflects the same sentiments.. When the King of Thailand announced that he wished to be addressed in the future as an Emperor, the representative of the United East India Company, wrote to his superiors: 'It is, after all, certain that his majesty wishes to be addressed by his subjects in the Siamese language as nothing more nor less than *'pro ponte suekka'*, which means nought but Supreme Lord. But we, to keep ourselves out of out of the line of fire, shall refer to him as 'His Majesty', leaving it to his discretion how he should interpret this'.[2] As this example shows, there is a solution to everything. About the same time, the company's representative in the Indian town of Negapatnam, a certain Van Dielen, used to receive his Indian clients in true local style, complete with temple dancers. This roused the indignation of the strict preacher in the town who wrote to Van Dielen's superiors: 'that director Van Dielen, in the presence of the other members of his board and their wives, did arrange such a feast of Belsdassar with the playing of cards and throwing of dice and did summon and admit such heathen whores and diabolic artists with the beating of drums and the playing of other pagan instruments, singing songs of damnation and felicitation, which they had dedicated to the devil but days before, combined with the foulest dances of prostitutes, ballets, masquerades and devilish spectacle'.[3] After an investigation into the affair, the preacher was dismissed. Van Dielen's superior commented: 'not all sources of offence are of the same nature but do vary greatly according to different occasions, customs, places, times and peoples and, if the greatest of caution is not observed, offence will often be taken rather than

---

2 *'Immer dit is seker dat sijn maijt, in de Siamse taale van zijn eijgene onderdanen niet anders aangesproken en genaamd werd dan pro ponte soekka, hetgene niet ander beduijt dan Opperste Heer. Maar wij, om ons eenerzijds buijten schoots te houden, noemen hem sijn maijesteijt, differerende de verdere uijtlegginge daarover aan haar eijgen discretie'*

3 *'dat 't opperhoofd van Dielen tot presentie van de andere raadtpersonen met hare vrouwen, daartoe aanstellende een expresse belsjazzarszars maeltyt tot kaartspelen, dobbelen suypen ende heeft ontboden ende toegelaten de heidense schandhoeren ende duyverskonstenaars met trommelen schellen ende andere pagodische instrumenten klinkende, singende vervloekte liederen ende gelukwenschende gesangen, die sij den duyvel daags te voren opgeoffert hebben, vermengt met de vuylste hoeredanse, baletten, mascaraden en duyvelsche vertooningen'*

given'.[4] *'s-Lands wijs, 's-lands eer,* indeed. The merchant had to be something of a chameleon. Dutch people who spend any time abroad do not retain their language and customs for long. The children and grandchildren of the tens of thousands of emigrants who left the country in the early fifties to start up elsewhere – particularly in Canada, Australia, New Zealand and Brazil – have little to betray their origins (unlike their counterparts from Germany or Greece) other than their surnames.

Dutch society, on the other hand, is very open to external influences. The intelligentsia grumble now and again about Americanization, and the detrimental efects of the 'McDonalds culture', but generally speaking there is little to stand in the way of such influences. Since the beginning of the fifties, the younger generations have followed American – and, to a lesser extent, British – trends very rapidly. They are increasingly exposed to them on television. Since the 1980s, the television cable network has reached even the most remote areas of the country so that most households can receive not only Dutch but also French, German and English programmes, plus a number of satellite channels, including MTV. This, in itself, is perhaps not so remarkable, but the Netherlands is also often a world leader when it comes to adopting international products and trends. For this reason, the country is frequently used by companies to try out new products.

These are, on the other hand, not always adopted totally wholesale, but are frequently adapted. A recent example is 'gabber house', a typical Dutch phenomenon which made the 'regular' techno music that has achieved such enormous popularity worldwide in the nineties sound mellow. 'Gabber' was created by the wilder elements among the football supporters, who were not interested in the melodious additions to the throbbing rhythm. Regular restaurant users encounter a similar phenomenon. Very few restaurants offer traditional Dutch cuisine. The hungry passer-by will see a wide range of pizzerias, Greek and 'Chinese-Indonesian' restaurants, which are increasingly be-

[198]

---

4 *'alle ergernissen sijn niet van een en dezelfde natuyr maar besondere gelegentheden, zeden, plaatsen, tijden en volkeren koomen darin groote veranderinge te veroorsaken, welke wanneer men deselve niet met alle voorsigtigheid aenmerkt, soo gebeurt 's dickmaels dat 't word in plaats van een gegeven een genomen ergernisse'*

ing joined by Indian, Turkish, Surinam, South American and Ethiopian establishments. 'Shoarmas', the meat snack from Israel, have also become very popular in recent years. This development is not restricted to the centres of large cities but is perhaps even more apparent in provincial towns. With a very few exceptions, these restaurants and snack bars aim at a wide public and not only at their own particular ethnic group.

The Dutch themselves, accustomed to an international cuisine, increasingly cook foreign dishes at home, using ingredients they can buy at any supermarket. Traditional Dutch cooking – stews, porridge and all kinds of dishes based on meat, potatoes and vegetables – is clearly on the decline. Pizzas and Asian rice dishes – particularly *nasi goreng*, an Indonesian meal made with fried rice – have practically become an indispensable part of the weekly menu.

Yet visitors from abroad who are served up dishes from their home country frequently notice a difference. It may be minimal, but it is there, nonetheless. The food may taste less spicy or perhaps a touch sweeter. It is difficult to explain how or why this happens, but restaurants do make concessions to the Dutch palate. This means that dishes must not contain a lot of spices, because their guests will soon find the food too hot. The traditional potato-based diet makes little use of herbs and spices. True cosmopolitan food-lovers are aware of this and give each other the addresses of places where such concessions are not made. These purists are, however, very much in the minority and most foreign dishes therefore acquire an unmistakable Dutch taste. As the food snob complains loudly of their blandness, you find yourself thinking 'Doe normaal, dan doe je gek genoeg'.

The best places to 'go native' are the bookshops with their shelves full of English and American publications. But nowadays they also have a wide assortment of foreign books recently translated into Dutch. In this way, the Dutch public has been introduced to Russian, African and South American writers. These translations are always given considerable attention in the serious media and, if the number of new translations appearing on the shelves is any indication, they clearly sell well. Many of them are available in cheap paperback series, costing around fifteen guilders a copy. The translations are always from the original language and not from the English version, because the Netherlands – with its traditional knowledge of foreign languages – has many competent translators. A typical example is Dr. August Willemsen, whose translations of the main works of Brazilian literature have made him one of the most well-known intellectuals in the country. It comes as no surprise that Willemsen is also a witty essayist on a wide variety of subjects ranging from his own profession to such diverse topics as alcoholism and Brazilian football.

Once again, translated foreign literature is not only available in the large city centres. Small bookshops out in the provinces also offer a wide selection. Foreign visitors who tune in to a Dutch television channel are often pleasantly surprised to discover that foreign programmes are not dubbed, as they are in Germany and France. All foreign series and films are broadcast in their original language with Dutch sub-titles. The same applies to the big screen, except in the case of Disney cartoons and other films intended for small children who are unable to read. The Dutch love to poke fun at their German neighbours, who dub everything; they make endless jokes about the cowboys or – even worse – Frank Sinatra, who babble away at them in German if they happen to hit upon a German channel while 'zapping' with the remote control.

It has regularly been predicted that this will all eventually lead to the decline of the Dutch language. A notable recent example was when education minister Jo Ritzen suggested that university lectures could perhaps better be given in English. It is also a common topic of conversation in cafés and bars. But until now, the language has shown no genuine signs of decay. Foreign-language media – such as a daily newspaper in English – have never really caught on. Ritzen's suggestion was met with broad disapproval and dropped. Legislation of the kind that exists in France, enforcing the use of neologisms rather than imported English words, such as bulldozer, hamburger or audio rack, would be unthinkable in the Netherlands.

Scientific researchers do have a tendency to publish in English, but that has more to do with increasing specialization. Since genuine colleagues are few and far between, it is necessary to be able to communicate with a broad international public. But in the immediate surroundings of the university or the laboratory, Dutch remains the working language and foreigners who stay here for any length of time without learning Dutch will find that this ultimately leads to isolation and considerably hinders their ability to function on a day-to-day basis. Although no one will force you to follow a language course, anyone who is unable to follow the discussion during some form of *overleg* or other will soon suffer the consequences.

This merchant spirit has another major characteristic – an aversion to nonsense and a love of hard facts. One of the most famous lines in Dutch literature, which comes from Multatuli's Max Havelaar, goes as follows: *'De lucht is geur en het is vier uur'*, 'The air is raw, the clock strikes four'. It is uttered by Batavus Droogstoppel, a partner in the company of Last & Co, Coffee Brokers. Droogstoppel is making a case for 'truth and common sense'. He says: 'Holland has remained Holland because our old folk attended to their business, and because they had the true faith. That's all there is to it!'. And later: 'I've no objection to verses in themselves. If you want words to form fours, it's all right with me! But don't say anything that isn't true. 'The air is raw, the clock strikes four'. I'll let that pass, if it really *is* raw, and if it really *is* four o'clock. But if it's a quarter to three, then I, who don't range my words in a line, will say: 'The air is raw, and it is a quarter to three'. But the versifier is bound to four o'clock by the *rawness* of the first line. For him, it has to be exactly four o'clock, or else the air mustn't be raw. And so he starts tampering with the truth. Either the weather has to be changed, or the time. And in that case, one of the two is false'.

[201]

Batavus Droogstoppel, coffee broker, is a caricature. He is clearly the 'bad guy', causing even his creator to exclaim with indignation at the end of the book: 'Halt, wretched spawn of sordid moneygrubbing and blasphemous cant! I created you … You grew into a monster under my pen … I loathe my own handiwork: choke in coffee and disappear!'. Caricature or not, there are still plenty of Droogstoppel-types around today. Multatuli's stereotype is built up from character traits that you frequently come across in Dutch society.

Elsewhere in Max Havelaar, Droogstoppel claims that he never has to ask the way anywhere twice, 'for I always know how to get to a place when I've been there once, because I always take such careful note of everything. I've made a habit of doing that in business.' The Dutch merchant spirit does indeed demand a sharp eye for the facts of a situation. All forms of pretence have to be exposed. You have to take care of business and not spend a cent too much. Everything else is pure fantasy. Dutch parents whose children do not take life seriously enough will be told: *'De zaken gaan voor het meisje'* , 'business comes before girls' or, to use a common English expression, 'business before pleasure'.

This means that many many conversations – no matter what the subject – soon take on a financial tone. *'Wat koop ik daarvoor?'* is a common response if someone is asked to help in some way or take part in some sort of activity. The question, 'What can I buy for that?', has taken on a general meaning, but its origins are clear – what will the person concerned get out of it? This attitude may lead to stinginess, but rarely to a fear of making investments that do not provide immediate profit. Van Dielen, the man who arranged such lavish parties in Negapatnam, was also prepared to donate funds for the building of Hindu temples. Even in the seventeenth century, they knew that goodwill could be very profitable.

ANYONE WHO GOES BANKRUPT RUINS HIS REPUTATION FOR GOOD

A debtor can count on little sympathy. Anyone who goes bankrupt ruins his reputation for good and will have great difficulty in winning back the confidence of his creditors. Until well into this century, the Reformed Church community in Friesland excluded bankrupts from Holy Communion, their most sacred religious ceremony.

Because he did not commit suicide after going bankrupt, as gentlemen were required to do in his circles, the family of Rotterdam old-clothes dealer Herman Heyermans Junior broke all contact with him. He subsequently moved to Amsterdam, where he became one of the country's greatest playwrights, frequently compared with Ibsen.

The reverse can also happen. Timber merchant Dirk Witte was also a songwriter with a talent that few have surpassed. His funeral was attended by the *crème de la crème* of the Dutch art and entertainment world. His family, however, were proud to observe that there were also many friends and colleagues from the timber trade. In spite of his hobby, Dirk has always kept a solid head on his shoulders.

'When I went to the bank, it was always to deposit money, not to take it out.' This was the response of the conservative father in the renowned Dutch television series *De Glazen Stad*, 'The Glass Town', when his son wished to borrow from the Rabobank cooperative to modernize his market gardening company. This is the stereotype of traditional Dutch dependability – you must not owe anyone anything. Yet, the Dutch economy could never have spread its wings so far if there had not been a powerful banking system to provide the funds. It is almost impossible to start up a business with your own money, particularly these days. The ING Bank recently ran a television commercial that was shown almost day and night in which a consignment of goods from San Francisco was given the go ahead at the last moment because the bank provided emergency credit after a single telephone call. Anyone who goes to a bank with a good idea and expects this kind of treatment, however, is in for an unpleasant surprise. The banks are cautious and suspicious. They always ask for security. They will look very critically at your proposed business plan and will not be swayed by your powers of persuasion and talent for business. Nor will a good bank provide credit on the basis of sufficient security alone. Banks also depend on continuity and therefore prefer long-term relationships. After all, no one benefits from the financial ruin of a client. Nevertheless, the ABN AMRO, the country's largest bank, had a poster made showing a young woman who was saying: 'I'm good for thirty-thousand guilders!'. This was her spending limit.

Whatever her limit, she would be well-known at the *Stichting Bureau Kredietregistratie* in Tiel, in the province of Gelderland. Set up by banks, insurance firms and trading companies, this central credit registration office stores information on the 4.6 million people who have or have had a credit facility of some kind, no matter how small or how large. A total of 8 million facilities are registered, including all credit card holders. The organization makes no judgement on the solvency of the persons on its register – the companies providing the credit do that. Anyone with a bad credit record will be refused further loans. The *Bureau Kredietregistratie* receives many delegations from abroad who come to see how the system works. It also takes great care to ensure that hackers do not gain access to its computer files.

Since the 1970s, the Dutch have become more daring about living on credit. A large part of the money they lend is used to buy consumer durables, like cars. Few can afford their own house without winning the national lottery, so most people with their own homes also have a heavy mortgage to go with it. A house is, of course, a long-term consumer durable, so many see it as an investment in the future.

In spite of this, a survey conducted in 1990 showed that the Dutch are still the most cautious borrowers in the European Union. Whether Dutch banks are also as reluctant to grant credit was not investigated.

So why is the girl on the poster 'good' for thirty-thousand guilders? The

ABN AMRO has a rule of thumb that an individual with a 'normal' lifestyle should have a fiftieth part of the total loan over each month. After paying all her monthly costs, such as the rent or mortgage, tax and insurance premiums and all the other expenses required to live her 'normal' life – which the bank estimates at about 950 guilders for a single person – the girl must therefore have six hundred guilders left. With that much to play with, you would be more likely to open a high-interest savings account – especially in a country with such low inflation as the Netherlands.

Significantly, most Dutch people are very careful about using their credit cards. They prefer to use their bankcards to pay electronically so that the money is automatically deducted from their current accounts. This means that they are not in debt for a single moment. In spite of this, a growing number of people are finding themselves in financial trouble. Particularly those at the bottom of the social scale are confronted with debts that they have no hope of paying off, even though the amount they owe may seem reasonably small to those who are better off. Anyone who buys household goods 'on tick', usually from mail-order firms, eventually finds themselves inundated with small monthly repayments. When this happens, there is a safety net. There are a large number of municipal credit banks who are prepared to take on the problem of clearing the debts. This generally means that the creditors have to settle for less than they are due. They usually agree to this because otherwise they would never see any of their money again. Government bodies, such as the tax department and the energy companies, prove to be the least willing to reach a settlement. The debtors themselves have to tighten their belts for a couple of years. The credit banks offer their help under strict conditions. They take responsibility for paying fixed costs, such as rent and energy bills. The debtors then have to live on what little is left. They also receive guidance with keeping the household budget. Anyone who refuses these conditions is left to their fate.

In the first five months of 1994, the average debt per person registered with the credit bank in The Hague was a little over 21,000 guilders, three or four thousand more than at the beginning of the decade. The total registered debt was 25 million guilders. According to a spokesman, the bank helped about 40 per cent of debtors who apply for assistance; the remainder are not prepared to accept the conditions. By way of comparison, an average net income in the Netherlands is seventeen or eighteen hundred guilders.

This might all lead one to conclude that brilliance is not easily recognized in the Netherlands, that the common soldier does not carry a field marshall's stick in his knapsack or that the paper delivery boy had better stifle any ambitions he may have to become a millionaire. Everyone is pushed upwards in a social mish-mash with the consistence of honey, sweet but sticky, so that no one is able to fight their way to the top. This is made even more difficult by the many Droogstoppels hanging around your ankles with their deeply entrenched narrow-mindedness. You really have to do your best in the Netherlands to end up as a down-and-out – by developing an addiction for hard drugs, for example – but it is equally difficult to work your way up from nothing to become a captain of industry. There is something in this, even if it is nothing more than that it is a regularly heard complaint. For the past two hundred years or so, every generation has had its prophets, who have raised their voices against the ossification and the lack of dynamism in society. Multatuli, after all, created Droogstoppel as a stereotype that would show the country's élite the less pleasant sides of their own character. Even the Proceedings of the *Tweede Kamer*, which have recorded the house's history since it was founded, contain repeated warnings against the in-built 'braking mechanism' in Dutch society. One of the main priorities of all the governments led by Ruud Lubbers was to increase the dynamism in society. The roots of this dynamism can be found in the spirit of entrepreneurship.

THEY HAVE A LOT TO DO

Asked how things are going, most Dutch people will answer that they are busy. They have a lot to do. They are always full of new plans. The attitude they wish to project is not one of calmness and leisure, but of great vigour and activity. Bosses across the country can often be heard to respond to enthusiastic employees coming to them with a new proposal: 'Write down the main points on a sheet of paper and put it on my desk'. The implication is that they do not have the time to read long and complicated arguments and that an idea of any importance can always be formulated in a few hundred words. The boss will then be the one to decide whether the idea has any merit. Lubbers and his successive governments tried to give added impetus to this vigorous approach. They initiated campaigns to encourage people to set up their own businesses. The 'starting entrepreneur' was the model citizen. They would identify a 'niche in the market' and find a way to fill it, benefiting not only themselves but also – by creating jobs – society at large. Even non-profitmaking organizations and government departments adopted this new 'market-oriented' approach. The jargon of the private sector penetrated the formerly closed world of the civil service. Courses in economics and business studies experienced a period of enormous growth. Yet the word around which the social debate centred was not 'entrepreneurship', it was 'management' – the ability to give dynamic leadership to an organization. Student associations seeking sponsors did not present themselves as tomorrow's entrepreneurs, but as tomorrow's managers. Captains of industry prefer to be seen as the enthusiastic managers of their companies than as directors who sign enormous contracts.

Every year, fifteen to twenty thousand of these 'starting entrepreneurs' set up new companies. This is not a very high percentage for a country with over fifteen million inhabitants. When it comes down to it, most Dutch people prefer to express their dynamism within an existing organization with a proven history of continuity.

In the 1990s, interest in commercial and management courses has declined in favour of disciplines such as psychology. This has led to complaints from the business sector that the younger generation has not had sufficient training in 'hard' subject areas, such as engineering, which will eventually lead to a shortage of technological know-how in the country.

There was an element of exaggeration in this fear, as a glance at any university, production hall, farm or motorway will show. If the country had a problem, it was certainly not with out-of-date factories, or that it had to work with ramshackle, obsolete machinery, which made it the laughing stock of more advanced neighbours. It is, however, true to say that the Netherlands is not a trendsetter in many areas. It is more likely to be follower of new technological developments, but the pioneers are likely to feel the Dutch breathing down their necks. Genuine innovations are rarely developed in the Netherlands – the last one of significance was the compact disc, which was rendered suitable for mass production at the Philips Laboratory in Eindhoven – but they are very quickly snapped up and put to use. Philips itself is a good example. The company was set up at the end of the nineteenth century to produce electric light bulbs, invented shortly before by the American inventor, Thomas Alva Edison. The main priority was commercial gain. The first major achievement of the company's founder, Anton Philips, was to win a contract to electrify the lighting in the palace of the Russian Tzar.

Today, Philips is going through a difficult period. Its CEO Jan Timmer blames the problems on a lack of dynamism. He is fighting a running battle with bureaucratization – a common problem in large Dutch companies – and in-built inertia.

Another primary concern is cost control. This is, of course, an ever-present problem for company directors, since unnecessary costs reduce profit. But Dutch managers devote particular attention to the problem. A saving today is almost always preferred to potential revenue in the near future. If income falls the response tends to be to cut back on expenditure. Planned investments are scrapped and less profitable activities are stopped, even if their prospects for the future are promising. This is called in Dutch *'de tering naar de nering zetten'*, not spending more than one makes or 'cutting the coat to suit the cloth'. It closely resembles the regime imposed by the municipal credit banks on their debtors. [207]

The national budget deficit is therefore a common subject of public debate. It is always seen as a matter of grave concern and ministers of finance devise policies aimed at providing a lasting solution to the problem. The response to serious economic setbacks is unfailingly to reduce expenditure and *never* to cover the shortfall by printing more money. Ex-businessman Hendrikus Colijn, prime minister during the economic crisis of the 1930s, believed that the country would only survive the depression by making financial adjustments. He pointedly rejected a Keynesian solution of government investments to get the private sector back up and running. The same applied to devaluation of the Dutch guilder. He held on to the gold standard until 1936, years longer than neighbouring countries like France and Great Britain. The strong guilder was a source of great pride to Colijn and when the Netherlands also abandoned the gold standard, he saw it as a capitulation.

The recession of the 1980s produced a new wave of cutbacks, but this time based on different arguments. The government claimed, to put it in simple terms, that a guilder spent by the government was a guilder that could not be invested by the private sector. Once again, the value of the guilder was protected jealously. Since then, inflation has been almost negligible, compared to the 1970s, when – much to everyone's concern – it sometimes rose to between six and eight percent a year.

When the economy recovered strongly in the second half of the eighties, the government saw no reason to put a stop to its policy of cutbacks. The parties that formed the new government in 1994 worked on the basic assumption that they would have to save a further twenty billion guilders. Reports on renewed economic growth and falling unemployment had no impact on their resolve. They could also feel the warm breath of the media in their necks, who were keen on exposing most proposed cutbacks as juggling with figures. The same media always devote considerable attention to *'meevallers'* and *'tegenvallers'*, unexpected extra revenue or costs, which the Ministry of Finance regularly brings to public attention. These are usually tax revenues or social security expenditures that were unforeseen in earlier prognoses. *Tegenvallers* are a powerful weapon for a minister of finance who wishes to push through more cutbacks; *meevallers* are a godsend for hard-pushed ministries, such as education and social affairs, who are under continual pressure to bring down costs.

Among the general public, a fairly broad consensus developed that the Netherlands was 'too expensive'. It was pricing itself out of the market because salaries were too high. Not that everyone actually ended up with such a large amount on their bank accounts every month – it was the high taxes and social security contributions that pushed costs up to such irresponsible heights. All kinds of complex models were devised to establish a link between increases and decreases in government spending and the rise and fall of unemployment in the private sector. Minister of finance and PvdA leader Wim Kok therefore announced in the summer of 1994, while engaged in the negotiations to form a new government, that the 18 to 20 billion guilders in cutbacks would lead to 350,000 new jobs in four years. Commentators observed that, since the early eighties, no self-respecting politician goes anywhere without their pocket calculator. They need it to draw up 'income scenarios' and 'cost-revenue analyses' and to calculate their impact on unemployment.

THE NAME BETRAYS ONE CAUSE OF THE PROBLEM

These handy calculators are known in the Netherlands as *'zakjapanners'*, 'pocket Japanese'. In many people's eyes, the name betrays one cause of the problem. From the eighties on, the industriousness and perseverance of the economies of South-East Asia was presented as an example to the idle Dutch. The Asians, it was claimed, are not out for personal gain, they wish only to achieve good results. Typical of these critics was that they did not draw attention to the low level of salaries paid in these countries, but focused on the mentality. Dutch commentators on the success of Japan suggested that it is largely due to the fact that most employees feel a sense of belonging to the companies they work for. They claimed that they recognized certain aspects of the Dutch consensus mentality in the way people deal with each other in the Far East. Several companies in the Netherlands experimented with Japanese organizational models, a phenomenon which eventually came to be known as 'Toyotization'.

Toyotization meant the formation of teams from various sectors of the company, whose task was to satisfy the demands of a certain group of customers, with quality once again the key word. This was bad news for the middle managers, who were largely organized along department and sector lines. Since they were largely responsible for monitoring the activities of others, they lost much of their *raison d'être*. After all, the multidisciplinary teams – comprising all levels from stock controller to engineer – held the responsibility themselves for creating the product the customer wanted by pooling their knowledge. The guidance and coordination formerly provided by the middle management was now replaced by *overleg*.

Few companies introduced complete Toyotization. Yet, in the nineties, almost all large companies have been reviewing the role and function of their middle management. Are all these managers and undermanagers actually doing anything worthwhile? Are they not, with their power and their right to say No and to modify ideas submitted by their subordinates, an obstacle to the dynamism that is so crucial? In short, are they worth their money?

With the renewed emphasis on dynamism, a second word became fashionable – flexibility. Companies, institutions and individuals were expected to respond more alertly to the demands of the moment. The successive Lubbers governments were convinced that this could best be achieved through the free market and, consequently initiated a fully-fledged policy of privatization. Where possible, government services had to be put back in private hands. This was particularly true of companies that had originally been taken over by the government because of their monopoly position in the market. The post, telegraph, telephone and other forms of electronic communications were privatized, as were the railways. Local authorities sold the subsidized housing they had built for the lower-income groups to housing associations who had been operating with the same aim in mind for decades. This, of course, opened up the market for competition.

But flexibility also means greater insecurity. There was less chance than ever before of people who started a new job staying in it for life. The custom I referred to earlier – where, until the late 1980s, employees with 40 years' service were automatically honoured by the Queen – was dropped without any fuss, the reason given being that such unquestioning loyalty was, after all, not so great an achievement. In addition, many Dutch people came to realize that education and training – no matter how extensive – were no guarantee that they could continue to function adequately for their entire working lives. Technology progressed at such a rate that it was impossible to keep up without attending regular refresher courses. A number of areas of expertise disappeared. Typographers – who once considered themselves the true aristocrats of the labouring classes – were replaced by computers. Only those who trained as graphic designers survived the technological revolution.

Training and retraining therefore became the order of the day. Since the 1980s, the Dutch have been engaged in a process of mass adjustment to a society that no longer offers – to them as individuals, to companies, to government departments or to non-profitmaking organizations – the continuity that was formerly accorded such importance. For many, this has been a painful experience. In a certain way, it has put them back in the same position as the herring fishermen six and seven hundred years ago. They sail, with their frail craft, on a stormy and unpredictable sea. But – in spite of its dangers – the fishermen, the merchants and the explorers never allowed the sea to daunt them.

Many Dutch people find something attractive about this new uncertainty. They like to show their dynamism and flexibility. They relish the challenge. But still, they heed the old seamen's motto: *'Kalmpjes aan, dan breekt het lijntje niet'*. Be careful and the line will not break. A good sailor is prepared to take risks but is never reckless. In uncharted waters, he will drop a line to plumb the depth. He will always resist the pull of the land, until he is certain that there are no dangerous currents. Because, after all, the most important thing is to get home safely.

If you are in any doubt about this, you should watch the KLM pilots – they are the masters of the soft landing.

Chapter 5

PRIVACY MINDED

'BE A PRINCE IN YOUR OWN SQUARE METRE !'

Reserve as a basic character trait. Caution in contact with strangers. Keeping emotions under control. Respect for the privacy of another. Freedom of choice and conformity combined. Money does not buy happiness. A relationship for spiritual contentment, work for self-respect. Loneliness. The restrictions imposed by 'gezelligheid'.

A café in the Netherlands can be a very sad place. There may be two or three men at the bar who would most probably like to talk, but there will be empty bar stools standing resolutely between them. Only the most talented of barmen can break through such loneliness. Most of them are content to serve up the drinks in silence.

In the Netherlands there is a distance between people. Literally. The Dutch will sit next to someone else only if there is no alternative. Even in the bus or train. If they are all packed together during the rush hour, they will pull in their stomachs, as if to say: 'I am touching you, but I don't really want to. I am trying to make myself as thin as possible. It's not my fault, I'm really doing my best'. Anyone who fails to observe this rather forced ritual is asking for trouble. They will be seen as another one of those dirty foreigners who rub themselves up against you in public places.

Physical contact is avoided as much as possible. People from cultures where there is less distance between people, such as the Arab countries, notice this immediately. They find that the people they talk to will back off continually until the minimum acceptable distance has been restored. A test conducted among my colleagues proved that this is about 70 centimetres. There was no significant difference between men and women. Yet lovers will stand in each others arms at the bus stop, kissing without embarrassment. They walk down the street with their arms around each other's waists. Or they will lie, bodies entwined, on the beach. If there are no empty seats left on the tram, a polite young man will stand up or he might allow his girlfriend to sit on his knee. No one minds this, but you will notice that they look away. It is not done to stare at such scenes of intimacy. Many people will even make it clear that they have not seen it at all.

Television pictures of foreign dignitaries embracing at the foot of the aircraft steps are greeted with amazement. Russian leaders even kiss their inferiors on such occasions. For many Dutch people this only confirms their suspicions that these people are not to be trusted. Decent people keep their distance. If they do not, then there is something going on. Couples in love – as long as they are heterosexual – are permitted to make an external show of their affection. In the most modern parts of the country, such as the more progressive parts of Amsterdam city centre, you may see two men walking hand in hand, but it is still very rare and not considered acceptable by most people. In any case, a couple will present themselves as such. The 70-centimetre barrier may no longer be between them, but it is a clear signal to others that, for them, it applies more than ever.

YOU DON'T TALK TO COMPLETE STRANGERS

The Dutch have a reputation as being a little dour and unapproachable. They will frequently agree with this view of themselves, but then add that, once the ice is broken – a very appropriate choice of expression – they are hospitable hosts and faithful friends. It is difficult to say the extent to which this is true. Everyone has their own character and some seek more contact than others. But there can be no denying that the way the Dutch communicate creates a barrier between them and people they do not know.

You simply don't talk to complete strangers. People in public places will not easily strike up a conversation with those around them, unless there is good reason. If you ask the way, or some other question that is not of a personal nature, you will receive a detailed answer. But it is very unlikely that you would be invited to join a group of strangers at a table in a café. In the trains, the passengers maintain a stony silence, with their faces buried in a newspaper or with their walkman cutting them off from those around them. There may be a buzz of conversation here and there, but it generally comes from groups of friends or people who work together.

This is all in sharp contrast to the picture I painted earlier of a society in permanent communication, in perpetual search of compromise. So why do people talk to each other so little? The Dutch will answer that they are minding their own affairs, not impinging on the privacy of others. They are afraid of being a nuisance. They will speak only if there is a common theme to bind the group together. If a train stops out in the middle of nowhere, and there is a delay of half an hour so that everyone's carefully arranged plans are thrown into disarray, conversations will soon start. The hot summer of 1994 also provided such an opportunity. Since Dutch houses are not built to withstand tropical temperatures, people fled into the open air and met neighbours they had perhaps not even greeted before. One thing led to another. Tables were set up in the street. Playing cards and drink were fetched from indoors. The media covered these unusual events with great interest. My own mother, who lives in an apartment block, told me enthusiastically of how she had spent an evening with the neighbours out on the grass field below. Normally she would not dare to visit them unannounced of an evening. After all, you don't want to disturb people.

But once the delayed train arrives at the station, or the weather starts to get cold again, the common theme disappears and the animated conversations and open-air gatherings come to an end.

Many Dutch people believe that this lack of contact with others is on the increase. Interviews with older people almost always contain complaints about it. The main theme – which comes in many variations – is that people used to be more united as a group. They helped each other. No one does that nowadays, everyone is too concerned with themselves.

The question is, what do they mean by this? The Dutch make a clear distinction between strangers – who are nothing to do with them – and friends. It is possible that, as time has passed, the circle of friends and relations has grown smaller. There is evidence to suggest that this may be true. With the exception of the mass migrations to the cities in the west of the country around the turn of the century, the Dutch traditionally tended to stay put. Families would live in the same villages and towns generation after generation. The enormous economic development since the end of the Second World War largely put a stop to that. I can still remember how my father and his five brothers would gather at their parents' house on a Sunday, together with their families. They were connected to other families in our provincial town by a complex web of relationships which meant that the circle of friends and relations was always large. Today, not a single Van der Horst of my generation still lives in the town. The family is now spread across the country and I have not seen the majority of my cousins for perhaps twenty years. I hear of them through the family grapevine. My own brother lives in a completely different part of the country (actually only fifty kilometres away, but to the people of this small country, that is a long way). This effectively prevents the development of close networks of relations, such as the family had in the fifties. This network was largely made up of separate families who all lived within a few streets of each other and whose parents had also known each other.

These extended family networks have been destroyed in the modern age and this makes the consequences of keeping one's distance even more marked. It is easier to become caught in a vicious circle of loneliness. Old women in particular fall prey to this. Their average life expectancy is 78 and, as in most countries, they tend to outlive their husbands. Behind their impeccable white net curtains, they endure their unhappiness in silence, because they find it difficult to express their emotions. They put on a brave face and hide their misery from outsiders. This is due partly to pride, partly to embarrassment and partly because they don't want to be nuisance. The obvious thing to do is to bring these lonely people together, and many attempts are made. They are, however, rarely successful because the loneliness is often partly founded on the desire to be left to one's own devices and not be dependent on anyone. The result is a contradiction that is not easy to solve and produces a feeling of powerlessness. There are countless organizations in the Netherlands prepared to provide assistance to people in trouble – but the average citizen has the tendency to leave them to their fate.

THE CARING SOCIETY

The Christian Democratic politician Elco Brinkman brought this problem to the political forefront in the 1980s. He invoked a vision of a caring society, in which everyone took responsibility for the welfare of their families and neighbours. Although he received a certain amount of support, his ideas also unleashed a storm of protest. Brinkman wished to make people dependent upon each other again. His ideas were a cover for a vicious policy of cutbacks. His primary concern was to erode the system of social provisions, or as his opponents called them, 'social rights'.

By way of illustration, Brinkman suggested that children should take elderly parents into their homes. This proposal was greeted with anxiety, particularly among older people themselves. They were afraid that they would have to 'go begging' from their own sons and daughters, that they would have to 'ask nicely and say please'. This was the worst thing that could happen to anyone.

Foreign visitors, particularly from Africa and Asia, are shocked when they see the old people's homes where younger generations can dispatch their parents and keep them out of sight. They consider this shameful evidence of a lack of love for one's parents and of a sense of responsibility. But this is not the philosophy behind the system. The homes give their residents the opportunity to live their lives according to their own norms. They do not need to adapt to the wishes of their children or vice versa. As elsewhere, the compromise culture plays a leading role in families. Older people wish to be taken seriously and not to spend the rest of their lives in a situation of permanent give and take. In spite of their age, they want to retain their independence and their privacy. This is impossible if they have a room in their children's house. Yet, in some ways, there is good reason for Asian and African visitors to respond to this system with such aversion. Many old people complain that a visit from their children every couple of months is not often enough, and that they do not see as much of their grandchildren as they would like. But they still consider their option of living in an old people's home a significant acquired right.

In spite of this, most Dutch people will try to postpone the day on which they move into one of these places. And the government provides them with every support. Most people agree that the elderly should stay independent as long as possible, preferably in their own homes. The prospect of moving to an old people's home is only seriously considered when, in spite of help with the cleaning and meals delivered to their doors, they are no longer able to fend for themselves. 'Oude bomen moet je niet verplanten'. You should not uproot old trees. People have the right to stay in their own homes and surroundings as long as possible.

In 1994, the elderly were led to believe that the government was planning to cut state pensions, a major right acquired in the 1950s, and felt that this would threaten their independence. In the general elections of that year, they voted *en masse* for two hastily set up political parties who supported old people's interests, which consequently won a total of 7 of the 150 seats in the new parliament. This was in spite of denials from most of the established parties that they intended to cut pensions. The fact that the parties of the outgoing coalition – the Christian Democrats and the social democrats – lost so many seats (also to the two liberal opposition parties) had a great deal to do with this *faux pas*. The older generations were afraid and they punished the cause of their fears – the established political leadership – with the only weapon at their disposal, their right to vote for someone else. No one just should just sit back and allow their independence to be threatened.

This protest also effectively brought to an end the – until then – brilliant political career of Elco Brinkman and his ideology of the 'caring society'. He led his party to its largest election defeat in its hundred-year history.

Taking all this into account, you ask yourself how that boy and girl who kiss each other completely without embarrassment at the bus stop ever managed to meet in the first place when everyone so jealously guards their own privacy. The answer is obvious – they started off as acquaintances, or rather, their two networks of family and friends came into contact. They found a themselves in a situation where they could talk about a common theme. And one thing led to another.

At least, this is how these things often get started. But love is blind and it is dangerous to generalize about how people meet each other. The whole country is covered with discothèques where young people in particular can meet for the first time. But these discos – and this is also true of most cafés and other places of entertainment – tend to attract youngsters from a certain sub-cultural group, whether they be the conventional 'Johnnies and Anitas' or the 'Altos', who embrace an alternative lifestyle to the bourgeois values of their parents. Their young guests will therefore probably meet new friends who at least have similar lifestyles, tastes in music and cultural preferences. In most cases, these preferences are international in nature and bear little resemblance to the traditional Dutch values I have described above. There is, for example, a small 'tango' sub-culture which extends across the whole country. Its members present an atmosphere of 'suffering to dance to', and the females can be recognized by their close-fitting black dresses and their tightly combed dark hair. In Rotterdam, the Johnnies and Anitas queue up nightly in front of the Baja, where a beach has been reproduced with sand and wooden boarding. The personnel, some of whom are American, explain that it is intended to portray Florida. Those who prefer harder rock music gather at the Nighttown and fraternity students join others who still pursue the yuppie ideals of the eighties in the old harbour, which has been transformed into a centre of entertainment. These different lifestyles all have their own kind of music, which also largely follows international trends.

Yet most communities still have a traditional café, where people of all ages and from all of these different sub-groups mix. These cafés are usually old and run-down, which is often the reason why they are so popular. Anyone visiting one of these establishments will discover that there is usually a large group of regulars, who may not always be prepared to accept a stranger in their midst. They will tell you that the bar is like a second home to them or express some similar sentiment. There are fixed norms and rules for behaviour in these places and it is not easy to become a fully-fledged member of the inner circle of regular clients.

[217]

THE EXPLOSIVE DEVELOPMENT OF CLUBS AND ASSOCIATIONS

Anyone who is not a part of some network of relations or other, giving them an opportunity to talk about matters of common interest, soon becomes lonely. This may be one of the reasons for the explosive development of clubs and associations in the Netherlands, particularly involving sports and hobbies at local level. Although the hobby or sport is the main reason for taking part, social contact is of more than secondary importance.

This system is becoming less and less effective. As the population becomes more mobile, it is increasingly difficult for individuals to build up networks of this kind. Spiritual leaders and social workers see loneliness as a serious social problem. Opponents of reductions in social security benefits often use the argument that the unemployed will then have less money to spend on subscriptions to clubs and will become isolated. In spite of their highly developed sense of privacy, most Dutch people are afraid of isolation. They prefer to function as part of a group and most believe, in the last instance, that life can only be lived to the full if shared with a partner.

Finding a partner is, however, not always an easy task. At least, it has become increasingly difficult in the past thirty years. Traditionally, as in the rest of Europe, the family was the basic unit in the Netherlands. You got married in your early twenties, had children, promised to be faithful 'till death did you part' and you kept your marriage vows. You did not have a lot of choice. Until the 1950s the social pressure on couples to stay together was enormous. The Roman Catholic Church did not officially recognize the annulment of marriages and, although the Protestant Church permitted divorce, few took advantage of the right. This was unquestionably connected to the fact that, in the Netherlands, the man was traditionally seen as the breadwinner, while his wife tended to the housekeeping and the children. This was so deeply embedded that, even as late as the 1950s, female civil servants automatically received an 'honorary discharge' when they got married. The cultural watershed of the 1960s – and, without doubt, the mass availability of the contraceptive pill after 1963, which allowed women to decide for themselves whether they wished to bear children – put an end to this traditional system of relationships. Living together without being married – previously considered little better than prostitution – became normal. Sex before marriage – until then a taboo subject – was generally accepted. Under new legislation, 'irreconcilable differences' were acceptable grounds for divorce, hitherto only granted if one of the partners admitted to adultery (a precondition that came to be known as 'de grote leugen', the great lie). The social security system guaranteed that partners without their own income would receive at least a minimum benefit, making it easier in practice for relationships to break up.

This change in the economic importance of the marriage contract was perhaps the most significant factor in the break up of the traditional system. In less prosperous times, economic security is an important part of what people experience as 'happiness'. In modern society, economic security is guaranteed for practically everyone. Consequently, other – less material – factors become more important, and relationships are assessed entirely on their emotional quality. The character of the partners and how they interrelate are far more important that how much either of them earns. The quality of the relationship is paramount. If it is not considered optimal, the partnership may break up.

Because of the national respect for privacy and, compared with Asian or African cultures, the loose contact with other family members, couples in the Netherlands become very dependent on each other. Staying together till death do you part is no small task when average life expectancy is between 75 and 80. Relationships have to last a very long time and the love has to be very strong if the partners are not to become bored with each other at some point. This is particularly true if you are not prepared to live a life of disappointment and if you are not satisfied with a partner who is a source of pleasure around the home, leads a regular life and brings in a reasonable salary every month.

BEAUTY FADES AWAY, AND THE UGLINESS REMAINS

Romantic love in its purest form has, more than ever, become the standard for happiness. Weddings themselves often have the character of a fairy-tale. Western fairy-tales traditionally end with the sentence 'And they lived happily ever after' and most modern Dutch couples will settle for nothing less. Ultimately, they apply the same norms as Goocheme Sallie, a popular film and stage character in the 1930s. The aged working class lad from the backstreets of Amsterdam sang a well-known song, with lyrics by Philip Pinkhof:

'Je bent niet mooi, je bent geen knappe vrouw.
Je nagels zijn voortdurend in de rouw.
Toch wil ik van geen ander weten.
Omdat ik zoveel van je houd.

Al ben je ook een beetje vreemd van ras
Toch ben ik danig met jou in m'n sas.
k'Wil van een ander nooit iets weten
Omdat ik zoveel van je houd.

Wat verdriet, mooi ben je niet
Vooral wanneer je kijft
Al ben' je geen plaat
Schoonheid vergaat.
Maar weet de lelijkheid die blijft,
daar moet je maar aan wenne.

Al zijn je kleren ook van satijn
en doe je niet mee aan de slanke lijn

Toch wil van geen ander weten.
Omdat ik zoveel van je hou

Al zijn je haren niet gepermanent
en is 't gebruik van zeep je onbekend.
Toch zou ik jou niet willen ruilen
voor zo een maag're modeprent'.

'You're not too pretty, you're not a beautiful woman,
And your nails are always dirty.
But I would never look at another
Because I love you so much.

Even though you're a bit of a strange lass
When I'm with you I feel like a king.
I would never look at another
Because I love you so much.

It's a pity, you're not so pretty
Especially when you nag.
You may not be a picture,
But beauty fades away.
And you just get used to
The ugliness that remains.

Even though your clothes are not of satin
And you're not much of one for dieting
I would never look at another
Because I love you so much.

Your hair may be in need of a perm
And a bath might not be out of turn
But I would never trade you
For some skinny dolly bird.'

The fact that fewer and fewer people succeed in finding a relationship that meets these high emotional requirements is illustrated by a phenomenon that has become commonplace in the last twenty years – the 'personal ad'. An increasing number of people place advertisements in newspapers and magazines stating that they are looking for a partner. There is no long tradition of seeking contact in this way in the Netherlands. Although these 'small ads' have always existed, they would formerly begin with such apologetic phrases as 'I am forced to use this impersonal means of communication …' Nowadays, however, the Saturday editions of the national papers contain one and a half to two pages full of these contact advertisements. Each of them publishes some 200,000 per year. The identity of the advertisers is kept anonymous by the use of letter numbers, to which interested parties address their replies. The paper then forwards them to the advertiser.

[221]

These advertisements paint a reasonably good picture of what people understand as 'happiness'. 'Doctor seeks Eve, no older than 40. Offers love, protection, peace and security in exchange for a warm and tender heart'. The Cindy Crawford type will demand 'A dip in the sea before breakfast, a run along the beach in the evening. Ideal: to watch the sun set together'. She is looking for a 'sensitive, optimistic, exciting and athletic man with a lively intellect'. 'Woman, 2 children, seeks child-friendly man who is smart, young at heart, humorous, doesn't like sport/watching television'. She herself loves 'culture, travelling, camping, swimming, walking, cycling, friends'. Another will present herself as 'sport-lover, beach, wine, woods, talk, togetherness'; she is looking for 'a versatile young man with brains and sensitivity'. Even the 'high-heels-and-leather lover' is looking for 'good conversation, trust and mutual respect'.

Or it may be: 'Me and you against the world. You: a woman of between 25 and 30, slim, attractive, controversial. Me: athletic, early 30s, creative profession, stimulated by new challenges – like you.'

'Every night when I go to sleep, I hope to see the woman of my dreams. Every morning when I wake up I hope to see her! (…) You are a charming, attractive and fun lady (25–30, university) who is looking for a serious partner with whom you can enjoy life in all its facets. Are you going to contact me, or are you going to just keep on dreaming?'

The same rules apply to homosexual relationships. Advertisements for gay men and women seeking contact are printed in the daily papers and differ little from those placed by heterosexuals. 'Independent young man, 35, seeks ditto for monogamic romantic relationship. If you know what you want, have both feet on the ground and have had enough of the gay scene, write to me (with a photo). Perhaps we can spend the cold winter evenings together'.

THERE ARE A LOT OF NICE PEOPLE OUT THERE

[222] One noticeable thing about these advertisements, they tend to emphasize the positive side of the advertiser's character. There are a lot of nice people out there. Very few of them make any reference to money or material possessions, or give any details of the advertiser's income. They do, however, contain a great deal of indirect information. People often state their educational qualifications or demand a certain level of education from their prospective partner. Ads in the progressive newspaper *De Volkskrant* frequently refer to a university or equivalent education. In the right-wing newspaper *De Telegraaf*, advertisers are more likely to present themselves as being 'in business' because the paper supports free enterprise, promoting the interests of the entrepreneur and the lifestyle that goes with it. Advertisers in the liberal NRC *Handelsblad* will often use the expression *enig niveau*. A difficult phrase to translate (it literally means 'a certain level'), it is an indication that they are looking for someone who can fulfil certain minimum social requirements. While this by no means conceals a secret desire for a life of luxury, their ideal partner will certainly not be found living in a subsidized rented flat on a 1950s estate. What they want is someone with a decent education – although, of course, an applicant with a university education may reasonably be expected to have a sizable income.

Other terms that occur frequently in contact ads are 'equality' and 'good conversation'. There is a general consensus that these requirements can be fulfilled only by a someone with a comparable education. This apparently reasonable demand is, however, a cover for an age old source of social differentiation – status. Since the Second World War, educational qualifications have in many respects replaced what former generations referred to as 'social standing'. There used to be an enormous gap between the gentleman farmer and his farm labourers, between entrepreneurs, shopkeepers and simple workers.

These differences would often be manifested in their manner of dress. The sons of shopkeepers did not marry factory girls, and a farmer's daughter would not dare to come home with a young farm labourer. It happened, of course, but it was asking for trouble. With the democratization of modern society, such attitudes have become unacceptable, but educational qualifications have emerged as a good substitute. The implicit assumption is that a university graduate will hardly be able to conduct a decent conversation with someone who has only had an intermediate technical education or has a diploma in home economics, let alone set up house on any equal basis. Intelligence and creativity are directly linked to educational achievement.

This, of course, says nothing at all about the countless relationships that develop without the help of the small ads. At the most, the advertisements reveal a little about the ideals of the people who place them. But, because they describe the ideal partner, they are an important source of information on what many Dutch people would like to see in the perfect relationship. The fact that, just as anywhere else in the world, *l'amour* plays the game according to its own rules, makes little difference. I myself have never been in love with anyone who conformed perfectly to my image of the ideal partner and I believe that this applies to most people.

It is therefore remarkable that the requirements continue to be so high. The fact that most Dutch people now live outside of the traditional family unit illustrates that, in spite of the unabated desire to form a partnership, they are less prepared than ever to make concessions. You might wonder whether this change is for better or for worse. The dramas of divorce have become an ever-present feature of modern society; but perhaps they are still preferable to the sorrow born silently by many partners in former generations as they preserved the pretence of a successful marriage.

WORK IS GOOD FOR ONE'S PERSONAL DEVELOPMENT

In addition to a relationship, the modern individual needs one other thing to be fulfilled as a person – a paid job. At least, there is a widely held consensus that work is good for one's personal development. It is a source of self-respect and of contact with others. People without work for any period of time find themselves 'on the margins of society' and feel that they 'no longer belong'. Full employment is therefore one of the main aims of all political parties. They may not agree on how it is to be achieved, but they are unanimous on the end itself.

Work has become a scarce commodity in the Netherlands. 57 per cent of people between the ages of 16 and 64 have a paid job – a total of about 6.5 million, including all those with part-time jobs (sometimes amounting to only a few hours a week). This means that, in a country with a population of over fifteen million, a little more than a third are in employment. The rest are at school, retired or living off some form of benefit. These figures are the source of grave concern in the Netherlands and it is widely believed that the number of people out of work is growing rapidly. This is, however, not the case. In 1970, 58 per cent of people between 16 and 64 had jobs. The difference lies in the percentage of people who wish to work. The Netherlands was traditionally a country where the husband was the breadwinner and the wife stayed at home. Partly as a result of the second wave of feminism, this situation has changed radically. An increasing number of women wish to make careers for themselves and are receiving the active support of the government.

Not that women were afraid to go out to work in previous generations. Most girls looked for jobs after they left school, making a contribution to the upkeep of the family and saving the rest for their *'uitzet'*. This was their 'bottom drawer', originally consisting of bed linen, but later covering the whole range of household goods that would give them a good start when they got married and gave up their jobs to look after their own home.

Until well into the 1970s, there was a particular type of school, the *Middelbare Meisjesschool*, which was originally intended for the daughters of well-off families, who would later marry the sons of the gentry, many of whom would have have had a university education. The future model wives were taught modern languages, cultural history and literature so that they would later be able to converse on a whole range of subjects – in French if necessary – but not too deeply, over a dinner that they had also prepared themselves. The girls who attended the MMS were not able to go on to university.

Very few women actually went to these schools. Most parents considered it unnecessary as their daughters would be getting married later anyway. This has now all changed dramatically.

PERSONAL RELATIONS ARE POLITICAL

This change was symbolized by what came to be known as the 'second feminist wave'. Female activists in the sixties noticed that they were often left to make the sandwiches while the men did the talking. At the beginning of the seventies, they emerged as a group with a wide variety of demands, which they presented under the motto: *'Het persoonlijke is politiek'*, 'personal relations are political'. They claimed that existing relations between the sexes – also between couples – were repressive for women. They said that keeping a household was also work, and demanded that men do their share. Their aim was to achieve a situation in which the percentage of men and women in paid em-

ployment reflected the demographic balance between the sexes. They pursued this aim through a policy of positive action. Best-selling author Maarten 't Hart noted that they were always concerned with higher positions and were not interested in the 'feminization of the dust-cart', but his reservations gathered little support. The image of the housewife changed. From a respected mother-figure who ran the home, she was degraded to a stupid drudge who sacrificed herself so that her husband – a 'fallocrat' and oppressor – could pursue his wonderful career. The feminist novelist Renate Dorrestein christened this sorry figure a *'Theemuts'*, a tea cosy. The second feminist wave never became a mass movement, but it acquired considerable support in leading circles and among the intelligentsia. A moderate form of positive action – exemplified by the policy of giving preference to women candidates if job applicants had identical qualifications – was introduced throughout the entire government apparatus. Public information campaigns encouraged girls to study for a trade or a career, claiming that *'een slimme meid is op haar toekomst voorbereid'*, a smart girl will prepare herself for the future. The media, across the political spectrum, expressed their support for the feminists' demands. Universities set up courses in 'Women's Studies'. Increasingly well-educated women started participating in the labour market. At present, about half of further education students are female, although they still tend to avoid the technical subjects. It has become very unusual for women to give up their jobs because they are getting married or going to move in with their partner. It still happens frequently when they decide to have children, but many couples wait until they are well into their thirties to start a family when it becomes a matter of 'now or never' for the woman. As a result of the pill and other means of contraception, the number of children per family has fallen sharply. Whereas a family with six children was normal in the 1930s, with nine or even twelve not considered particularly exceptional, two is now seen as the norm. Recently, a new group has appeared on the labour market – mothers whose children are old enough to look after themselves at home. The statistics therefore reflect not so much increasing unemployment as a rise in the number of people who wish to work – more people than jobs can be created.

The pressure this places on the benefit system is compounded by the belief – which is becoming increasingly popular across the political spectrum – that many of the unemployed do not make sufficient effort to look for work, but prefer to live off their benefits, sitting 'on their lazy butts' all day in front of the television. The government takes a wide range of measures to restrict access to benefits. Every now and then, there are scandals as employers are unable to find labour for seasonal work. A recurrent example of this is the harvesting of asparagus, heavy work which is so badly paid that, even when compared with the lowest of benefits, it is not worth the effort.

At the same time there is an extensive circuit of 'black' work – work performed outside the official channels and for which no tax or social security contributions are paid. The 'black' rate for domestic cleaners is ƒ 12.50 an hour; the 'white' rate is twice this and more if they work longer than eight hours a week, because then their employer has to pay even higher taxes and social security contributions. A growing number of social security inspectors try to catch people on benefit who are also working on the side, while the government dreams up all kinds of incentives to encourage people to seek paid employment.

Whatever the causes, for every job vacancy there are ten applicants. This is a misleading statistic; it means in practice that anyone who loses their job will spend at least a few months searching for something else. Any longer and they are in trouble. Experience has shown that people who are unemployed for more than two years have little chance of ever finding another job – if for no other reason than that their own desperation eventually gets the better of them. These people form the hard core that accounts for slightly less than a third of the total number of unemployed.

The government attempts to create jobs by cutting back on its expenditure, based on the rather simplistic belief that every guilder that is not taxed is free to be reinvested in the private sector and will therefore provide more work. The coalition led by Prime Minister Wim Kok, which took office in the summer of 1994, hoped that it could create 350,000 new jobs by cutting back on government expenditure where possible and keeping salary increases to a minimum. Between 1994 and 1998, the number of people looking for work was expected to grow by 300,000 – most of them young school-leavers – leaving a balance of 50,000 vacancies to help reduce unemployment. A public debate arose as to whether such a meagre result was worth the sacrifices involved. Some commentators, including the sociologist and ex-labour politician Marcel van Dam, claimed that unemployment was a fact of life in modern societies with their high levels of prosperity and automation and that there was little to be done about it. If it was so important that everyone had a job, the only solution was to shorten the working week. Another possible solution was to guarantee a basic income for everyone, leaving it up to the individual to decide whether they wished to supplement this by taking on paid employment. The level of the basic income could be established through a broad-based process of democratic *overleg*. This solution would also save a lot of bureaucratic red tape, because it would replace the current complex system of benefits which already supports everyone without paid employment (except homeless drug addicts, because it is impossible to receive any kind of benefit in the Netherlands unless you have a permanent address).

Although this line of thought is slowly gaining ground, it is still indignantly rejected by the majority of Dutch people, who see it as condoning laziness and surrendering a traditional social ideal – you cannot just leave people to fall by the wayside, effectively denying them the right to develop themselves as persons by working for a living. For most people, the ideas of work and self-respect are still far too closely linked for such a solution to be acceptable.

Men and women in the Netherlands today therefore have to acquire for themselves two scarce commodities – an emotionally satisfying relationship and a paid job. In this respect, the most successful are the *'tweeverdieners'*, couples who both have jobs. If their relationship is also sound, they are in luck. Furthermore, since it is still assumed that salary levels have to be sufficiently high to maintain a family, working couples have more financial room to manoeuvre. They can afford a holiday in Thailand or the Dominican Republic (exotic, faraway places are becoming increasingly popular) or a mortgage on a house. The interest on mortgage repayments is tax deductible and the traditional aversion to lending money for the acquisition of material possessions does not extend to the buying of a house. The belief that a house will increase in value over time is deeply entrenched and is not affected by temporary dips in the property market.

YOU CAN BE YOURSELF BEHIND YOUR OWN FRONT DOOR

A decent home of their own is one of the main priorities for most Dutch people. You can be yourself behind your own front door. As soon as young people have their own source of income – their first job or a student grant – they start thinking seriously about leaving home. From humble beginnings – a room or a single-floor flat – they will gradually move on to better things as their income increases. A new word has even appeared in the Dutch language to describe this process: *'wooncarrière'*, literally a 'residential career'.

Through a wide variety of consumer surveys, a picture has developed of what Dutch people see as their ideal home. This is not a flat, but a house of their own – preferably detached, but a semi-detached or terraced house will do – with a front and back garden. In most cases, the wish remains unfulfilled because, just as with a job or a satisfying relationship, such houses are difficult to come by. The Netherlands is small and, with the exception of Bangladesh, is the most densely populated country in the world. Due to lack of space, house builders are forced to construct high-rise apartment blocks, particularly in the urbanized areas in the west. Since the 1970s, however, low-rise housing has once again become fashionable. The designers of new estates have discovered that – with a little creativity – they can fit as many people into the same surface area in 'regular' houses as they previously did in four or five-storey apartment blocks. After all, there had to be sufficient space between these blocks if the estate was to offer reasonable living conditions for its residents. 'Hong Kong'-type solutions, with high-rise blocks built shoulder-to-shoulder, were never a realistic alternative.

Many of the people living in flats or upper-floor maisonettes dream of a house with a garden. It is difficult to say why this is. If you ask them, they will say that a garden is 'nice for the children' or that it is 'pleasant to have a bit of greenery outside the door', but there is often a municipal park nearby that would fulfil this function. It is possible that they are nostalgic for their agricultural roots, but this is unlikely – gardens are generally used for decoration, rather than for growing vegetables. Perhaps a patch of land in front of and behind the house fulfils some deep-lying desire to extend one's own private terrain, the place where you can 'be yourself'.

Being yourself is a problem that was described perfectly seventy years ago by songwriter Dirk Witte. His lyrics have now become a part of the classic Dutch repertoire:

> *'Je leeft maar heel kort, maar een enkele keer.*
> *En als je straks ánders wilt, kun je niet meer.*
> *Mens, durf te leven.*
> *Vraag niet elke dag van je korte bestaan:*
> *Hoe hebben m'n pa en m'n grootpa gedaan?*
> *Hoe doet er m'n neef en hoe doet er m'n vrind?*
> *En wie weet, hoe of dat nou m'n buurman weer vindt?*
> *En – wat heeft 'Het Fatsoen' voor geschreven?*
> *Mens, durf te leven!*
> *De mensen bepalen de kleur van je das*
> *De vorm van je hoed, en de snit van je jas*
> *En – van je leven.*
> *Ze wijzen de paadjes, waarlangs je mag gaan*
> *En roepen 'of foei' als je even blijft staan.*
> *Ze kiezen je toekomst en kiezen je werk.*
> *Ze zoeken een kroeg voor je uit en een kerk*
> *En wat j' aan de armen moet geven.*
> *mens, is dat leven?*
> *De mensen – ze schrijven je leefregels voor*
> *Ze geven je raad en ze roepen in koor:*
> *Zó moet je leven!*
> *Met die mag je omgaan, maar die is te min.*
> *Met die moet je trouwen – al heb je geen zin.*
> *En dáár moet je wonen, dat eist je fatsoen.*
> *En je wordt genegeerd als je 't anders zou doen.*

Alsof je iets ergs had misdreven.
Mens, is dat leven?
Het leven is heerlijk, het leven is mooi.
Maar – vlieg uit in de lucht en kruip niet in een kooi.
Mens, durf te leven.
Je kop in de hoogte, je neus in de wind.
En lap aan je laars, hoe een ander het vindt.
Hou een hart vol wan warmte en van liefde in je borst.
Maar wees op je vierkante meter een Vorst!

Wat je zoekt, kan geen ander je geven.
Mens, durf te leven!'

'You only live once and life is so short,
If you change your mind later, it's already too late.
So live your life to the full.
Don't ask every day of this short existence
How would my dad or my granddad do that?
Or how would my cousin and my friend do it?
And who knows what the neighbours would think?
And what is the 'Right Thing To Do'?
Live your life to the full!
Others tell you the colour of your tie,
The shape of your hat, the cut of your coat,
And – of your life.
They tell you which paths you are permitted to wander
And call you to heel if you stop for a while.
They choose your work and your future,
The pub where you drink, the church where you pray,
And what you should give to the poor.
Do you call that living?
The others – they write the rules
They give you advice and they call as one:
This is how you should live!
They say: here is a friend, but this one is no good
And you should marry this one – whether you want to or not.

Go and live there – decency requires it..
And then they ignore you if you do it your own way,
As if it were a terrible crime.
Do you call that living?
Life is a fine and a wonderful thing.
But spread your wings and don't get trapped in a cage.
Live your life to the full.
Keep your head high, your nose to the wind,
And don't give a damn what others may think.
Fill your heart with love and with warmth..
And be a prince in your own square metre!
No one can give you what you are looking for.
Live your life to the full!

[231]

Don't give a damn what others may think. It clearly takes courage to 'live your life to the full'. It brings nothing but trouble. The 'others' will soon be on your back. You do not behave according to their rules and the fact that this rubs them up the wrong way is clear from the uniformity of their small gardens and that the furnishings of their houses are often so predictable. Who are they, these 'others'? A few years after the success of *'Mens, durf te leven'*, singer Louis Davids enthralled packed theatres with a portrayal of his audience. His words have lost little of their power over the passage of time:

Dat is die kleine man, die kleine burgerman
Zo'n hele kleine man met een confectiepakkie an
De man die niks verdragen kan, blijft altijd onder Jan
Zo'n hongerlijer, zenuwelijer van een kleine man

That is the little man, the small and decent man,
The very little man wearing his off-the-peg suit,
The weedy little man who never has the upper hand,
The poverty-stricken, nerve-wracked, little, little man.

Davids was honoured with the nickname *'Die Grote Kleine Man'*, the Great Little Man. The entire song can be encapsulated with the words: 'The little man carries the can':

'Dempsey gaat weer aan het boksen en krijgt weer 'n dik miljoen
Om zich 'n kwartiertje te laten stompen
En zijn tegenstander, als ie wint, een half miljoentje meer
Want die kereltjes die laten zich niet lompen!
Wie snakt er naar zo'n baan, zou, kreeg ie het gedaan,
Voor twee tientjes al zijn kiezen uit zijn kaken laten slaan?

Dat is die kleine man, die kleine burgerman
Zo'n doodgewone man met 'n confectiepakkie an
De man met zo een uitgesneden linnen frontje an
Zo'n zenuwelijer, hongerlijer van een kleine man

We verzorgen onze medeburgers tegenwoordig best:
Als je niet werkt krijg je achttien gulden premie.
En dan zijn er veel slampampers die zijn liever lui dan moe
Want die denken: nou achttien piek, die neem ie!

Ze schelden allemaal op patroon en kapitaal
En wie is weer de dupe van dat vrijheidsideaal?

Dat is die kleine man, die kleine burgerman
Zo'n hele kleine man met een confectiepakkie an
Eén met zo'n imitatie-jaeger onderbroekie an
Zo'n minimumlijer, zenuwelijer van een kleine man'.

'Dempsey earns more than a million when he steps back in the ring,
For fifteen minutes of punching and pain.
And his opponent, if he wins, gets half a million more,
You can't pull the wool over a fighter's eyes!
Who would want a job like that, getting paid
A few guilders to have their teeth smashed in?

That is the little man, the small and decent man,
The very little man wearing his off-the-peg suit,
The little man with a dicky on his chest,

The poverty-stricken, nerve-wracked, little, little man.

These days we take good care of our fellow man
If you can't get a job, they give you a handout of eighteen guilders.
And there are lot of layabouts who prefer to be lazy than tired
Who think: eighteen guilders for nothing, I won't say No to that!

They all complain about the bosses and their capital
But who is the real victim of that ideal of freedom?

That is the little man, the small and decent man,
The very little man wearing his off-the-peg suit,
The little, little man in the Jaeger-copy underpants,
The poverty-stricken, nerve-wracked, little, little man.

There are several other verses to the song but, without an explanation of
Dutch society in the thirties, they would be incomprehensible to the reader.
They show the Little Man to be a monument to jealousy. He believes himself
to be the victim of everyone who does not wear an off-the-peg suit, from vice-
admirals to unemployed good-for-nothings, from the idle rich in their villas
to overpaid sporting heroes. He is the stereotype of the resentful, lower mid-
dle-class citizen, the *petit-bourgeois* who rejects everything that is not a part of
his narrow world. In retrospect, it is not so surprising that lyricist Jacques van
Tol hosted a pro-Nazi radio programme which included an anti-Semitic version of his most successful work. After the war, the 'little men' treated him in
typical fashion – he remained one of the country's most productive song-
writers, but his name was never mentioned.

It is also typical that the *'Kleine Man'* is still widely seen as a brilliant apo-
logia for the hard-working loner. Singers who include it in their repertoire can
count on loud applause before they have sung the first note. Yet the basic
characteristic of the little man is that he does not dare to live his life to the full.
He feels that his square metre is under threat, but he never uses that scarce
space to create something unique. Everything he does complies with what
Dirk Witte refers to as *'Het Fatsoen'*, what commonly passes for Decency, the
'Right Thing To Do'. Anyone who wishes to be decent imposes considerable
restrictions on their behaviour. Witte himself was a 'decent' man – he ran the

family timber business. His songs may have been something of an escape valve for the enforced decency within which he had to live his life. That is why they were accepted. A decent man may make unconventional statements now and then, as long as they do not affect his daily behaviour. And if that does happen, punishment is swift and merciless, as Witte himself was aware: 'And then they ignore you if you do it your own way'. The price of non-conformism is isolation. Like Big Brother, 'they' are watching you.

They may be watching you, but they are not very likely to take any steps against unconventional behaviour, either collectively or as individuals. They have too much respect for another's privacy. The media regularly report stories of children living in large towns and cities who have been abused by their parents for years while the neighbours simply pretended not to know anything was going on. Or perhaps they genuinely did not notice anything strange. People in the Netherlands have a blind spot for what others do in the privacy of their own homes. The neighbours will often be heard to say: 'We never had much contact with that family anyway'.

It would have been a different story if the abuse had occurred in public. Firm measures would certainly have been taken. One of the main characteristics of *Fatsoen*, Decency, is that 'you don't wash your dirty linen in public'. It was not uncommon in the past for a teacher or a scoutmaster to give up his job without all the usual farewell receptions and speeches in praise of their years of faithful service. Everyone would know that they had been caught playing around with the children.

For the past fifteen years or so, however, it has become increasingly acceptable to wash the dirty linen in public. Offenders against public morality are dealt with by the courts and find themselves the centre of what can be very extensive publicity. Since the sixties, when the church began to lose its hold over people's lives and petit-bourgeois values began to crumble, the balance has been swinging against the *'Kleine Man'* in favour of *'Mens, durf te leven'*. Anyone who watches the crowds in the Kalverstraat, the Rembrandtsplein or the Nieuwedijk in Amsterdam, with their weird and wonderful clothing, will not need convincing of this. Especially if they then discover that a junkie has broken into their car. *Fatsoen* is clearly nowhere to be seen.

'Fatsoen' shares a common root with many similar words in other languages. It is clearly linked to the English 'fashion', and in eighteenth and nineteenth century texts you sometimes find it used in this way, to describe

clothing. But it now has a far wider application. The definition in the Van Dale, is one of the longer entries: 'Everything that is considered to belong in the realm of common decency and acceptable behaviour, whether in the moral or the formal sense (i.e. good manners in the widest meaning of the term), and particularly what is understood as conventional'. A very careful choice of words! The use of the passive form cleverly evades the question of who decides where the limits of decency lie. It is also very clear that *fatsoen* has a great deal to do with appearances, otherwise the concept would not be described by a word that originally referred only to clothing. It is concerned with the way people behave in public. You can walk around naked in your own home, if you so wish, as long as the curtains are drawn. In other words, it is a system of norms and rules of behaviour which have developed as part of the collective process. If you want to belong, you have to abide by these norms, or at least appear to do so to the outside world.

Older people often complain that traditional *Fatsoen* is on the way out. This may, however, not be entirely true; *Fatsoen* is not so much being eroded as fragmented. Society is being divided up into a plurality of collective 'spaces', each with its own form of *fatsoen*. This is entirely compatible with the basic social principle that each group should be given its own space in which to develop as it pleases. Staying with the example of walking around naked, a good illustration of this is nude bathing. When it became popular in the 1970s, most bathing resorts set up nudist beaches. Wearing a swimsuit is not optional on these beaches, it is forbidden by general consensus. It is also inadvisable to sit up on the dunes fully clothed and ogle the naked bodies running around in front of you. You will soon receive a visit from a delegation of 'heavies', whose muscles are all the more impressive for being totally exposed. They will inform you in no uncertain terms that you are offending the *Fatsoen* of the beach. You either play by the rules, or you stay away – there is no middle way.

These naked defenders of decency have something in common with the residents of the small town of Staphorst, in the Province of Overijssel. These people, who are strict Calvinists, are very serious about observing the Sabbath as a sacred day of rest. Even driving a car is considered to be in conflict with the Will of God. The faithful do not wish to be confronted with such sinful behaviour as they walk to the church for morning and evening service. They therefore walk along the middle of the street and do not get out of the way of any vehicles that may chance to come along. If drivers sound their horns or try to accelerate past, there is a good chance that the locals will defend their beliefs with their fists. The people of Staphorst, like the nude swimmers, do not wish others to offend their *Fatsoen*.

Anyone who lives in a community with many practising Christians who still like to see the Sabbath observed would be ill-advised to cut their grass or repair their car in the street on a Sunday. Do the car in the garage, but don't make too much noise. Of course, it is everyone's right to do as they please and the radicalism that still rules in Staphorst is rare. Nevertheless, most Dutch people have a mental signal that is triggered if they fear that their actions are likely to give offence. This places considerable limitations on individual behaviour in its more extreme forms. An Asian anthropologist suggested that so many Dutch people leave their curtains open in the evening to show passers-by that, inside too, nothing is going on that may cause offence. This is clear evidence that the Dutch have a strong tendency to conformity and, if true, it is bad news for those from the '*Mens, durf te leven*' school. Then you would be better off humming to yourself in secret or joining a sub-culture that does not demand such extreme individualism. That should not be too difficult. Even sado-masochists have a magazine through which they can contact fellow SM enthusiasts. The magazine is, however, sent to them in a plain envelope. That is perhaps understandable, but the same applies to the Gay-Krant – with a circulation of over 26,000, the world's most widely read magazine for homosexuals. In spite of the fact that homosexuality is broadly accepted in the Netherlands and that the law forbids discrimination against gays, most readers consider it safer if the postman or the neighbours do not know that they are subscribers.

No one wants to risk giving offence. You never know who might turn out to be the little man in the off-the-peg suit. With such a wide variety of clothing available these days it has become very difficult to spot him at first glance.

YOU DON´T WANT TO BURDEN OTHERS WITH YOUR OWN EMOTIONS

In this way, the princes – and princesses – impose restrictions on themselves in their own square metre. Outside they are even more cautious. And this has important consequences when it comes to expressing their feelings. You don't want to burden others too much with your own emotions.

When my father died, it was up to me – as the eldest son – to say a few words at the cremation. I drew up a short speech summarizing the basic principles by which my father had lived and explaining why the cremation service was not religious in character, in spite of my father's Catholic upbringing. He had foresworn his faith in the sixties. Since many of the people who attended the service would probably not have seen my father for many years, I thought it a good idea to ask a number of friends and colleagues for their comments on what I intended to say. This proved to be a bad idea. Few of them were willing to comply with such an extraordinary request. They did not even know how they should respond. I frequently ignore certain accepted norms of behaviour, but this time I had gone too far. I was inviting people to enter a private world in which they clearly felt that they did not belong. I was giving them access to my emotions, but that also meant I was forcing the door behind which they kept their own concealed. I was making an unexpected attack on very sensitive terrain.

This made my mother study my speech even more closely. Not because she wished to influence what I said, but because she wanted to know what was coming. She, too, did not want to burst into tears during the cremation service.

It was a solemn occasion. It was permitted to show one's grief, but not with outbursts of sobbing. In such situations, you have to keep a 'stiff upper lip' and show that you are completely in control of yourself. In doing so, you not only show respect for yourself, but also for others who would perhaps not know how to respond to outward displays of grief. We in our family had always been suspicious of the true depth of sorrow or of joy, disliking people who cried or laughed too loudly, believing them guilty of melodramatic or theatrical behaviour. The service went entirely according to plan. There was an atmosphere of silent dignity and we all kept our tears to ourselves.

Even by Dutch standards, this perhaps went a little too far. We Van der Horsts have perhaps hidden our emotions away behind a particularly thick wall. Many Dutch readers will then be a little perplexed when they read the story of my father's funeral, but the mechanism behind it will be familiar to them. You should be economical in expressing your emotions and shield them from others because they are private. And, at the same time, you do not want to burden others with them. They belong in your own square metre and not 'out there'.

This is perhaps not entirely true. You may be able to express your feelings – in a controlled way – in a safe environment. For example, to someone in a professional capacity. In the past, this was the monopoly of preachers and priests. Listening, offering consolation and good advice was – and still is – the main component of the service they provide. This is why they are rarely praised for the quality of their liturgical talents. Their strength lies in their ability to alleviate suffering, their wisdom and the moderation they practice in their contact with others.

But secularization is well advanced in Dutch society. The Netherlands now has the greatest concentration of psychiatrists in the world. You can permit a psychiatrist to enter your own square metre in the same way that you can admit a plasterer, painter or electrician to allow them to do their work. These people do not bring in their personalities, but knowledge of their chosen trade. So the psychiatrist always has a box of tissues at the ready – here you can and may cry as much as you please.

Nevertheless, Dutch society is full of unexpressed sorrow. This causes psychological damage that does not heal overnight. A famous photographer, who lost two children in a road accident, found respite from his grief when he visited the Sahel. He was able to talk about the tragedy there without people being shocked. They knew what it was like to lose their children and they treated grief as a perfectly natural phenomenon. The Dutch tend to leave people alone with their sorrow and loss, as though they do not dare to touch it. And those who are suffering keep their feelings to themselves. This makes grieving a long and lonely process.

In recent years, a number of extremely successful television programmes seem to have undermined this aversion to outward displays of emotion. There are dating shows in which, by playing a sort of game, the contestants choose a partner to go on holiday with. On their return, they reappear on the show and tell the studio audience and the viewers how it all went. By far the most popular show of this type tried to bring together couples who had broken up and to turn long-standing animosity into friendship. The host acted as a conciliator. He did not actually enter the homes of the people he was hoping to reconcile, but would take them to a caravan nearby where they would be shown a videofilm of the other partner, who would declare their love for the injured party or promise to mend his ways. Tears would flow freely and the final reconciliation would take place in the studio in front of the live audience. All appearances to the contrary, the success of these shows actually reinforces the Dutch tradition of not burdening others with your problems. The 'victims' do not expose their suffering or joy to a small number of individuals who are physically present, but to an anonymous unknown mass of people. There is no interaction. This is television as therapy. Sorrow can be expressed openly, public reconciliation can take place, joy and happiness need no longer be suppressed, while the others, the onlookers – even though there may be millions of them – remain at a distance. The television proves to be a perfect escape valve for emotions that would otherwise stay bottled up. And the members of the audience, in their turn, need not be embarrassed about this public show of emotion. For them, too, there is no opportunity to interact. They can satisfy their curiosity without having to suffer the consequences. [239] They do not have to look the other way, as they do when the see the couple kissing at the bus stop or when the neighbours start fighting on the stairs. Suffering and happiness may be expressed, as long as it is at a distance.

FRIENDSHIP RARELY PROVIDES A SAFETY NET FOR SURVIVAL

The programme that reconciles all those enemies has a snappy title: All You Need Is Love. As I said before, happiness is a matter of satisfying immaterial needs and this is the basis of a genuine relationship. Friendship rarely provides a safety net for survival. People who find themselves in financial problems will not easily turn to their friends for a loan. You might go on holiday with friends, you will visit each other's homes, but the friendship should not become entangled with material debts. Furthermore, the door of the Dutch home is not always open, even for the closest of friends. Many people dislike visitors who arrive uninvited. It messes up their plans and, since they were not expecting guests, they generally have nothing to offer them and feel that they are failing in their duty as hosts. In practice, it will generally not be as bad as I suggest, but the principle remains the same.

In contrast to many other peoples, the Dutch never allow for a possible unexpected extra mouth to feed at the table. It is simply 'not done' to turn up uninvited at a friend's house around dinner time and afternoon visitors will be expected to leave again around five, because the evening meal is traditionally eaten between six and seven. If they stay any later, the hosts will start to feel uncomfortable. They cannot start cooking until the guests have left. If they do, it is tantamount to inviting them to dinner and they do not have enough food to do that.

The first way to solve this problem is to try and make it clear to your guests that it is time for them to go. You can do this primarily by allowing each topic of conversation to run dry, by remaining silent instead of responding. Some very direct people might then stand in front of the window and say: 'Well, it's dried up now, you can be on your way' – especially if the sun has been shining all day. If this does not shift the more tenacious of guests, the invitation to dinner will then follow, but it will not come from the heart. People only visit each other at dinner time in the Netherlands if they have been expressly invited to do so. The invitation will then generally be for a clearly stated time. You must not be late, and certainly not cancel half an hour before, because a dinner invitation is a serious matter. It means breaking one's normal routine, extra shopping and a lot of work. For these reasons, there is always something a little festive about having people to dinner. You cannot serve them just any old dish. It must at least be a little more elaborate than your average daily meal. Other types of invitation – 'Drop round for a drink this evening' means from eight o'clock on, after dinner – should also be taken seriously, if a specific day or time is mentioned. Only when a Dutch acquaintance leaves you with 'Wij zien elkaar' – 'I'll see you around' – or 'Wij moeten snel eens een afspraak maken' – 'We'll have to make a date to meet some time soon' – can you be sure that you can safely take your leave with no strings attached.

And so the Dutch live their lives in the quiet privacy of their own square metre. 'Home' is one of their most cherished concepts. A well-known television commercial shows a car driving down a motorway somewhere in Europe past enormous signs showing an arrow and the words 'Naar huis' – this way home. Home is where the soup is. And the coffee. If you want to see the ideal Dutch family in action, watch the coffee commercials. They exude an atmosphere of safety and stability. They show slight changes in traditional role patterns. The son of the family comes home from delivering the newspapers and his father – not his mother! – is preparing breakfast. He pours his son a cup of fresh coffee. In another commercial, a young father is as tired as his young wife from their futile efforts to rock the baby to sleep. Time for coffee! Yet another shows a mother and father – this time in their forties – who have just finished helping their daughter to move into her first rented room. Mother wipes away a tear, but is clearly proud. The daughter's first step towards independence is to switch on her own coffee machine. Once the coffee is on, the situation becomes gezellig.

Gezelligheid is another Dutch word that defies translation. It describes an atmosphere that the Dutch proudly believe is unique to them. The word itself is closely related to *gezelschap*, company. It is a form of behaviour, of communication, which keeps the people involved together because they appreciate it and it makes them feel good. *Ongezellig* behaviour on the part of one of the participants can ruin the atmosphere entirely. And the chance is always there because in a café or at a party, it is no longer necessary to search for a consensus. People are there for fun. They can and do stand up for their opinions. Controversial statements can be heard from all corners. The danger then is that the *gezelligheid* will be disrupted if someone does not permit another to voice their opinions and attacks them personally.

[241]

My mother and father used to visit my grandparents every Sunday. My uncles and their families were also expected to appear, and each of them took two cigars for my grandfather. Everyone was given a cup of coffee and then they would settle down to argue about social problems. They never talked about family matters, that would be too close. I was a small child at the time, but I remember my father rising to his feet and – as if he were addressing a mass gathering – declaring: 'The tram is a prehistoric means of transport'. He said it very emphatically, making it clear that he would tolerate no objection to this clearly true statement, but my uncles nevertheless entered into a heated argument with him on the subject. I saw my aunts looking at their spouses, warning them not to go too far, but they did not intervene.

I remember another occasion when this happened. It was in the fifties, when the Cold War was at its height. My father had just made another of his controversial statements.

'Then', said my uncle Anton, 'you are a Communist'.

'Of course I'm not a Communist'.

'You *are* a Communist'.

Then my grandmother intervened. 'Easy now, boys', she said 'There's someone sick in bed next door'. She used to tell us children that , too, when we were making too much noise.

Then my aunt Eugenie, uncle Anton's wife, said: 'Give it a rest, Anton, let's keep it *gezellig*'. All of my aunts forbade my uncles from talking about politics at family gatherings, because we were all there for the *gezelligheid*. My mother said once, after we had returned from a funeral: 'It's terrible really, but it's always so *gezellig* afterwards'.

Gezelligheid is a common good and everyone has a moral duty to preserve it. The main component is communication, contact between two or more persons, often – depending on the nature of the occasion and of the people taking part – facilitated by the consumption of coffee, tea, alcohol or even weed (passing a joint around is a very successful means of breaking the ice). Anyone who disrupts this *gezelligheid*, this togetherness, is in for trouble, as the seventeenth century biography of admiral Michiel de Ruyter clearly illustrates:

'Once, on a horse-drawn barge, someone uttered scandalous things in his presence against the Government and he responded with great severity, saying that he was a servant of the Land and that he could not tolerate such language. He ordered the speaker to be silent and, after several warnings, told him that if he did not cease his slanderous accusations, he would order the captain to put him ashore. When all this was to no avail, he seized the troublemaker, picked him up and, strong as he was, set him overboard not far from the land, where he concealed himself'.

The admiral, who had a Schwarzkopf-type reputation throughout Europe, could be a little short-tempered. Those who disrupt the *gezelligheid* these days need not fear that they will be manhandled, except in a café where the drink has been flowing a little too freely. They will, however, be studiously ignored and will notice that it is increasingly difficult for them to draw up a chair and join in the conversation around the table. They have not respected the principle of 'each to his own' and such behaviour is not easily forgiven.

Be warned – De Ruyter did not set the man overboard because of his opinions, but because of the way he presented them. Someone like that did not belong in the saloon of a barge, where the whole group had to spend may hours cooped up together and *gezelligheid* was the best remedy for boredom. The admiral wanted only to prevent the atmosphere from being ruined. In spite of his personal piety – he read theological books for pleasure – his biographer claims that he was not a quibbler. 'He was always loath to hear other forms of Christianity, or even those who live outside of Christendom, being condemned wholesale. He preferred to reserve judgement. Although he saw no reason for hope, since there is no salvation without Christ, he himself not only observed that this was true, but also recognized an unfathomable deepness.

Wishing to be charitable in judgement of both, he left the matter to the Will of God. He was also greatly displeased when those who were misguided in their religious beliefs were the subject of mockery and scorn.'

The *gezelligheid* that is found among groups of friends on café terraces is a continuation of the harmony that ought to reign in the household. The Dutch word for living room, *huiskamer*, itself suggests a cosy, homely atmosphere. Once the stove has been lit, the room is *gezellig*. '*Zet die TV nou eens af en laten we gezellig naar bed gaan*', people will say to their partners. 'Switch off the television for a change and let's go bed'. The use of the word *gezellig* is intended to make the suggestion sound more enjoyable than what the other person is do- ing at the time. Similarly: '*Wees eens gezellig en leg dat boek weg*', 'Put your book down and be a bit sociable'.

Gezellig can also be used to describe a room or a home. Some houses may be furnished in modern styles, with their cool colours and sharp contrasts, while others – perhaps with more traditional interiors – are really '*gezellig*'. *De Rotterdammer*, the now defunct daily newspaper, advertised itself as '*Een gezellige krant!*', believing that it, in doing so, it would create the right homely image to attract the Protestant families at which it was aimed.

Kees van Kooten and Wim de Bie, two of the Netherlands' best known ca- baret artists, produced the perfect description of *gezelligheid* in their song '1948'. Ironically enough, it is set to the music of Leonard Cohen's 'Alone Again'. The loneliness is there, but in a very different form.

'*Buiten huilt de wind om 't huis*
Maar de kachel staat te snorren op vier
Er hangt een lapje voor de brievenbus
En in de tochtigste kieren zit papier
Wij waren heel erg arm
En niemand hield van ons.
Maar we hadden thee en nog geen tv
Maar wel radio en lange vingers
We gingen nog in bad
Haartjes nat, nog even op
Totdat vader zei: 'Vooruit naar bed'
Dan kregen we een kruik mee
Gezichten op 't behang

Maar niet echt van binnen bang
Toen was geluk heel gewoon.

Buiten huilt de wind om 't huis
Maar moeder breit een warme sjaal
En het ganzenbord op tafel stond er
De volgende morgen nog helemaal
Ook gingen wij naar 't bos
Daar zijn we toen verdwaald

Van de weg geraakt, carrière gemaakt
Heel die pannekoekensmaak vergeten'.

'Outside the wind is howling round the house
But the stove is switched up to four.
There's a flap in front of the letter box
And the draughts are stuffed with paper.
We were very poor
And no one loved us,
But we had tea and no TV,
Just the radio and sponge fingers.
We all had a bath, got our hair wet
And were allowed to stay up for a while
Until father said: 'Off to bed',
Then we were given a hot water bottle.
There were faces on the wallpaper
But we weren't really scared, back then
When we were always happy.

Outside the wind is howling round the house
But mother is knitting a warm scarf
And the board game was still on the table
Untouched the following morning.
And we went to the woods
Where we got ourselves lost,
Couldn't get back and made our careers
And forgot the taste of the pancakes.

The italics in the last four lines are mine. To the Dutch, the woods often represent wild and untamed nature, even though most woods in the Netherlands today have been planted. In the woods, the trees are high. You can see little sky and nothing of the horizon that is familiar out in the open polders. The woods are a strange world, where you soon lose your sense of direction. *'Iemand het bos insturen'*, to send someone 'into the woods', means to let them down or abandon them.

The woods signify insecurity and danger. Van Kooten and De Bie described the lost haven of *gezelligheid*, from which they have been exiled as they have pursued their careers. They are a living testimony to *'Mens, durf te leven'*. [245] They went their own way. But, with hindsight, they realize that they have lost their ways and that the *gezelligheid* has gone forever. That feeling of complete safety and continuity has dissipated for good into the mists of time. They now have to survive in the cold light of reality. The warmth – so often associated with *gezelligheid* and, as is shown by the references to the stove, the water bottle and the scarf, one of the main attributes of this paradise lost – is the price they have paid for success and freedom.

It is this that stops people from turning their back on the *gezelligheid*, and going out into the wide world, or at least giving the princedom on their square metre the appearance of an absolute monarchy.

THE AIR IS PERMEATED BY THE STIFLING SMELL OF SPROUTS

Yet much modern literature deals with attempts to escape hearth and home, traditions and all forms of *gezelligheid*, which are now seen as suffocating. This passage is taken from the first and still best known work of this genre, *De Avonden* – The Evenings – written by Gerard Reve and published in 1947:

'While she cleared the table, his father went to lie down on the divan, decided to take off his shoes, sat for moment staring in front of him and then stood up and walked to the bookcase. Just before he reached it, he slipped, his left leg shot up in the air, but he regained his balance. 'Whoops!' shouted his mother. 'He's alright', Frits said. 'You don't need to yell so.'

His father took a book out of the bookcase, went back and lay on the divan, and pushed his free hand through his hair. 'Uh oh, the stove', said his mother. She looked at the fire and added: 'It's burning away fine in there. Don't touch it. Just leave it as it is, with the kettle keeping it open.' She showed them how the aluminium kettle had to rest against the top of the flap of the stove, so that it stayed open a little. 'Otherwise it will all be burned up within an hour', she explained. She went into the kitchen.

Frits looked at the clock. 'Everything is lost', he thought. 'Everything is ruined. It is ten past three. But the evening will make up for a lot.'

Reve paints a similar picture to Van Kooten and De Bie, but to him it is an oppressive prison, in which the bars are formed by narrow-mindedness, hypocrisy and fear of the unknown. And the air is permeated with the stifling smell of sprouts. Sprouts are a kind of miniature cabbage with a slightly bitter taste, and most children hate them. If they are boiled for a long time, a penetrating odour fills the whole house. The smell is a reminder that the vegetable is as good as tasteless (boiled for only a few minutes, sprouts are delicious, but this is the modern method of cooking them. Traditionally, they were left on until all the taste had been boiled out of them), that what little taste they do have is bitter. It recalls their sallow green colour, so representative of the colourless nature of existence itself. The smell of sprouts can be invoked by the uninspired words of a colourless politician, the cliché-ridden reports of a burned-out media commentator or the exaggerated caution of a company director. Where *gezelligheid* reigns, there are always those who believe they can detect the smell of sprouts. For them, it is not liberating, but confining. The unwritten rules no longer help you to be yourself in company, but enforce uniformity in thought and deed. All colour fades. You feel that you would like to give everyone a 'good kick in the butt'. Silently, you revolt against what you now see as *lulligheid*. *Lullig* is yet another of those Dutch words that covers a multitude of meanings in English. The Dutch-English Van Dale charmingly translates it as 'shitty, cruddy, crappy', but *lullig* extends to a whole range of unpleasant aspects of human nature. If you accuse someone of being *lullig*, you may consider them feeble, stupid, mad, lacking in character, nasty or irritating. The word crops up in a wide variety of common Dutch expressions, such as '*Doe niet zo lullig*' – Don't be so stupid, feeble, etc. – or: '*Zo'n een grote vent op een vouwfiets is een lullig gezicht*' – A large man like that looks so silly/stupid etc. on a fold-up bike. *Lulligheid kent geen tijd*: this is how the well-known columnist Nico Scheepmaker paraphrased the expression *Gezelligheid kent geen tijd*, roughly equivalent to the English 'pleasant hours fly past'.

Van Kooten and De Bie – as we can learn from their biography – consciously escaped the *gezelligheid*. They acquired an unassailable reputation as 'slayers of sacred cows'. No self-respecting intellectual would dare miss one of their TV shows. Van Kooten's books are bestsellers. At least until the early nineties, the duo were genuine trendsetters and any leading figure or type that had been the target of their satire was never seen in quite the same light again.

If people like this produce an ode to *gezelligheid*, it is a testimony to the lasting attraction of the phenomenon. You have to be of good stock if you want to develop sufficient momentum to escape its pull. The protagonists in the 'smell-of-sprouts' literature rarely come to a good end, while well-intentioned organizations of all persuasions try to lure people who have fallen outside the safety net of decent society – in practice, drug addicts of various kinds – back into the fold by arranging '*huiskamerprojecten*', 'living room projects'. They set up centres, with tea and coffee and someone to listen to your problems – the main attributes of *gezelligheid*. These are not hostels or treatment centres. They simply create the conditions for mutual contact in an atmosphere of safety and security provided by the visitors themselves. Treatment is the next step, which will only be taken on the visitor's own initiative.

As elsewhere in the world, junkies are clearly on the lowest rung of the social ladder. Or, even worse, they have been kicked off even that lowly perch and are completely on the ground. They are the outcasts of Dutch society and the general opinion is that they have only themselves to blame. More than half of the country's prison population are addicts.

You can see them shuffling through the centres of the larger cities, looking for whatever they can pick up from the street, the waste bins or the passers-by. The latter respond with anxiety and aversion. Yet the junkies seldom pose a genuine threat. They exude physical deterioration and are too far gone to make any effective attempt at relieving anyone of their possessions. It is those who have not yet fallen prey to a life on the streets, but who prefer drugs to a good meal – the still invisible cases – that are the main perpetrators of drugs-related crime. The junkies are almost indistinguishable from another group that is becoming an increasingly familiar sight on the streets, people with severe psychological problems who choose not to be admitted to a psychiatric institution. Compulsory treatment can only be imposed, by order of the local mayor, if it can be proved beyond doubt that the person concerned presents a danger to himself (or herself) and those around him. The evidence must be indisputable, as is illustrated by a tragic case that occurred in 1993. A disturbed man, of whom the whole street was afraid, beat a twelve-year-old girl to death with a club. The situation had been allowed to go this far because there had been too much respect for his privacy, for his right to behave as he wished. The murder led to much debate on the limits of acceptable behaviour. The ultimate conclusion was that all the organizations involved had been working at cross purposes and, consequently, the signs that something was amiss had not been picked up in time. The issue of whether people should be 'taken out of circulation' at an earlier stage was hardly discussed at all. For the Dutch, it goes against the grain to restrict people's freedom of movement for their own good.

Once again, the cultural revolution of the sixties only helped to reinforce this attitude. For a while, anti-psychiatry – which considered society sick, rather than the people who lived in it – was relatively popular. At the same time, new legislation gave psychiatric patients more rights. Psychiatric institutions adopted the spirit of the new law and now largely accept only patients who have consented to treatment themselves. Compulsory admission is now permitted, as I said above, only if the patient is clearly a danger to himself and those around him. That is why people who are clearly disturbed can be seen shuffling around the shopping centres in the larger cities. They are the equivalent of the American 'bag ladies'. Critics claim that this respect for the rights of the individual is simply a means of justifying cutbacks in psychiatric care – after all, it means that institutions have to deal with fewer patients. This siltation provoked the following cynical observation from Hans Slijpen, social worker with the Utrecht police, about the country's largest shopping mall, the *Hoog Catharijne*. Speaking in the daily newspaper *Trouw* on 24 September 1994, he said: 'In the Hoog Catharijne, they not only find shelter, anonymity, freedom and fellow addicts, they also have a team of 'nurses', dressed in the blue uniform of the police. The Hoog Catharijne is sometimes just like a mental home, with all the necessary facilities. Addicts get sent here. There are staff and other patients. They can take their pills and their injections.'

Slijpen's remarks were made in connection with the tragic case of Anna, an incontinent woman who suffered from religious mania and heard voices in her head which forbade her to wash. She 'lived' for years in the Hoog Catharijne. The psychiatrists did not consider her sufficiently disturbed to be admitted to an institution and the courts decided that she was not a threat to herself or public order. But she smelled so badly that the junkies who lived in the shopping centre tried to drive her out. The story in *Trouw* continues: 'A few weeks later, something happened which the police team had been afraid of for months – the addicts decided to take the law into their own hands. One day, the woman was found covered in bruises and cigarette burns.' Hans Slijpen feared that this was only a first warning. 'It was then decided that Anna could finally be admitted. She was down at the police station when the authorization came through. She was a complete wreck, in such a bad way that she was taken straight to hospital, where she was kept in for a while.'

I do not like having to write of such cases. Nor are they typical of the way the Dutch treat each other. Yet I, who live in the centre of a large city, have the impression that this is not an isolated incident. On the street and at the railway station, I come across too many disturbed wretches whose human rights are clearly being scrupulously denied – except by others whose life is on streets: the junkies, tramps, street prostitutes and petty criminals who maintain a rigid pecking order and come down hard on the weakest wherever they show their faces. The problem is, help is available, but it first has to be requested in clear and unequivocal terms. The request must never be non-verbal. Anyone, dressed in rags and unwashed, who stands mumbling at the entrance to the station, looks for half-eaten hamburgers in rubbish bins or sleeps on the metal grids outside the city hall – I am talking about two cases I know of – will not receive any support. Such behaviour is not seen as an *actual* cry for help. And I am just as guilty of ignoring them as the rest of the passers-by. After all, we think, we pay our (very high) taxes and there are institutions for people like these.

For the same reason, there is no system of compulsory treatment to cure addicts of their habit in the Netherlands, as there is in Singapore, for example. Of course, there are plenty of people, both in the cafés and in the political arena, who demand the introduction of such a system but so far their arguments have had little success. The 'helping hand' must not be imposed from outside, it must be asked for. There are countless organizations which offer help to addicts, but they do not force people to make use of their services. They have an intake procedure and the initiative has to come from the addicts themselves. They come and go when they please. The strictest punishment for those who run away is that they are categorized as hopeless cases the next time they ask to be taken in.

This has nothing to do with the fact that drug addicts make regular appearances in the country's criminal courts. They are there for pickpocketing, burglary or breaking into cars (no one leaves their radio in the car in the city.

That is simply asking for trouble). But being treated as a criminal is a completely different to being treated for an addiction.

The drugs problem – just to put the situation in perspective, crack did not appear on the streets until 1994 – places a heavy burden on the shoulders of Dutch society. At least, that is what most people feel. This is exacerbated by the fact that no one seems to have a workable solution to the problem.

If this burden is as heavy as it appears and people still respect the right of addicts to decide for themselves when they need help, while at the same time – if statistics are to be believed – feeling less safe on the streets than ever before, it once again shows just how careful the Dutch are about interfering in another person's private affairs.

They will not offer a helping hand unless asked to do so. This applies as much to individuals as to organizations. The initiative never comes from the helper. The most surly of passers-by will show you the way when you are lost, if you ask. But you can stand shivering in the rain for half an hour, while the wind keeps threatening to blow away the map in your hand, and no one will ask you if they can help. People in need of assistance or information have to go in search of it for themselves. There is a whole complex network of government bodies, associations and organizations set up purely to help people in a wide variety of ways. But you have to find them yourself. Rotterdam even has a Help and Information Centre to guide people through this labyrinth. You only find the right place by being referred to it. But once you are there, you will receive their every cooperation. Some organizations are so keen to be of assistance that they try to help people they can actually do very little for. This is particularly true of bodies that provide grants of various kinds. Grants are particularly suited to this way of working, because they usually give people a helping hand in some way or another but are provided only on request. Not wishing to send people away empty-handed, these organizations frequently refer unsuccessful applicants to other bodies where they might have more luck. These will then most likely give the client the same treatment. This polite form of rejection is known as 'van het kastje naar de muur sturen', sending people from pillar to post. It eventually drives unsuccessful applicants to distraction, especially those who do not understand the reasons for it. They think that they are being tricked and 'aan het lijntje gehouden'. This expression, literally 'dangled on the end of a line', means that a decision that is important to someone is continually postponed in the hope that they will give up and not come back. This is a very effective way of not having to provide a service without actually refusing outright. For foreigners who are not familiar with Dutch society, this frequently leads to a lot of unnecessarily wasted time. They apply to some organization or other for a grant of for assistance. They are told that their proposal or application is very interesting but unfortunately falls outside the criteria for acceptance. They are then given a list of other organizations that might be able to accommodate them. If this happens more than once, it is likely no one is genuinely interested in the proposal. There is only one way to find out – ask what is wrong with it, what the weak points are, why it is unacceptable. You will need a thick skin if you go this far, because this service will be provided with equal enthusiasm, most probably in no uncertain terms and with no respect for your feelings. After all, you did *ask* for it. It is, however, worth exposing yourself to such possible humiliation. You may finally realize that, until now, you have been chasing an illusion. Or, perhaps, a number of feasible alternatives will emerge.

A similar attitude is observable in many teachers, particularly at university level. With a few exceptions, who are frequently considered eccentric, they are generally unwilling to declare their student's achievements below par. They prefer to precede criticism with praise and therefore emphasize those areas in which the student in question has done well before moving on to make a number of critical remarks. It is very likely that the kind words are a sugar coating intended make the bitter pill a little easier to swallow.

In the business world, managers and other bosses have bitter pills aplenty to dish out. The problem for the recipient is to see through the sugar coating to the true meaning as soon as possible because, in the end, the pill will have to swallowed anyway. 'Perhaps', your superior will say, 'Perhaps it is time for us to go our separate ways'. Or: 'Perhaps your undeniable talents can be put to better use elsewhere'. But ask 'Where?' and you will receive a vague reply.

I speak from experience. While I was still a student, I was thrown out of a free-lance job. This happened very unexpectedly and was, I thought at the time, totally unjustified. Now – sadder, wiser and older – I can recognize the signs that I failed to see at the time. My colleagues had accompanied their praise for my work with small criticisms – and the criticisms were always the same.

My boss tried to cheer me up. Perhaps I could realize my potential elsewhere.

'But your company is the only one in the country in this field', I replied. 'And you take on the staff. That doesn't give me much of a chance.'

'Where there's a will, there's a way', he said. 'Look at Beckenbauer (he was a famed German footballer at the time). He doesn't keep to any pre-planned pattern of play. He goes his own way. He is as stubborn as a mule. But it is he who gets that vital goal.'

'So, if you were the manager of the German national team, you would never have selected Beckenbauer?'

Touché, I thought. But the boss lost no time in escorting me personally to the door. I have never seen him again. Once a particular course of action has been decided upon, there is no going back. The discussion may continue, but only to explain the decision in greater detail. Anyone who responds emotionally or with the slightest signs of aggression only gives the other an opportunity to bring the whole painful experience to an end. The rules of the game have been broken. My boss wished only that he could fire me in an atmosphere that was as *gezellig* as possible. I ruined that for him.

Perhaps Beckenbauer would never have been selected for the Dutch national team. The antics of the Brazilian footballer Romario during his time as a player in the Netherlands bear witness to that. Romario comes from a culture where the people at the top live by a different set of rules. They can ignore the laws that apply to the mass of the people and generally get away with it. They celebrate this almost unlimited freedom by adopting a particularly brash kind of individualism. This made Romario – who played sublimely during the 1994 World Cup – totally unsuitable for the Dutch premier division club PSV. The Brazilian followed his own rules when it came to training and other agreements with the club. He more than made up for this with his dazzling performances in games, but never became the undisputed hero of the fans. His criticisms of the manager, his fellow players and the club directors – superficial in his eyes – eventually proved to be very fundamental. PSV and Romario parted company, and the star went to Barcelona. At the Spanish club he encountered similar problems with the Dutch manager, Johan Cruyff.

De kruik gaat net zo lang naar te water, tot zij barst, say the Dutch. The water jug goes so often to the well that it finally breaks. And then you are in trouble. You can try and preserve *gezelligheid* to the very last moment, but you cannot achieve the impossible. The contact is broken. You find yourself on the street.

You go to a bar and stare at the wall. Across the road, on the other corner, there's another bar. One drink follows another. The barman puts them in front of you with a curt *'Alstublief'*. It is sometimes not easy to be in Holland. What use is it then being a prince in your own square metre?

Chapter 6

A DEBT OF HONOUR

THE DUTCH AND THEIR ETHNIC MINORITIES

Growing ethnic diversity. The empire and the collective guilty conscience. Increasing racial tension. The Netherlands as a haven for immigrants. Integration versus adaptation.

On one Saturday every summer, the Coolsingel in Rotterdam is transformed into a tropical boulevard. The weather usually enters into the spirit of things and the temperature rises way above the twenty degree mark. An enormous crowd stands expectantly along the side of the road. They are waiting for the Antillean carnival. Traditionally, the high point of the festivities takes place in front of the city hall. The mayor stands up on the balcony, his chain of office around his neck, watching the parade

The parade varies – it is different every year – between one and a half and two kilometres long. An enormous convoy of trucks carries the cream of Dutch salsa, merengue and kaseko bands through the streets of the city. In between the trucks, dance groups give sparkling performances, usually exotic dances from their home countries, far away across the sea. There are also a lot of traditional carnival floats – most with a theme and a some of them with a beauty queen waving to the crowd. In recent years, African groups have also taken part in the procession.

In the evening, the carnival continues in gigantic halls, but Rotterdam's white population is hardly represented. The widely varied coloured minority groups in the city have their own centres of entertainment, which are relatively separate from those of the rest of the population.

During the Summer Carnival, Rotterdam shows a friendly, multicultural face. This smile can, however, also turn into a menacing grimace. When, for example, 13 percent of the seats in the municipal elections go to xenophobic parties with fascist tendencies, whose members equate a non-Dutch back-ground with crime, drug abuse and social security fraud, and accuse the 'for-eigners' of stealing 'our' jobs.

During a survey carried out by the Social and Cultural Planning Office in 1993, 50 per cent of those asked said that 'too many people of other nationa-lities lived in the Netherlands'. On the question of whether they would like to live next door to people of other nationalities, the participants in the survey were split roughly down the middle. Only 13 per cent of people, however, found the presence of foreigners in the country a problem. Two years pre-viously, 43 per cent of Dutch people thought that there were too many for-eigners living in the country. Other figures confirmed this trend of decreasing tolerance. In 1985, 20 per cent of people said that Dutch families – however you may define 'Dutch' – should be given priority in the allocation of muni-cipal housing. By 1993, this had risen to 36 per cent.

What can be said about this? It is tempting to turn the figures around and say that almost two thirds of Dutch people consider it normal that families of foreign origin have as much right to a house as they do; or that 87 per cent of people do not consider the presence of 'foreigners' a problem and half do not believe that there are too many of them walking around on Dutch soil. Com-pared to some countries, the Netherlands is a haven of tolerance. The Dutch are keen to point the finger at Germany, where revived racial violence in the nineties has already cost several lives. Racial attacks occur very rarely in the Netherlands. On the other hand, there is very little difference between the Ne-therlands and their neighbours to the east when it comes to voting for extreme right-wing parties. In the last parliamentary elections in 1994, they even managed to win three seats, while in Germany, the five percent threshold is an effective obstacle to the presence of radical splinter groups in the representa-tive organs of government. In the most recent national elections in Germany, extreme right-wing parties received half the percentage of votes of their counterparts in the Netherlands.

RACISM IS A SPIRITUAL INCONVENIENCE
TO 'RIGHT-THINKING' PEOPLE

Faced with German racism, the Dutch tend to invoke the ghost of Hitler, im-plicitly casting themselves as the good guys. Similar developments in other

European countries, such as the success of the *Front National* in France or the participation of the neo-fascists in government in Italy generally result, however, in little more than concerned articles in the left-wing media. Does this mean that the Netherlands is losing its reputation for tolerance?

There is certainly a widely held conviction that the recent rise of the extreme right in the Netherlands is not a 'normal' development. This is illustrated, on the one hand, by the explosive proliferation of anti-racism groups, complete with telephone numbers which you can call to report, for example, racist graffiti; and, on the other hand, by the mental acrobatics performed by 'right-thinking' people to overcome the spiritual inconvenience caused by obvious racial hatred. In their view, people who dislike foreigners or vote for extreme right parties are actually protesting about other social problems: unemployment, inner-city decay or their lack of confidence in the government. Anyone who complains about the 'filthy Turks' in the street therefore really means that it is about time something was done about renovating the houses in the area. It is very difficult to establish the truth of such reasoning. It is, after all, an interpretation and not based on empirical fact – any more, for that matter, than the standpoint that anyone who talks about the filthy Turks actually means filthy Turks and nothing more.

It is important in examining this phenomenon to bear in mind that liberalism, tolerance and respect for human rights may have gained a solid foothold in many European countries, but that parallel currents still exist in which intolerance and xenophobia are the order of the day. Before the Second World War, political parties which advocated such ideas enjoyed considerable (in some cases, very considerable) support in most Western European countries. Their leaders were admitted to the top levels of serious political and social debate.

During the Second World War, the extreme right proved itself to be capable of such shocking atrocities that all of the countries occupied by the Nazis were practically free of this political disease for several decades. But now half a century has passed since the liberation. Those who experienced the war at first hand are old and increasingly in the minority. For the majority of the population, the Second World War is history, part of the collective memory. This has had the effect of weakening, so to speak, the deterrent effect of Auschwitz. The power now enjoyed by the extreme right is not so very far removed from the position it was in before Hitler sent his armies out to conquer Europe. This is also true of the Netherlands, although it must not be forgotten that, before the war, the pillar system was still very strong and provided an effective counter to extreme-right ideas. The pillars have now crumbled but, in national terms, the racist political parties have not yet equalled the four per cent of the votes that the National Socialist Movement managed to scrape together with great difficulty in the 1930s.

A PROBLEM OF SOCIAL ADAPTATION

The problem may be one of social adaptation. The Netherlands is becoming more multiracial – more 'colourful', as the anti-racists put it. For the past thirty years, the country has become a haven for immigrants, most of whom have settled in the centres of the larger towns and cities. Although only 7 per cent of the population is of non-Dutch origin, it appears to be more because they are concentrated in certain areas. In 2015, this percentage will most likely have doubled. At the same time, they are gradually integrating with the original Dutch population. At present 11 per cent of marriages are interracial. There are, of course, no records of those who live together or who have relationships of other kinds. Dutch people may be a little alarmed to see a minaret rise up among the church towers of their town, but in twenty years or so they may be used to it; and especially if a form of Islam develops with specifically Dutch characteristics. The first signs of this are already appearing. One of the country's leading imams, for example, goes by the name of Abdoelwalid *van Bommel*.

Alle begin is moeilijk. Every beginning is hard. This is the first time that the Netherlands has been confronted with a group of immigrants from completely different cultures than those in Western Europe. The Dutch used to refer to its colonies proudly as 'the tropical Netherlands'. Now they see this 'tropical Netherlands' at the end of the street and it is taking a bit of getting used to.

MORE THAN JUST CHINESE-INDONESIAN RESTAURANTS

The collective memory of the tropical Netherlands and the colonies is still with us at all levels. It helps to determine the way in which the Dutch respond to foreigners, ethnic minorities, immigrants, non-Dutch nationals or whatever other name is given to them. No one consciously makes the connection, but for unprejudiced outsiders, it is clearly visible. The empire has left us with more than just a Chinese-Indonesian restaurant in every village.

The use of the word 'empire' is not an exaggeration. Until 1949, the Netherlands was the world's third colonial power, after Britain and France. This was due to its possession of the Dutch East Indies, now Indonesia, a group of islands in South-East Asia that cover a surface area larger than the entire continent of Europe. The Netherlands also ruled six small islands in the Caribbean and Suriname (formerly also known as Dutch Guyana), a large country to the north of Brazil but which had a population of only a few hundred thousand. It was the East Indies, with its population of 50 million (it is now four times that) that made the Netherlands a large colonial power. King Abdul Aziz, the creator of Saudi Arabia, asked his Dutch counterpart Queen Wilhelmina for advice, because he considered her the ruler of the most important Moslem kingdom in the world. After all, she was the sovereign of the fifty-million Indonesians, shiploads of whom made the pilgrimage to Mecca every year.

Possession of the Dutch East Indies was a source of great national pride. The majority of Dutch people believed that their fellow countrymen out there in *'Insulinde'* (Multatuli's name for the colony) or the *'Gordel van Smaragd'*, the Emerald Band, were doing a good job. They protected the people against the tyranny of the local chiefs and brought progress and civilization. There was a general assumption that the local population were grateful for the Dutch rule over their land. The Javan, it was commonly said, was the most kind-hearted being on the face of the earth. Reports of independence movements and nationalist leaders were therefore taken with a pinch of salt. They were rejected as isolated pockets of unrest which had not yet fully understood the beneficial nature of Dutch rule. They were completely isolated and of no significance whatsoever.

ALL GOOD INTENTIONS ENDED UP IN DISASTER

It was not so surprising that the Dutch public interpreted the situation so incorrectly. There were never more than 80,000 Dutch people in the colony at any one time. As a consequence of the development of mass tourism, more Dutch people have set foot in Indonesia since 1980 than in all the centuries before. Previous generations had to rely on hearsay and information filtered through the colonial sieve. The severing of the ties between the two countries was therefore an extremely traumatic experience. It created wounds that have still not healed fifty years later. Relations with Suriname, which became independent in 1975, are equally traumatic. Consequently, most people believe that the Dutch did not handle the process of decolonization at all well. All good intentions ended up in disaster.

The basis for the Dutch colonial empire was laid in the Golden Age by the United East India and the West India Companies. As we have seen, these were trading companies whose main purpose was to ship foreign goods of all kinds to Europe. They tried to acquire an import monopoly, and did not flinch from [259] the use of weapons to achieve this aim. The East India Company, for example, occupied the entire coastal area of Ceylon (now Sri Lanka) effectively cutting off access to the sea for the island's ruling monarchy and thereby ensuring its monopoly position. A minority group known as the 'Dutch Burghers' still lives in this coastal region and their Dutch surnames bear witness to the fact that their ancestors were company employees who married local girls. (Racism did not exist at this time. It only developed later when the Europeans realized that military superiority alone did not justify the subjugation of other races and began to believe that they were also morally and intellectually superior.)

Batavia (now Djakarta), where the East India Company had its headquarters, was also a multiracial city and the colonial élite were very much an integral part of the community.

Local rulers were not particularly enthusiastic about the trade monopoly that the East India Company imposed upon them. This frequently led to armed conflicts, which they generally lost. As a consequence of these wars, the territory governed by the Company steadily expanded, even though it was still very small compared to the area covered by present-day Indonesia. Threequarters of that was conquered – or, as colonial sources preferred to put it, pacified – only in the last half of the nineteenth century and the first fourteen years of the present century by the KNIL, the Royal Netherlands Indies Army. This was often accompanied by such cruelty, violence and bloodshed that it bears comparison with Vietnam.

The East India Company went bankrupt in 1799, after which the Dutch state took on its debts, possessions and political responsibilities.

The West India Company concentrated its activities in North and South

America. Initially, it focused on officially sanctioned piracy – known as *kaapvaart*, privateering – against Spain, with whom the Netherlands was at war until 1648. Every Dutch child learns the song of Piet Hein, who conquered the silver fleet. It has even become a favourite of football supporters. The company was also involved in normal trade, but that demanded greater efforts in the Americas than in Asia. Any reasonably well-advanced civilizations that the company could perhaps have done business with had been completely wiped out by the Spaniards in the decades following Columbus' discovery of the continent. The land was suitable in many areas for the cultivation of tropical crops (in the seventeenth and eighteenth centuries, sugar was in great demand) but there was no one there to grow them. The Spaniards and Portuguese had solved this problem by setting up plantations. Initially they enslaved the local population and, later, imported black slaves from West Africa. To take part in the sugar trade, the West India Company therefore had to get its hands on a number of plantations. It competed with the French, British and Danes to occupy a whole array of islands in the Caribbean. It also conquered the northeast of Brazil, driving out the Portuguese, and appointed Prince Maurits van Nassau-Siegen, second cousin to the Stadholder of the time, as governor.

Johan Maurits ruled like a Renaissance prince. He governed as fairly as he was able, became a patron of the arts, aimed to invest in the country and its people and dreamed of a new Netherlands on the Brazilian coast. This was, however, not to the liking of the company directors in Amsterdam, who were concerned more with the pursuit of profit. After seven years, Maurits resigned, an embittered man. In the years that followed, the company's power in the area was destroyed by a popular uprising in favour of the Portuguese. The prince, however, still has a place – as Mauricio – in the Brazilian folk memory and belongs in the nation's pantheon.

Eventually the company achieved permanent access to sugar plantations. Under the provisions of a peace agreement with Britain which brought an end to a trade war between the two countries, Suriname was exchanged for the trading post of New Amsterdam, which had already fallen into the hands of the Duke of York. The Duke decided to underline the new situation by giving the settlement a new name. New Amsterdam became New York.

At the end of the sixteenth century, privateers from Middelburg once returned home with a slave ship. The local people were so shocked that they immediately freed all the slaves. They and their fellow countrymen soon, however, became accustomed to the sight. The West India Company accounted for a considerable share of the slave trade from the very beginning. This meant that outposts had to be set up on the West African coast. Small areas were conquered and forts built on them with large dungeons where the slaves could be imprisoned until the ships arrived. The main settlement was Elmina on the Gold Coast, where families with Dutch surnames live to this day. The deserted fort still rises above the rooftops of the town and tourists are shown the secret staircase between the governor's bedroom and the quarters of the female slaves.

It is difficult to say how many slaves were transported to America on Dutch ships. Not does it matter. It is sufficient to know that they were stowed in their hundreds in the holds of slow sailing ships; and that the voyage was so harrowing that they needed a couple of months rest on the island of Curaçao (known appropriately as the 'slave plantation') before the company branded them like cattle and put them up for sale on the slave market. The mortality rate during the ocean crossing was very high – and was taken into account in the selling price, which was about ten times higher than was paid for the unfortunate wretches on the African coast. Despite modern claims to the contrary, the slave trade was not particularly profitable. The death rate must therefore have been very high.

It was not necessary for the Dutch slave traders to round up their human merchandise themselves. Along the West African coast there were large, well-organized kingdoms, where slavery was already a large-scale phenomenon. Supply and demand therefore came together. The fortress at Elmina appears now and again on the television in programmes documenting the excesses of the period. The substantial part played by the Netherlands in the slave trade is considered a dark chapter in the country's history. But unlike their competitors for the gains to be made from the 'middle passage', the Dutch slave traders did not have to contend with opposition to their activities at home. In England, a mass anti-slavery movement grew up during the eighteenth century. During its radical period, the French Revolution abolished the entire system. In the Netherlands, no such movements developed and parliament abolished slavery in two steps – in the East Indies in 1859 and in the Caribbean colonies in 1864 – compensating the owners for their 'losses'. Anyone wishing to go into the slave trade now faces a maximum prison sentence of twelve years.

There are, however, signs here and there of a guilty conscience. In the eighteenth century a free black inhabitant of what is now Ghana became renowned when he was awarded a doctorate in theology by Leiden University. His thesis was a defence of slavery. And one of the last companies in the Netherlands to specialize in the buying and selling of human beings was known by the extremely neutral name of '*Middelburgsche Commercie Compagnie*'. No one defends the moral acceptability of street lighting. It is only when customs or institutions acquire a moral foundation that they become controversial.

The development of racist ideologies in the nineteenth century had a great deal to do with this phenomenon. White Europeans – including the Dutch – had to reconcile their position as colonial rulers with the fundamental Christian idea that all men are equal before God. Anyone who traded in other peoples or deprived them of their basic human rights in some other way, therefore had to come up with some good arguments. One of these was to 'prove' that they were of an inferior species, or at least different in some way. Consequently, the trade in Africans was frequently justified by reference to the biblical story of Noah, the builder of the Ark and the forefather of all mankind. Noah had cursed his son Ham. Clearly enough, the Africans were the descendants of Ham. The various pseudo-scientific attempts to link genetic differences between races to greater or lesser intelligence are another example of this kind of reasoning.

There is also a non-racist form of justification for European colonial rule which enjoyed considerable support in the Netherlands. It was closely related to Kipling's famous concept of the 'white man's burden'. The Europeans brought civilization to the world, nurturing and educating barbarian peoples until they achieved a level of development comparable to that of their mentors. Until that level was actually reached, European domination remained a necessary evil. The campaigns of conquest undertaken by the KNIL in the Indonesian islands from 1870 on were in part officially justified as crusades against the slavery practised by uncivilized local rulers. According to the official propaganda, the entire campaign was a war of liberation.

At the same time, colonialism became an increasingly 'white' affair. This was largely due to the arrival of the spouses. In the days of sailing ships, a journey from Amsterdam to the East Indies and back could take a year and a half. It was considered normal if a third of the crew embarked on their final voyage to eternal life on the way. The death rate in the colonial outposts was also high, because the newcomers were very susceptible to tropical diseases. The Dutch made this problem even worse by set-tling in places that reminded them of home – marshy river deltas. Batavia looked very much like a Dutch city, complete with canals and bridges, and provided a perfect habitat for malaria-carrying mosquitoes. Im-mediately after the conquest of North-East Brazil, the Dutch moved the centre of government from the town of Olinda – which, like the Afri-can slave forts, has now been de-clared a monument to mankind by Unesco – to the fishing village of Re-

18TH+19TH CENTURY | 20TH CENTURY

cife, which was situated lower down on a nearby river estuary. Recife now has a population of millions and is still regularly disrupted by floods.

These were not the kind of places to send women. The United East India Company did experiment with *'compagniesdochters'*, women recruited from the dregs of Dutch society, but those that survived the journey did nothing to add to the moral element in the far-flung outposts of the empire. Moreover, the colonial masters had little need of 'consolation' from home when there were mistresses aplenty available to them from among the slaves. The colonial system as a whole contained a clear element of structural rape.

The construction of the Suez Canal and the arrival of steam-powered ships made the journey shorter and less hazardous. This made the tropics a safer bet for well-brought-up young women looking for a secure future. The colonial masters – themselves changed now that the greater chances of survival made colonial service more than just a desperate refuge for bankrupts and others who were well advised, for one reason or another, not to show their faces in the known world – wanted to find a nice girl of good stock and get married. The arrival of these fresh young spouses resulted in a powerful 'Europeanization' of the colonies. They fiercely took on their local competitors, the unofficial native wives (known in Indonesia as *njais)* and mistresses of their husbands. They also tried to lay siege to the *'sociëteiten'*, the gentlemen's clubs where far too much strong liquor was consumed, but with considerably less success.

They had little choice in this – the colonies were still a man's world. European wives ran their households but their status depended entirely on the position and reputation of their husbands. They were wives and mothers, and nothing more. They therefore had to keep their husbands on the straight and narrow as far as possible, at least in the eyes of the outside world.

Bumi Manusia (Earth of Mankind) – written by Indonesian author Pramoedja Ananta Toer and the first part of what will probably develop into the definitive Indonesian novel cycle – tells the story of how a *njai* is robbed of her child after the death of her old-fashioned and therefore not officially married master by his white Dutch family. The novel is a condensation of historical fact and makes a direct link between such incidents and the development of Indonesian nationalism.

In this way, an element of racial segregation crept into colonial society.

ETHICAL POLITICS

In 1899, the liberal politician Conrad van Deventer published an article in the political-cultural monthly magazine *De Gids* that caused great uproar. The article was entitled *'Een Eereschuld'*, A Debt of Honour, and introduced a new concept of 'ethical politics'.

Van Deventer showed clearly with facts and figures that the Netherlands had always exploited the East Indies, sucking the colony dry. He argued that the Dutch therefore had a debt of honour that current generations were morally bound to repay. One of his suggestions was that, from then on, the colonies should be governed in the interests of the local population, so that, in time they would be ready to rule themselves independently. Much of what he proposed closely resembled what we today call 'development policy'.

Van Deventer was not alone. He was part of a group of intellectuals at and around the University of Leiden, which offered a course of study for colonial administrators. The course included Indonesian languages and law, which contained an increasing element of anthropology as the science itself developed. Their great hero was the brilliant scholar Christiaan Snouck Hurgronje, an *uomo universale*, who had built up an enormous and widely varied base of knowledge on the Orient around an Arabian course offered by the university. Snouck Hurgronje had genuine admiration for the cultures of the East Indies and there are indications that he secretly converted to Islam. He impressed upon his students – the future colonial administrators – that they should not only learn about the native cultures, but respect and even admire them, and that the colonies should be structured on the basis of this respect rather than on the pursuit of profit. The inheritor of his spiritual legacy, Cornelis van Vollenhoven, codified the *adat* – the indigenous Indonesian legal systems – and argued throughout his life that the government of the colonies should stick as closely to the *adat* as possible.

Public opinion in the Netherlands had been prepared for this approach to the country's colonial responsibilities by Multatuli – who I already mentioned earlier – and his long-standing bestseller 'Max Havelaar or the Coffee Auctions of the Dutch Trading Company'. In the novel, through the eyes of Batavus Droogstoppel, Multatuli portrays the Netherlands as a small-minded and hypocritical colonial master, which wishes only to earn as much as it can from its power in the East Indies. Max Havelaar, the noble leading figure, is ruined because he defends the oppressed natives and his superiors simply drop him like a stone. The story is practically identical to what happened to Multatuli himself. It should, however, be noted that the novel is not a plea for emancipation of the native people from the colonial yoke, but for more paternalistic government on the part of the Netherlands. The traditional native chiefs, whom Havelaar – as an official in the colonial service – must keep under control, are held primarily responsible for the exploitation of their people; the colonial bureaucracy is guilty only indirectly. One of the crucial passages in the book is a speech given by Havelaar to the chiefs of Lebak, the division for which he is responsible. He, the Dutchman, explains to them how they should rule wisely on the basis of their own principles. He, Max Havelaar, clearly knew better than the traditional chiefs before him.

General van Heutz, the commander of the KNIL, renowned for the extreme aggression with which it performed its duties, was responsible for a number of activities which would most certainly qualify as war crimes according to the standards applied in Nuremburg and Tokyo. He was also a faithful supporter of ethical politics. Snouck Hurgronje's advice to Van Heutz was such that he must surely count as one of the founding fathers of psychological warfare. And, if the local population proved to be less than enthusiastic about the tactics of ethical politics, the artillery was always primed and ready.

Yet the advocates of ethical politics were serious and their concern was genuine. Colonial business interests, infuriated by the administrators educated at Leiden, set up a rival faculty at Utrecht. The *adat*, so respected by the ethical bureaucrats, had stood in the way of capitalist development for too long. Whether the bureaucrats genuinely respected the *adat* is still a matter of debate today. They certainly respected Van Vollenhoven and his studies, as well as the hundreds of pleas he made – anonymously – for ethical politics in the *Nieuw Rotterdamsche Courant*, the paper read by the intelligentsia. But Van Vollenhoven himself visited the East Indies once only, for a few weeks. Other than that his ideas were based on information that reached him from the colony in Leiden. Modern research has shown that the local population often had a different interpretation of the *adat* – which was not a written set of laws but was passed on by word of mouth – than the well-intentioned colonial officials who had studied under Van Vollenhoven. When that happened, it was generally believed to be the locals who were misguided.

In the meantime, the Dutch public had come to believe that they did indeed owe a debt of honour to the colony, and it was gradually prepared for independence. The key word was 'gradually' – even the most progressive supporters of ethical politics believed that this process would take generations. The response to the nationalist movements was therefore rather contorted. Radical leaders were interned in the Boven-Digoel camp in New Guinea, where the indigenous population still lived in the Stone Age and censorship was imposed to keep a firm grip on the opposition press.

More moderate nationalists argued for a relationship between the Netherlands and Indonesia in which the latter was permitted internal self-rule. The Dutch government rejected this proposal and appointed governor-generals who had not been infected by the ethical-political virus.

After the attack on Pearl Harbour, the Netherlands declared war on Japan. The whole house of cards in the East Indies collapsed within three months. Most of the eighty-thousand Dutch people in the colony looked on with amazement as the local population, rather than rallying behind the Dutch flag, waited with a certain enthusiasm to see how they would be treated by the new occupiers. When the Japanese arrived they gave the budding nationalism a free reign, in as far as the nationalist leaders identified with their war aims. But at the same time, the occupying armies proved themselves capable of terrible atrocities. They looted the country and terrorized the people. The Dutch colonists were interned, with the men and women in separate camps, where there was great lack of food and other basic facilities.

[267]

When the Japanese capitulated after the bombing of Hiroshima and Nagasaki, their occupation of Indonesia was still intact. The nationalist leaders Sukarno and Hatta took advantage of the power vacuum to declare independence. This came as a great surprise to the inmates of the internment camps, who had assumed they would simply carry on where they left off. They soon discovered that they were safer where they were than outside, because radical nationalists were hunting down their former colonial masters. The government in the Netherlands – where the occupiers had also been driven out – declared that the nationalist leaders, who had after all cooperated with the Japanese, were just as much traitors as those at home who had collaborated with the Nazis. They sent in an expeditionary force to restore order. The intention was not to re-establish colonial rule – an independent Indonesia was acceptable as long as it was on Dutch terms. The Dutch government envisaged a loose federation of autonomous areas where the *adat* and local customs would be fully respected. This led to an extra four years of war in the region. Under great pressure from the international community, the Netherlands entered into negotiations with the new republic, but little progress was made. On two occasions the expeditionary force was ordered to conduct an offensive, known euphemistically as 'police actions'. It was a bloody affair, in which the Dutch also proved capable of cruel reprisals. Eventually the United Nations as good as forced the Netherlands to cast Indonesia loose. For the sake of appearances, Sukarno and his nationalists agreed to a federation, of which their republic would be a part. But in the years following independence, they simply annexed the remaining states.

Sukarno had to agree to New Guinea staying in Dutch hands. Formally it was a trust territory of the United Nations. The new Indonesian president pursued a policy of confrontation to bring the region under his power and finally succeeded in 1963 when the UN once again made it clear that it would no longer support any further obstinacy on the part of the Netherlands. The Dutch foreign minister, the conservative and extreme anti-Communist Joseph Luns, was so enraged that he later refused a request to send a Dutch battalion to South Vietnam on the grounds that the Netherlands no longer had a role to play in Asia.

The dismantling of the East Indies provided the Netherlands with its first two genuine minority groups. A large part – about 250,000 – of the *Indo's*, people of mixed Dutch-Indonesian descent, fled to the Netherlands. They had developed a complete identity of their own – particularly in and around Batavia – complete with a unique version of the Dutch language and, with a few exceptions, had remained loyal to the colonial regime. Afraid of reprisals, they now sought refuge in what they considered their fatherland.

Once in the Netherlands, the Indos did their best to accentuate the Dutch side of their identity. In fact, they had little choice. They were initially housed in camps and boarding houses where social workers gave them a rather harsh introduction to Dutch norms and values. Many of their instructors, for example, tried to persuade them to abandon their rice-based diet and those who served up traditional Dutch potatoes with the evening meal were given priority in the allocation of houses. The Indos tolerated this because they had chosen to live in the Netherlands and tried to bring their children up to be as Dutch as possible. In spite of this, the entire community has suffered to this day from a debilitating homesickness for what has become an idealized image of their home country. This is known in Malay as *tempoe doeloe*, the 'olden days'.

In every large town or city in the Netherlands, you will regularly see posters announcing a *pasar malam* (evening market) or a *pasar dalam* (covered market). The venue is usually a local sports centre and the markets offer a broad cultural programme, so that the *tempoe doeloe* can be created for a short time, within the restrictions imposed upon it by Dutch society and the cold maritime climate. The younger generations are in the process of rediscovering their Indonesian roots. They are very critical of the way their parents and grandparents were received in the fifties and seek to develop new ties with Indonesia.

THE MOLUCCANS FELT BETRAYED AND USED BY THE DUTCH

Around the same time as the Indos, the Moluccans also arrived in the country. These were soldiers from the Moluccan Islands, who had fought in the KNIL and their families. They came to the Netherlands not out of choice, but because they had obeyed the orders of their military superiors to do so. On arriving on Dutch soil, they were immediately demobilized, much to their surprise and anger. The Christian community on the minute island of Ambon had traditionally made a sizable contribution to the colonial army. The loyalty of the Moluccan soldiers to their Dutch masters was, if anything, stronger than that of the Indos and Indonesian independence held little promise for them. On Ambon itself, there was a separatist movement that received the support of the Dutch regime, which did not make the situation any easier. Hence, the orders to embark for the Netherlands and the subsequent demobilization. On Ambon itself, a Republic of the South Moluccas had been declared, but this was very short-lived.

The Moluccans felt betrayed and used by the Dutch. They refused to leave the camps set up for them in the Netherlands and the men continued to consider themselves soldiers. They resisted any attempt to integrate them into Dutch society and embraced the ideal of the Republic of the South Moluccas. A government-in-exile was hastily formed and received loyal and very disciplined support.

The Dutch government was unequivocal in its rejection of this ideal, and generally continued to pursue a policy of integration. This led to occasional conflict with the exiled community and, in the sixties, the Dutch looked on in amazement as the Moluccans consistently refused to exchange their now leaky barrack homes in the camps for nice houses outside. Even the more moderate elements finally agreed to move only on the condition that they were housed together in separate communities. The acceptance of decent housing would be taken as a sign that their stay in the Netherlands was no longer temporary and that the men had finally accepted their discharge from the army. They still considered themselves soldiers – they were very disciplined and did not use violence against the Dutch authorities. But they refused to give an inch.

In the seventies, a new generation of Moluccans emerged that employed completely different weapons. Inspired by the liberation movements of the sixties and organizations like the PLO, radical splinter groups adopted terrorist tactics. It started with the taking of hostages in the Indonesian Embassy. Later, they hijacked a train full of passengers and, on one occasion, a children's day-care centre. The first fatalities occurred. The Dutch government responded invariably by setting up a crisis centre, complete with psychologists and psychiatrists, and holding consultations with the terrorists which, in one case, lasted three weeks. This wore the terrorists down and enabled them to be overpowered by élite commando units from the Dutch army.

The Moluccan community was firm in its rejection of these terrorist activities, but took advantage of the incidents – which attracted the attention of the world – to demand understanding for their situation. They referred to the terrorists as *'onze jongens'*, our lads. This was vague and subject to a wide variety of interpretations. The Moluccans failed to recruit support for their ideal outside their own community but, on the other hand, the terrorist attacks did not provoke anti-Moluccan sentiments of any consequence among wider Dutch society. The Moluccans themselves disappeared from public view. Statistics show that the newer generations have been reasonably successful in finding a place for themselves in society without entirely losing their identity. In the seventies, the communities that grew up when the moderate elements moved out of the camps suffered from typical 'ghetto-related' problems, such as drug abuse and unemployment, but these have now become less acute. The old soldiers – now old men – who still refused to accept their enforced demobilization, allowed the last of the barracks to be renovated in the 1990s, from which the conclusion could be drawn that they were no longer seen as temporary accommodation. The tenacity of these old fighters received sympathetic treatment in the media. The ideal of the Republic of the South Moluccas lives on – as does the government-in-exile – but it is increasingly taking on the characteristics of an 'official' ideal, a kind of 'Kingdom of Heaven' which only the good and the righteous can enter. And, with the passing of time, the Dutch public have become convinced that the Netherlands did, indeed, betray the Moluccans.

The Netherlands' colonial past in Indonesia can still evoke strong emotions from time to time. When Lou de Jong, the author of the official history of the Netherlands, wrote the sections on the war with the Japanese and the subsequent Indonesian fight for independence, he was overwhelmed with criticism. For the first and only time, he found himself pressurized from outside to change the text. He had to tone down references to Dutch war crimes during the period, using less controversial terms like 'excesses'. In 1994, novelist Graa Broomsma was taken to court for comparing the Dutch expeditionary force to Indonesia between 1945 and 1949 with the SS. He won the case easily on the grounds of freedom of expression. It is, however, significant that this was not a civil lawsuit, but a criminal case brought by the Public Prosecutor.

Just how sensitive the colonial past is can be seen from the experiences of essayist Rudy Kousbroek, a consistent critic of the *tempoe doeloe* legend. Kousbroek was interned by the Japanese in a camp during the Second World War. He never tires of insisting – notably in his compilation *'Het Oost-Indisch kampsyndroom'* – that the conditions inside the camps were no worse than those outside. He notes that the memoirs of other ex-prisoners frequently refer to the fact that they were given the same treatment by their Japanese captors as they dished out to the 'coolies', the indigenous Indonesian population. The prisoners complained particularly that they had to greet their captors with a traditional Japanese bow. This was an unacceptable affront to their white (i.e. racist) sense of superiority. Kousbroek also points out that nowhere in the camp literature is there any reference to the Indonesian victims of the Japanese terror.

Kousbroek's criticisms are very far-reaching, but the arguments against him are equally vociferous and the entire debate seldom touches the essentials of the problem. Fifty years on, the wounds are still open and raw, and the truth about what happened in those terrible years is surrounded by taboo and myth, making it impossible to look back on the period with any genuine objectivity. It has, without doubt, left deep scars on all those involved and perhaps on the country as a whole.

The history of decolonization in the Caribbean is no more edifying. The colonial authorities had learned their lesson from Indonesia – they would not make the same mistakes again. Dutch colonial possessions in the region were modest – Curaçao, Aruba and Bonaire, three small islands off the coast of Venezuela with a total of less than two hundred thousand inhabitants; Sint Eustatius, Saba and half of Sint Maarten, three minute islands to the south of the Dominican Republic and Puerto Rico. These together constituted the Netherlands Antilles. Lastly, on the coast of Guyana, was Suriname, a region of wild jungle with an urban enclave in Paramaribo, which was surrounded by

[272]

THE NETHERLANDS, AS A MODERN COUNTRY, FELT A LITTLE ASHAMED

After the Second World War, the Netherlands did in the Caribbean what it had intended to do in Indonesia – it gave the colonies self-rule. This was laid down in the Charter for the Kingdom, which divided the country into three parts. The Netherlands itself was responsible for foreign affairs and defence for all three. The other two parts, Suriname and the Antilles, sent a minister to represent their interests in the Dutch cabinet but, other than that, had complete freedom to go their own way.

The reformers of the sixties derived great inspiration from colonial liberation movements. The younger generation, kicking against the conservatism of their parents, identified more with nation-builders such as Julius Nyerere, Kenneth Kaunda and Nelson Mandela – who was already world-renowned – than with the ethicists of the colonial period. And the General Assembly of the United Nations – full of representatives of recently decolonized countries – was keen on reminding the Dutch delegation that the tricolour with the horizontal red, white and blue stripes was still flying in the Caribbean. And the Netherlands, as a modern country, felt a little ashamed.

Events in Curaçao reinforced this feeling. Anti-government demonstrations in 1969 ended in a riot in which the business centre was looted. The government in The Hague – with the support of the social democratic opposition – ordered Dutch Marines to be sent in to restore order. This was met with a great deal of criticism at home and abroad. The use of Dutch troops to call a bunch of poor and desperate wretches to heel was inconsistent with the country's image of itself as a modern democratic society. And particularly at the end of the 1960s, when so many young people in Europe had a poster of Che Guevara hanging over their beds. Joop den Uijl, the social democratic leader, realized more clearly than ever that Dutch colonial possessions had to be relinquished as soon as possible. He vowed that, if he were to become prime minister, he would at least guarantee the independence of Suriname. Shortly after, he became prime minister.

THE 'UMBRELLA STRUCTURE' OF THE KINGDOM HAD ITS ADVANTAGES

In Suriname and the Antilles, however, the response to the Charter was generally favourable. If the Queen visited the overseas territories, she was greeted by enthusiastic crowds. In the Surinamese parliament, independence was demanded only by a small splinter party, consisting of intellectuals who had studied in the Netherlands and had been introduced to nationalism and modern theories on the Third World. The riots in Willemstad were directed against government corruption and low salaries, not against the Dutch flag.

The 'umbrella structure' of the Kingdom had its advantages. The Netherlands repaid its debt of honour by making sizable contributions to the former colonies, where the standard of living was significantly lower. Per capita income in the Antilles is now approximately half that in the Netherlands.

On the other hand, the government in The Hague made little effort to monitor how these funds were allocated. It was assumed that this would occur according to Dutch norms. And, what is more, they had abandoned the paternalism of their predecessors, who had the débâcle of Indonesia on their consciences.

The Antilles and Suriname are essentially Caribbean societies. An exemplary democratic constitution conceals a system of nepotism and corruption, where electoral support is provided in exchange for favours and tangible benefits. Politicians who do not take part in this system, lose their power. This offers considerable scope for corrupt practices.

By clever negotiation, the élites in the Antilles successfully resisted attempts by the government in The Hague to give the territories greater independence, until the Dutch politicians finally gave up. Aruba managed to negotiate itself a separate status in the Kingdom, apart from the Antilles. Since 1990, The Hague has accepted that the Caribbean territories are a permanent part of the Kingdom.

The elite in Suriname did permit themselves to be talked into independence, partly on the basis of the pledge that they would receive a bonus of several billion guilders if it did take the step. The Surinamese parliament accepted the offer by a majority of one and a referendum was effectively ruled out.

Suriname is a multiracial society. After the black slaves were given their freedom, they exchanged forced labour on the plantations for a usually poverty-stricken existence in Paramaribo. To replace them the government recruited contract workers, first in India and then, when the British authorities imposed a ban on this, in Java. The plantations finally folded because these imported workers did not renew their contracts. Consequently, the population became a mixture of an approximately equal number of Creoles of African ancestry and Hindus, together with a smaller group of Javans. There were also even smaller groups of Chinese, native Indians and 'maroons', the descendants of black slaves who had escaped into the jungle. The various groups lived closely together and the political parties generally followed the same lines. The government, however, was a multiracial coalition. The system bore great similarities to the Dutch 'pillar' structure, with the pillars representing racial rather than religious groups.

BIMRI – A NEW CITY OF MIRACLES

The divisions in this society were so sharp that many people feared they would erupt into violence if the Netherlands withdrew. When it became clear in 1975 that independence was inevitable, half of the people 'voted with their feet' – they bought tickets to Schiphol before they had to exchange their Dutch passports for Surinamese ones. The Creoles in particular headed for a new city of miracles whose fame had spread across the Atlantic Ocean – *Bimri*, where they knew that a golden future awaited them.

Bimri is a distortion of *Bijlmermeer*, a polder to the southeast of Amsterdam, on which apartment blocks were built shoulder-to-shoulder at the end of the sixties. Parks were laid out between the blocks and there was a strict separation of motorized and pedestrian traffic. Gigantic parking garages were built to accommodate the cars of Amsterdammers who would use their increased prosperity to rent one of these attractive and roomy flats. But the

[274]

people of the city found the Bijlmer too impersonal and too far away. It became a second choice for them. People who wanted to settle in Amsterdam were often given a flat in the Bijlmer, but generally considered it a temporary solution. For most Dutch residents, the flats were a first step towards finding something better closer to the city centre.

When the Surinamese immigrants started to arrive in their thousands, they therefore had little trouble in obtaining a flat in Bimri. Until they found jobs, they were eligible for a social security benefit. The government had also introduced rent rebates for the slightly more expensive new homes, so that they were accessible for people on lower incomes. Bimri soon became Suriname's second largest city.

The Hindus preferred The Hague, far from the Creoles. Many Creoles also settled in the *Oud-West* district of Rotterdam, where it was also easy to find a place to live because the housing was run-down and badly in need of renovation – and therefore no longer met the requirements of the increasingly prosperous local population. Consequently whole areas grew up within the major cities with an overwhelmingly immigrant population. The 'foreign' atmosphere of these districts was intensified by the fact that the local authorities followed the example of their predecessors in the colonies and made no concerted effort to impose their culture and language on the minorities under their jurisdiction. This is not surprising for a society founded on the basic principle of 'sovereignty in one's own domain'. Seen in this light, the respect shown by Van Vollenhoven for the *adat* and Snouck Hurgronje for Oriental cultures was perhaps more typical of the ethnocentricity of the Dutch than they themselves realized.

THEY HAD TO FIND THEMSELVES A PLACE ON THE LABOUR MARKET

The new arrivals had to find themselves a place on the labour market. They thought that this would not be too much of a problem because there was work for everyone – more than the Dutch themselves could handle.

The labour market had indeed come under pressure during the boom of the sixties. Salaries had increased considerably, and with them the purchasing power of the less prosperous groups in society. Yet it remained difficult for employers to recruit personnel, especially for unskilled work. Drastic salary increases might have solved the problem, or the involvement of women in the labour market on a large scale – which had been tried successfully in Finland. Dutch employees, however, chose a different option. In cooperation with the government, they began recruiting in the Middle East and North Africa, in particular in Morocco and Turkey. In doing so, they were following in the footsteps of their German counterparts, who were also faced with labour shortages.

In Morocco and Turkey, on the other hand, there was high unemployment. The Netherlands set up recruitment agencies in the two countries, agreeing with Germany that they should not get in each other's way. Since Germany had already been recruiting in the larger cities, the Netherlands focused on the rural areas. Consequently, there was an influx of Berbers and people from Eastern Turkey, most of whom intended to save as much as they could in a couple of years and start their own businesses back at home. This new wave of immigrants came directly from their traditional rural communities to the world of the large Western European city.

MOST GUEST WORKERS EVENTUALLY BROUGHT THEIR FAMILIES OVER

These immigrants were known as *'gastarbeiders'*, guest workers. They were given lodgings in boarding houses and quickly learned a painful lesson – although the wages were far higher than at home, so were the prices. This thwarted their plans to save. Furthermore, life in a completely strange culture, far from their homes and families, proved more difficult than they had imagined. This was exacerbated by the fact that they were more or less stuck in their new environment. Most guest workers eventually brought their families over. The Dutch government could hardly object to this; the preservation of family values has always been one of the battle cries of Christian politicians, and social democrats – considering their ideological beliefs – could not object to workers wishing to be reunited with their families. This led to the development of relatively permanent Turkish and Moroccan communities, even though surveys have shown that the dream of returning to their home countries has never faded. They have increasingly come to accept, however, that it will never be anything more than a dream.

In 1973, the first oil crisis put an abrupt end to the myth of permanent prosperity. Europe experienced a series of economic recessions and unemployment returned. At the same time, labour intensive industries, such as textiles and shipbuilding, found themselves competing with cheaper rivals in the developing countries. Automation and digitalization also began to take their toll. The impact on the immigrant population was far-reaching. Unemployment among immigrant groups is now double the national average. In Rotterdam, where the more than hundred thousand immigrants make up a fifth of the population, they account for 36 per cent of those registered as unemployed. Living on social security benefits means a lower income. Going back home is not a realistic option because the economic situation is frequently worse than it was before they left. Generations have now grown up who consider the Netherlands more as their home than Morocco or Turkey. What was originally seen as a temporary solution to a labour problem has become a permanent migration.

The influx of immigrants from Suriname occurred after the first oil crisis. Going back was also not an option for them, because their worst fears had been realized. The democratic government that took over when the Dutch left in 1975 soon degenerated into a morass of corruption and nepotism. In 1980, the army seized power and the country acquired a genuine military dictator in the form of sergeant Desi Bouterse. When Bouterse personally took part in the murder of political opponents, the Netherlands stopped payment of the independence bonus and Suriname got caught up in the downward spiral of pauperization.

Democracy was restored – with the discredited leaders of the first independent government once again in power – but the army remains a powerful force in the background. Thus the decolonization of Suriname also ended in a trauma.

The Surinamese immigrants also registered for work on a labour market that was having trouble accommodating all those already looking. As with the minorities from Morocco and Turkey, they found themselves faced with the prospect of unemployment.

The ability of minority groups to compete for jobs has proved limited. When it comes down to it, most employers prefer to take on Dutch employees. Article 1 of the Constitution forbids discrimination of this nature, but prospective employers always have sufficient other reasons for rejecting a candidate. Furthermore, although discrimination plays a role in this situation, it is not the whole story. Many members of minority groups do not have the qualifications required to find employment in an economy which demands an increasingly high level of education and training from its workers. This is often one reason for their being rejected for jobs. The same applies to their children, even though most of the younger generation have grown up in the Netherlands.

[278]

Anyone who studies education statistics will be put in mind of the Third World. A small number of people from the minority groups are successful in pushing their way through to the higher levels of Dutch society. They complete a university education with honours and become absorbed in the middle classes. But below them, then there is a great gap. Very few members of immigrant groups study vocational subjects at intermediate level, and the drop-out rate is high. It would appear that only the most intelligent are able to survive the Dutch education system. The large majority seem to come up against an insurmountable hurdle at some point.

This hurdle is related to Dutch culture and traditions. These immigrant groups find themselves in a society based on *overleg*, where each group is left to its own devices and help is given only to those who ask for it. This is not the way things are done in Turkey or Morocco. Or in Suriname. Generally speaking, the minority groups from the Islamic countries have a strong patriarchal culture, with great respect for parental authority, where having one's own opinions is often seen as a form of contradiction. The Hindus also have a strong family structure.

This is less true of the Creoles and the Antillians. The slaveholders did not permit close family ties to develop on the plantations, since they could pose a threat to their absolute power. Consequently, a culture of rapidly changing relationships developed, with children the responsibility of the mother. Creole and Antillian families are still frequently headed by very strong women, who are responsible not only for the household but also for the income. Survival in Suriname is a matter of being able to improvise and acquire small personal advantages wherever possible. This requires forming continually changing alliances with others. In the political sector, it is a matter of 'I'll support you and you find me a job in the bureaucracy'.

It is therefore difficult for these groups to operate effectively in a society dominated by Dutch values. This is compounded if you do not speak the language very well and miss many of the subtleties of what is said. It can lead to a great deal of misunderstanding if you are talking to someone who is seeking a compromise which is satisfactory to everyone concerned, while you are trying to extract a favour or make a deal.

Children from minority groups were surprised when they first went to a Dutch school. The lessons often started with a group discussion, in which the teacher acted almost as their equal. He or she seemed interested in what the pupils had to say, rather than simply teaching them what was in the books. The teaching methods included a lot of working on their own or in groups, and searching for solutions together. It was not the intention that the pupils should purely reproduce the truth as it was written in the school books. Teachers had a tendency to assess children on the basis of their creativity and ability to think for themselves. This was a stark contrast to their own cultures, where the children mainly had to imitate what they were taught as well as they could; where there was a strong belief that an opinion of one's own could only be developed from a great experience of life; and where children were expected to keep quiet and show respect for their elders. And if you do not understand the language, because you still speak Turkish, Berber or Sranan Tongo at home, it is even more difficult to adapt.

Rather than organizing introductory courses for the new immigrants, the Ministry of Education and Science responded initially by providing teaching in their own language and culture, recruiting teachers from their home countries. This was partly induced by some vague idea of sovereignty in one's own domain; but it was also a response to the desire to return home: the generations that grew up in the Netherlands would also have to be able to survive if the dream ever came true.

In addition, the government encouraged the minorities to form their own organizations, and developed an extensive system of grants. As a result all kinds of bodies were set up to represent minority interests, staffed by the élite few who had had a good education. They projected themselves as representatives of what the Dutch government considered as their particular group, whether they had actually gained a reasonable level of support among their own people or not.

For good or for bad, these leaders defended the interests of their 'grass-roots members'. They tackled real and imagined discrimination and were fierce defenders of their language and culture. They demanded positive action and a policy of preference to put and end to the disadvantaged position of their people on the labour market. In this, they were following closely in the footsteps of the feminists, who had had relative success with similar tactics.

Their efforts met with a favourable response from the official channels in the Netherlands. After all, discrimination and distinction according to race or ethnic origin were to be deplored. It was laid down in Article 1 of the Constitution, and with good reason. And, of course, the Netherlands had clearly and publicly broken with its own colonial past.

The dominant generations of the seventies wanted nothing to do with what their predecessors had found normal and acceptable during the colonial period. They had been taught to equate colonialism with the contemptible ideology of imperialism, and believed that the Netherlands should be ashamed of its part in it. Furthermore, discrimination in its many forms was a reminder not only of colonialism but of the persecution of the Jews in the Second World War, which the Dutch – it was now largely agreed – had not resisted with sufficient force. Thirdly, there was the bad example being set by their distant relations in South Africa, the Afrikaners.

The Afrikaners had their origins in the only genuine settlement of any size during the era of the United East India Company – the Cape Colony. It was set up as a supply post for ships on their way to the East Indies. The company therefore needed a strip of land around the port, where crops could be grown. Like Ceylon, the colony had been lost to the British, but the local population had preserved its character and developed its own language, Afrikaans, which was closely related to Dutch.

The Afrikaners preserved their identity by holding on tightly to their faith. They gave it a very specific interpretation, believing that – because they had access to the Divine Truth – they were the Chosen People. This placed them apart from their black neighbours, the descendants of the sinner Ham, with whom they had to share their land. This eventually led to the ideology of apartheid, which – since contact with the Netherlands had remained close – was in effect a racial variant of Abraham Kuyper's pillar system. Paul Kruger, the president of the Afrikaners, who had waged a desperate war against the British around the turn of the century, was also a great hero in the Netherlands. Solidarity with the Afrikaners was enormous. Nearly every town – large and small – in the Netherlands has a district dating from that time, where all the streets are named after Kruger and his generals. There will sometimes be a clearly more recent name among them, a *Steve Bikoplein* or something similar, which has replaced the original Afrikaner name. In the seventies and eighties, the ANC had largely taken the place of the Afrikaners in the national imagination. During his first visit to the Netherlands – shortly after this release – Nelson Mandela was greeted by tens of thousands of cheering people, just as [281] Paul Kruger had been in 1901. In taking to the streets to welcome Mandela, these people were closing what they considered to be a shameful chapter in their history.

THIS WAS NOT ENOUGH FOR THE PEOPLE OF BIMRI

After protests from minority groups, most media stopped reporting the ethnic origins of people arrested by the police, because it was considered irrelevant and, besides, they never carried headlines such as 'Dutch burglar escapes from police'. The police also found themselves forced to go to great lengths to describe non-Dutch suspects, if they were not to be accused of racism.

But this was not enough for the people in Bimri and other similar areas. The children failed at school, where the culture was so alien to them. Job applications were rejected, frequently because applicants – whose spoken Dutch was reasonably good – were unable to put together a halfway decent letter, and fell foul of the spelling traps that are so common in the Dutch language. The minorities in these areas were left further and further behind. They had insufficient in-built resilience to drag themselves up and out; they found themselves trapped in a society where temptations are rife but prospects are few.

There are many ways of making a situation like this bearable on a personal level. But there are two extremes: you can withdraw as far as possible into your own traditions and become isolated from society at large, or you can throw caution to the wind and rid yourself of all inhibition. Most immigrants choose a solution somewhere in the middle of this spectrum, making them, in principle, 'invisible'. But those who choose one or other of the extremes become extremely conspicuous.

For many Turks and Moroccans, the traditional Islamic beliefs from home give them something safe to hold on to. They reject Dutch society – with its mini-skirts and sex programmes on TV, its drink and drugs – as a 'den of iniquity'. Islam, with its three hundred thousand followers, has become the second religion of the Netherlands and the traditional headscarf worn by Moslem women is making a strong comeback.

The same applies to those who throw off all their inhibitions. At first glance, it may appear that 'anything goes' in Dutch society. Women in sexy clothes are looking for sex. You need have no respect for public property. Ticket inspectors in the tram are few and far between, so you can travel free. And if you do get caught breaking any rules, the punishment will be light. No one expects an outward show of respect – and they treat you like dirt anyway, because there are no jobs to be found. Terrible conflicts arise at home, particularly in patriarchal households, because children continually have to switch between a home life in which parental rule is absolute and the outside world where they are expected to have their own opinions and show initiative. The fathers' authority is not supported by society, at least not in the way to which they are accustomed. This can often lead to serious crises, which makes the younger generations of immigrants susceptible to the temptations of the wild life, of drugs and the world of crime of which they are a part. Anyone who chooses this path is also very visible. A stoned Creole playing with a knife on the number 3 tram is soon seen by his fellow passengers as representative of his whole community. The same applies to the bent little women with their headscarves and their faded raincoats. These people are different, but not in the same way as the Javans, the 'most kind-hearted beings on the face of the earth'. This is a difference that strikes fear in the hearts of 'normal' citizens. One of the Netherlands best known cabaret performers, Wim Kan, wrote a song in the early eighties to describe this fear. He called it *'Khomeini op het behang'*, 'Khomeini on the wallpaper'. The minority organizations were clearly right to protest about the ethnic stigmatization caused by reporting the racial origins of police suspects.

Since the seventies a whole anthology of urban myths has grown up around the ethnic minorities. They are based on an incomplete knowledge of their customs, but they never give specific dates and times. One of the most tenacious of these myths is that 'they' slaughter sheep in their homes. The next-door neighbour has a friend who has blood dripping over her balcony or even through the ceiling because the Moroccans in the flat above are slaughtering sheep. And there are plenty more where that came from. The other neighbour has a brother whose children can't get jobs because the 'foreigners' always get first choice. It's no use asking the local council for a house, because the foreigners (or, more often these days, the asylum-seekers) are given priority. More and more of them are arriving and the council doesn't want to discriminate. Or there is the one about a cousin or some other distant relative who was told by a policeman that there was no point in reporting a crime committed by a foreigner because 'even if we arrest him, he'll be walking around as free as a bird within the hour'. The same is often said about junkies – in spite of the fact that the police insist that all crimes are reported. And, of course, the old favourite – foreigners live like kings from the social security. They get child benefits for ten children, all of whom live back in Morocco.

[283]

The tenacity of these urban myths bears testimony to the tension that exists between the various groups that comprise present-day Dutch society. The official policy of tolerance seems to have little or no parallel in society at large. There is much fear and suspicion and no one knows how best to respond, or just how deep it really goes, because statements that may be interpreted as racist are strictly taboo. They are often preceded with such disclaimers as 'I don't like to discriminate, but...' People who protest about the building of a mosque at the end of their street, tend to base their arguments on the lack of parking space or the extra noise. They will even claim that the mosque will lead to a concentration of Moslems in one area, providing fertile feeding ground for racism and discrimination, which they themselves – of course – abhor.

This undercurrent of racism was long ignored by officialdom. The comparison was quickly made with Nazism and you simply didn't communicate with fascists. There was no place for racism in Dutch society.

'You know who gets discriminated against in this country? The Dutch, that's who.' This became a well-known complaint in many a local café, once the alcohol had undermined the plaintiff's sense of historical perspective – and, perhaps too often, long before. In the seventies, the Creoles from Suriname were the favourite 'bogey men' of the bar-room politicians. That honour has now largely been taken over by the Turks and Moroccans. They are evidently considered even stranger and more of a threat. This perhaps has something to do with reports of anti-Western Islamic leaders in countries like Iran. The headscarf is then soon associated with the *chador* and those who wear it seen as Khomeini's fifth column; or it represents the first sign of the Islamic 'fundamentalism' which will 'take over' here before we know it. This fear is widespread and has penetrated even the more progressive circles. It is difficult to explain in discussion circles that have been influenced strongly by feminism that the wearing of a headscarf may be a carefully considered choice, signifying the wearer's submission to the authority of God, not to that of men – that, on the contrary, it is expressly intended to displease the latter.

This is not necessarily bad news for those who wish to combat racism. It means that discrimination is based on prejudice and fear of all that is different and unknown, rather than a well-considered belief in the intrinsic superiority of the white race. Prejudices disintegrate more easily than ideologies. They can be tackled with concrete facts and good examples, with summer carnivals and other enjoyable experiences. A walk down the West Kruiskade in Rotterdam or the Hobbemastraat in The Hague also makes one more hopeful. Both are in the middle of working-class areas with large ethnic populations and are lined with shops run by Turks, Moroccans and Surinamese. Setting up a business – an impossible dream in their own countries – seems to have proved possible in the Netherlands. The shops were initially aimed at their own groups, but the circle of customers is getting wider all the time. More and more Dutch people are discovering, that the best lamb, for example, can be bought from the Turkish or Moroccan butcher. The cuisine of the minorities is also achieving wider popularity. It is becoming increasingly normal to go to the Surinamese snack bar on the corner for a *roti* if you don't fancy cooking for yourself. As a consequence, a middle class of small businessmen is developing within the minority groups. It has not yet progressed far enough to make up the lost ground, but it does offer prospects for the future. Moreover, this potential is not imposed from outside, it is 'home-grown'. It represents a process of self-emancipation that is developing without the help of the countless representative organizations or the Dutch government, with all its good intentions.

Nevertheless, the politicians and the authorities seem to be adopting a less cautious attitude to minority groups; their arguments are beginning to sound more and more like those heard around the tables in the local bars and cafés.

BIMRI´S NIGHT OF TRAGEDY

Fifteen years after the first mass migration from Suriname, opinions on the Bijlmermeer were sharply divided. Many people were frightened of Bimri. Junkies hung around the graffiti-ridden metro stations that connected it to the city. The police had conducted a large-scale clean-up operation in the city centre and many addicts had sought refuge in the Bijlmer, where the large, dark parking garages provided shelter. Bimri's design provided excellent opportunities for anti-social behaviour. The architecture made social control difficult. People had to walk down long corridors, sometimes hundreds of metres long, to get to their flats. The windows offered a poor view of the small parks between the enormous complexes. A single drunk could easily terrorize a whole block by, for example, destroying lifts or kicking in doors. The public areas consequently became run-down and neglected. Reports drawn up on the situation offered little hope. The housing associations that owned the apartment blocks concluded that the Bijlmer had been a terrible mistake of planning. They decided that two of the blocks were in such a bad state of decay that they would have to be demolished.

This was one face of Bimri. But at the same time, the town had a number of other, more hopeful facets. Despite all appearances to the contrary, a complete social network had developed that was unseen by the authorities and the official welfare bodies. Bimri's answer to the Rotterdam Summer Carnival was the gigantic Kwakoe Festival, which had started as a tournament for Surinamese football teams and now attracted hundreds of thousands of visitors every year. On Sundays, swinging music and joyful singing could be heard coming from many of the local meeting places. It was the sound not of raucous parties, but of church services. Bimri had developed into a very religious town, but the churches had little in common with official Calvinism. They more closely resembled Pentecostal communities, which do exist in the Netherlands but, compared to the congregations in Bimri, practice their faith with considerable reserve. Bimri also became a centre for followers of the Afro-Surinamese *winti* religion. Mediums had even made contact with Dutch *wintis*, including those of Jews gassed by the Nazis who had originally lived in Amsterdam-Zuid, which is adjacent to the Bijlmer. In this way, Bimri acquired its own understanding of the drama of Mokum.

But this informal social structure was invisible to the passing visitor, standing apprehensively among the graffiti on a run-down metro station. They saw only the drugs that were being passed from hand to hand. They saw the broken streetlights and were afraid of being mugged in the deserted footpaths between the blocks. The real Bimri did not show its face so easily. It would take something out of the ordinary for that to happen.

On 4 October 1992, an El Al Boeing cargo plane developed problems while approaching Schiphol. The pilot flew in great circles above Amsterdam in search of a free runway. Twice, the plane roared across the city centre. There was clearly something seriously wrong, serious enough to be mentioned on the radio news. The pilot was apparently having trouble lining the plane up with the runway. At the third attempt the Boeing lost height rapidly. It bore down on Bimri at enormous speed and crashed through one of the apartment blocks, De Kruitberg. It was a Sunday evening, around seven o'clock. Prime time. The whole country was watching Studio Sport. CNN brought news of the crash a little before the Dutch NOS. That Sunday evening, the whole country watched the drama unfold in front of their eyes. The flames rose high in the air above the Kruitberg, which had been partially demolished. Frightened people from the whole of Bimri rushed to the scene of the crash. No one would be able to survive this inferno, hundreds must have died. The television showed the whole thing live – the flames, the fire brigade working frantically to get it under control, the desperate family members and the hastily set up crisis centre, the police trying to keep onlookers at a distance and the shocked mayor of the city. Eye witnesses were interviewed. It soon became clear that the people living in the Kruitberg were largely Surinamese of Ghanian. But no one knew how many there were. The reporters said that, in addition to the official residents, there could have been a lot of other people living there, illegal immigrants who had gone underground and earned a living in the informal sector, the 'black' economy. There were soon rumours of a thousand dead, most of whom were not registered anywhere.

It took several days to recover all the bodies. After a week or so had passed, the authorities said that the death toll had been at least 250. A wave of emotion and sympathy swept through the country. For that first week, Bimri's night of tragedy was headline news. The television broadcast a moving memorial service, where the speakers included not only the prime minister but also the leaders of all the minority groups in Bimri. At the end of the service, the Mayor of Amsterdam led a procession of twenty thousand people to the Kruitberg to lay flowers at the scene of the tragedy. It was accompanied by effusive expressions of grief and religious faith from the various ethnic groups, while television reporters explained the various ways in which the different cultures expressed their sorrow. The tragedy had left a great impression on everyone and the nation was united around the victims. It actually made you feel good to be a part of it. The Netherlands was proud of this display of mass solidarity and grief.

The authorities pledged their full support for the victims, including, of course, those living in the immediate vicinity of the Kruitberg who had been psychologically traumatized by the disaster. They also promised residence permits to all illegal immigrants living in the destroyed blocks. The people concerned were told to report to the Aliens Police. It had, by this time, become clear that the final death toll of the crash had been a little more than sixty. The Aliens Police were, however, overwhelmed by nearly two thousand people who claimed to have been living in the Kruitberg. It was a multifarious and, as time wore on, increasingly aggressive crowd. Reporters discovered that many had come from as far as Paris in busloads to take advantage of this 'chance of a lifetime'. It took a long time for the crowds to be dispersed. Eventually, about fifty people who had lived in the Kruitberg were given residence permits.

This incident, however, reversed the sympathetic mood of the nation. It confirmed all the prejudices that the emotional pictures of the crash had covered with a veneer of sentiment. The image of Bimri as full of good people, people sharing the suffering of their fellow residents, evaporated overnight.

Where did all these people come from? As most of the other members of the European Union, the Netherlands had become more of a haven for immigrants than ever. Development experts had a very clear explanation for this – if the wealth will not go to the people, the people will come to the wealth. A global process of migration was under way towards places that could offer work and economic security and the Netherlands was one of the favoured destinations.

Like most of the rich countries, however, the Netherlands had closed its borders to foreigners without money. They were not given residence permits or allowed to take up paid employment. Exceptions were made for people who were persecuted by the authorities in their own countries for political reasons and who could prove that their lives would be in danger if they returned. These people were granted political asylum, which in effect gave them the same status as Dutch citizens, with the exception of the right to vote. In practice, however, political asylum is very rarely granted.

People who had relationships with Dutch citizens are also entitled to a residence permit, but it only becomes permanent if the relationship lasted longer than three years. The other alternative is to go underground, a feasible option in a democracy with reasonably open borders. Once you have entered the country – on a tourist visa, for example – you will be left alone by the authorities. Unless, of course, you do something to attract the attention of the police, such as being caught using public transport without a ticket.

[288]

The government closed more and more loopholes in the law. They tightened up the conditions for family reunification. The official procedures were long and difficult. Yet the impression was gradually gaining ground that the Netherlands was a besieged stronghold, surrounded by hordes of poverty-stricken down-and-outs who wanted to eat at the richly laid table of a developed industrial society.

Illegal immigrants provided manpower for the black economy. Textile workshops sprung up across the country where they worked for very low wages. Farmers and market gardeners hired them to harvest their crops. They found work in the catering industry. A hard-working, low-paid underclass developed in the Netherlands whose importance for the economy is impossible to estimate. Prostitution also acquired a more international character. Now and then, scandals would rise to the surface. Young girls from Latin America and Asia were apparently being treated as slaves by brothel owners. The following sex advertisements were taken at random from *De Telegraaf* of 7 October 1994: 'TEAP BANDAL, South American girls', 'CHINESE teenage girl (18) and irresistible blonde', 'Sweet THAI girls in luxury surroundings. Take a bubble bath or a Thai body-massage. Also Thai dominatrice and SM room.' There are one and a half pages of these advertisements, all with address and/or telephone number.

The whole illegal circuit was front page news after the Bijlmer disaster. It became clear that, in addition to the Turks, Moroccans and Surinamese, there were also large groups of Ghanians living in Amsterdam. Not to mention South Americans, including thousands of Brazilians who had fled the crisis in their own country. A large number of Pakistanis had found their way to the Netherlands and, after the fall of the Iron Curtain, they were joined by Russians, Poles and, especially, Romanians. The channels for receiving asylum-seekers were soon more or less clogged up.

People who register as political refugees become involved in a procedure set up by the Ministry of Justice to determine whether their claims are correct and whether the persecution is sufficiently severe to justify asylum. This is based on the implicit assumption that the majority of applicants are 'economic', rather than genuine political, refugees. The term 'economic refugee' has acquired strong negative connotations since the eighties. It refers to people who wish to take unfair advantage of the opportunities offered by the Netherlands. Now and then, a voice of protest may be heard, suggesting that – as a prosperous industrial country – the Netherlands should admit at least a quota of immigrants, but these are soon lost in the general verbal onslaught to the contrary. Politicians and the government respond firmly with the conviction that 'these people should build up their own countries' or that they should be 'helped at home'. It is worth mentioning at this point that most migrants do not come from countries with which the Dutch government has a development aid relationship of any magnitude.

Frits Bolkestein, the parliamentary leader of the conservative-liberal *Volkspartij voor Vrijheid en Democratie* (vvd), was the first politician to genuinely concern himself with what was already the favourite topic of conversation in so many bars and cafés across the country. The Netherlands was not a haven for immigrants, he insisted. He demanded that the borders be closed and – in the same breath – that foreigners already in the country should learn to adapt to Dutch society. He claimed that the policy pursued up until then had been too soft and it was time to adopt a harder line. His arguments received an immediate response. State secretary for justice Aad Kosto did what he could to close all the loopholes in the immigration legislation, resulting in a series of very tough measures. The conditions under which asylum-seekers could appeal against rejected applications were considerably tightened up. Dutch judges – who are proud of their reputation for being independent, meticulous and hard-headed – responded by studying the cases that came before them in even greater detail. And, true to the principle that, if in doubt they should choose the side of the defendant, they granted more applications than they had done previously.

Another loophole that was closed up was the 'love connection'. Anyone wishing to start a relationship with a Dutch national had to apply for a permit from the Dutch Embassy in their own country. The Dutch partner also had to meet certain requirements. They had to have decent accommodation and a gross personal income of at least four thousand guilders a month. This is well above the minimum wage and the level of social security benefits. The measures were designed to put an end to marriages of convenience. Certain Dutch citizens, particularly those in the drugs world, were earning a sizable bit on the side by marrying foreigners wishing to settle in the Netherlands. Once they had their residence permit, the couple would divorce. The new requirements for a house and a reasonable income were intended to make it more difficult for people to get permits in this way; but any regulation that restricts the choice of a foreign partner to those in paid employment is certainly open to question. The new law, however, passed through parliament without any problems and with hardly a voice raised in protest from among the general public.

The media also became less and less cautious about linking social problems to the composition of the population. They went back to stating the ethnic background of police suspects and published detailed reports of Moroccan and Antillian youth gangs who made the streets unsafe in the major cities. They laid heavy emphasis on the fact that these young people had not become criminals because of their ethnic backgrounds but because they did no know how to make a life for themselves in a culture so different from their own. But generally, the blame was seen as laying not with society but with the people themselves. This reflected a new hardness that was also manifesting itself in other areas of social life, such as the extensive cutbacks in the system of social security benefits. People had to solve their problems themselves as best they could and – you might think – the large majority of those in minority groups were living quiet lives and not causing any difficulties at all.

In government circles, a new school of thought developed that was a radical departure from the established practice. The minorities had been 'smothered to death' and now found themselves in a position of dependency. Conditions had to be imposed on them to shake them up and get them to stand on their own feet. People who did not want to learn Dutch, for example,

[290]

would never be given a permanent residence permit. This new approach exposed a number of painful shortcomings. There were too few opportunities for foreigners to learn Dutch and those that did exist were often voluntary organizations. There was clearly great interest from the minorities for Dutch courses, but most of them were placed on waiting lists, which only demoralized them all the more. It is all very well setting conditions, but society has to provide the facilities for meeting them. •

THE EXAMPLE OF THE OLD SYSTEM OF PILLARIZATION

In 1994, the government decided that, from then on, it would sign an 'integration contract' with all newcomers. It was not clear exactly what this would entail, but it would include the rights and duties of both parties. Newcomers would be able to take the government to court if it failed to provide the facilities required to allow them to fulfil the conditions for residence (for example, learning the language).

None of this affects in any way the right of minority groups to preserve their own language and culture; this is not under discussion. On the contrary, many politicians – particularly Christian Democrats, hold up to minority groups the example of the old system of pillarization. There is no need, they say, to integrate as individuals, but as a group. Moslems and Hindus are starting to take advantage of the education legislation, setting up schools based on their own systems of belief using funds provided by the Ministry of Education. The ministry gives the schools complete freedom to choose its own form of religious instruction, although school inspectors do monitor whether the schools meet the same requirements as all others operating within the state system. Liberals and social democrats are less enthusiastic about the possible revival of the pillar system, which they see as a form of historical regression.

This has led to a debate among Dutch intellectuals, politicians and other leading figures, showing that ethical politics is still very much alive. The Dutch discuss among themselves how minorities can best be prepared for their independence – no longer political, but economic and personal. They wish to repay the debt of honour, but decide for themselves how they should go about it. In the meantime, the minorities go their own way, pursuing their own emancipation without the help of all the good intentions and formal structures of their hosts.

The Rotterdam Summer Carnival is the best example of this kind of initiative. It is well worth seeing. Every year, it is held on the last Saturday in July. No one knows how they do it, but the sun always shines. Low sky or not.

*

Epilogue

RAGING WATERS AND AN ANGRY WORLD

This, Dirceu, is the story of the Low Sky and the fifteen million people who live beneath it. For some reason, I find myself thinking of the stickers your company gives to its customers: 'Brazil – all you need is love' and 'Brazil – we'll support you ever more'. Here in the Netherlands, we would never drive around with slogans like these on our bumpers. We are a little too afraid to promote our country with such enthusiasm. It can all too easily be interpreted as exaggeration and goes beyond the standards of 'normal' behaviour.

I hope I have been able to explain a little of who we are, the way we behave with each other and with outsiders and the reflexes that determine how we live. I do not pretend to have given a definitive description of the Dutch national character – that would be far too difficult a task. It has even recently become the subject of debate on the opinion pages of the national newspapers. The tone of the debate suggests that we are reviewing our concept of patriotism.

This is related to the fact that the face of the Netherlands is changing. European unification is progressing slowly and with difficulty, but is ultimately irreversible. The Netherlands is even cooperating on the abolition of that symbol of national pride and reliability, the guilder, in favour of the ecu, the coinage of the single European currency. You then find yourself wondering what distinguishes your own country from the other members of the Union, what qualities you have that are unique. And you wonder whether a small country like the Netherlands does not need some kind of recognizable 'binding agent' to hold it together.

The results of the debate were a little disappointing. Qualities defined as 'typically Dutch' proved to be little different than those that you would find in any humane society. The Dutch are apparently democratic, tolerant and peace-loving by nature, preferring cooperation to conflict. A glance at modern Dutch society would appear to confirm this assumption, but it is going a little far to explain this in terms of some sort of national character, to believe that the Dutch simply have such admirable attributes in their blood. This, at least, is what the opponents of the above-mentioned 'new patriotism' claimed.

Yet the entire debate does say something about the national character. The general democratic disposition and the respect for consultation and compromise are an echo of the late nineteenth and early twentieth centuries, when the Netherlands proudly guarded its neutrality and watched the power struggles of the great powers with a certain arrogance that bordered on pity. The Dutch considered themselves far too sensible to be tempted by shallow emotion and ambition. They were satisfied with themselves and with their orderly little country. They promoted the advance of civilization through mutual consultation – that kept them busy enough.

But patriotism returns with a vengeance when a country has its back against the wall. The Dutch found themselves in this position at the beginning of 1995. The eternal enemy, the water, once again showed its awesome strength. This time it did not, as in 1953, come through the front door. There were no hurricane-force storms and the North Sea was calm. Completely without warning, unprecedented volumes of water came rushing down the Maas and the Rijn, the two major rivers feeding the delta that covers most of the country. The water level reached record levels and it looked as though the river dykes would not hold. This was not because they were too low, but because – and this was news to many Dutch people – they worked like sponges. If the water level remained high for too long, the dykes would become saturated and collapse, giving the river water free reign.

The area particularly under threat was a strip of land of varying width that runs between the two rivers, practically cutting the country in two from east to west. In the middle of January, the water level had risen so high that the authorities decided to evacuate the population in the danger areas. 75,000 people in the Betuwe, in the west of the country, were ordered to leave their homes immediately. As the threat of flooding spread, they were followed by thousands more. The entire operation went off without a hitch. The police kept motorways free for the evacuees and the evacuated areas were sealed off hermetically from the outside world to keep out looters. It was a wonderful adventure. The commercial television organized a successful charity show for the victims, who had departed in their middle-of-the-range family saloons, pulling trailers with some of their more treasured possessions, to set up camp in the relative luxury of large sports halls and the like in the safer areas. Reporters descended on them *en masse* to record the emotions of these displaced persons. But, despite their efforts, it simple refused to develop into a genuine disaster. They had to go to great lengths to find people who would shed their tears or express their fears in public.

YET THE NATION WAS UNITED

Yet the nation was united in a way it had not been for many years. A feeling of elevated pride hung over the land. The government immediately announced an extensive programme of dyke reinforcement, to be known as the second Delta Plan, to ensure that 'this never happened again'. When the water level had returned to normal, the evacuees – by this time swollen to 200,000 – returned to their homes in their own cars or in special trains, with the same discipline they had shown when they left. They were welcomed home by a letter from the local council, which included instructions on how to get their lives back to normal, accompanied – in some cases – by a bunch of flowers. Every household was to receive compensation of five hundred guilders. Separate compensation schemes were devised for farmers and companies. The national consensus was complete and the dykes were to be reinforced. The rest was just details.

[295]

The near-disaster revived the debate on the national character. It had been a perfect illustration of the way the Dutch stand together in the face of adversity. And how, through a combination of improvisation, determination and unity, they ultimately regain control of the situation. How fortunate are those born in the wet deltalands.

A few months later, the Dutch were confronted with a disaster of another kind: the fall of Srebrenica. Srebrenica was one of the 'safe areas' set up in Bosnia to protect the Moslem population against the 'ethnic cleansing' of the Bosnian Serbs, who had the region in an iron grip. A battalion of Dutch UN troops, known as 'Dutchbat', had tried to keep the warring parties apart. The battalion – according to UN instructions – was lightly armed and had little authority to respond to direct aggression. The Serb generals rode around in stolen Dutch jeeps, even using them when they came to negotiate with Dutchbat's commanding officers.

It was a perfectly natural step for the Netherlands to contribute troops to the peacekeeping operation in Bosnia. The country is a supporter of inter-national arbitration as a means of solving conflict and is, consequently, a committed and active member of the United Nations. The Dutch army had taken part in peacekeeping operations earlier in Lebanon and Cambodia and, after the fall of the Berlin Wall and the end of the Cold War, the government decided to reorganize the army specifically to participate in such operations. An 'air mobile brigade' was formed and recruitment advertisements were shown on the television, showing Dutch lads in mountainous (and therefore very 'foreign') regions, 'defending' a dam. The copywriter's message was unstated but clear: 'Join the Army – and help to keep the world a peaceful place'.

Dutchbat, however, was confronted with uncompromising Serbs who were uninterested in working on a peace plan and who displayed completely different behaviour at the negotiating table than the Dutch normally expect. Diplomat and politician Hans van der Broek had already experienced this during his final days as foreign minister. As representative of the European Union for Yugoslavia, he had made a long series of agreements with the combatants in the former republic, which were usually broken within 24 hours. The average Dutchbat soldier had increasing difficulty justifying their presence in this cruel civil war. 'Why can't we just let them sort it out for themselves?', they complained to the people at home.

THE DAYS THAT FOLLOWED WERE SHAMEFUL

Then the Bosnian Serbs, under general Ratko Mladic, took over the enclave of Srebrenica without encountering any resistance to speak of. Dutchbat did not fight back. It was not equipped to do so and, in any case, its mandate from the UN did not permit retaliation. Furthermore, the Serbs had taken several hundred Dutch soldiers hostage. The days that followed were shameful. While Dutchbat looked on, the Serbs separated the Moslem men from the women and children. The latter were packed into overfull buses and taken to the front, where they were dumped near the Moslem lines and told to walk the rest of the way. The men disappeared into detention centres for 'interrogation'. Television pictures were shown worldwide of Dutch soldiers in their blue UN helmets witnessing this selection process without raising a finger in protest.

The response to these events in the Netherlands was remarkably calm. Foreign minister Hans van Mierlo stated on television that the Serbs held all the cards, that he was forced to negotiate without 'small change'. And that the first priority was to get all the Dutch soldiers home from Srebrenica safely.

In the meantime, there was increasing evidence of atrocities committed against the refugees by the Serb forces. In response to this, the Dutch soldiers were ordered not to say anything that they had seen because loose talk might endanger the lives of their comrades who were still being held. Only Jan Pronk, the development minister, dared to speak out. He spoke of 'genocide' and called on the world community – not the Netherlands on its own – to respond with a hard hand. His remarks provoked an immediate wave of criticism in the Netherlands and Pronk was accused of putting the lives of the hostages in danger. The hostages, meanwhile, returned to the Netherlands in small groups, because the Serbs had a tendency to release their captives in dribs and drabs. A whole contingent of psychologists were at the ready to help the hostages to come to terms with their undoubtedly traumatic experiences. The first group to arrive back at the Soesterberg air base were given a heroes' welcome.

There were a few discordant voices. Some commentators suggested that the attention lavished on the 'boys in Bosnia' was disproportionate to that paid to the tens of thousands of Moslems driven out of the enclave – while under the 'protection' of Dutchbat – and now at the mercy of rapists and murderers. Such remarks met with an indignant response from the general public. From the fourth day of the crisis, De Telegraaf expressly no longer led with news from Bosnia. The editors, who know the way the public thinks better than anyone, did not want to upset their readership any more than was necessary. The other papers continued to lead with details of the disturbing developments in the Balkans, but support for the government and for Dutchbat did not falter. There was a general feeling that we had done our best and were not to blame for the failure. The only priority now was to get the boys home in one piece. It all put one in mind of the 'injured innocent'.

The events in Srebrenica explicitly did not lead to reflections on the national character or on the nature of patriotism and its consequences. A more widespread reaction was that we should turn our backs on these global hornets' nests. The Netherlands was surrounded by an angry world and it was best to have as little to do with it as possible. There were no demonstrations or letter-writing campaigns organized in protest. The nation proved to be very much able to face the other way when the pictures got too shocking.

One Dutch soldier was actually killed in Srebrenica. This led Alain Franco, the correspondent in the Netherlands for the French newspaper *Le Monde*, to make the following, rather uncomplimentary, comment: "The death of the Dutch UN soldier Raviv van Renssen was a great shock to everybody. We are not used to one of our boys being killed in action', said a diplomat who is to take over responsibility for media and cultural affairs in Paris next week. The country was right to be shocked. The Netherlands fortunately has little experience in these matters. The people are not used to their soldiers being sent home in bodybags, burials with military honours and having the sorrow and grief of the family broadcast into their living rooms. And the government would like to keep it that way. 'We are a small country, and we have limited resources', a top official at the foreign ministry told me. 'We do not possess great power like France or Great Britain, so there is little we can do.' *La belle affaire!* The Netherlands, the smallest of the large European countries and the largest of the small, which so much wants to play a role on the international stage, has got an attack of cold feet.' Franco advised the Netherlands to adopt a less ambitious foreign policy, if it is not prepared to take risks.

The tragedy of Srebrenica thus became the opposite of the near-disaster during the winter. A united front can be made to fight the raging waters, but when the angry world outside comes knocking, we can do little more than wring our hands in desperation.

You might wonder, of course, if it wasn't all true. That, given the circumstances, Dutchbat did everything they could. Or that it takes more practical courage for a soldier to hold his fire than to let loose in frustration or to perform two or three acts of heroism before being overrun by the Serbs. That would certainly have resulted in more burials with military honours. It may have saved our face internationally, but neither the government nor the general staff were prepared to sacrifice human lives on such a gesture. Van Mierlo was right – the Serbs held all the cards. Such situations call, above all, for self-control and extremely clear thinking. There is a positive side to the fact that Dutch soldiers are not prepared to sacrifice their young lives for the first cause that comes along.

These are, however, not the kind of qualities that a nation wishes to be reminded of. Perhaps that is why, after the fall of Srebrenica, no one took the opportunity to use it to analyze the Dutch character. Yet, Dirceu, I think – when it comes down to it – that this all comes very close to what you meant when you told your daughter: 'You must not stay here. The sky is too low.'

Behind our dykes, under our low sky, we feel safe against the raging waters and the angry world around us. Here, in our small country, we try to make sure everything is organized as well as possible. In the last instance, the Dutch are not a nation of adventurers. They prefer to stay at home, where they are in control and it is safe. Perhaps that is our main character trait, from which all others follow.

TRANSLATOR'S NOTE

As one of those people who was – and still is, even after more than fifteen years – 'surprised at the Dutch and the way they live', I would like to thank Han van der Horst for giving me the opportunity to translate 'The Low Sky'. It was a genuine 'labour of love'. Not only was it a pleasure and a challenge to try and reproduce in English his compact and witty style (if you should find the book neither of these things, the fault is therefore mine), it also taught me a great deal about the people who have become so much a part of my life.

No matter how long you stay in this country, keep this book with you. It will genuinely help you to understand the Dutch who can make you feel so welcome and, at the same time, such a stranger. And if, at times, even that fails, just forget about it, have another cup of coffee and enjoy yourself. *Laten wij het vooral gezellig houden.*

ANDY BROWN